Praise for Joan Gussow's
This Organic Life

"You will forget that education is the purpose of this book, because it moves so much like a novel. However, you will find yourself stopping and jotting down little bits of information and recipes along the way. Well written, poignant and packed with facts.

—*The Washington Post*

"Joan Gussow provides us with delicious inspiration by picking from her garden and cooking seasonally. She is an enlightened nutritionist who understands that our health and the health of the planet begins with stewardship of the earth."

—Alice Waters

"Will give heart and nourishment to anyone with a garden that seems beyond help."

—*The Chicago Tribune*

"[Gussow] makes a compelling argument—both ecological and moral—for growing our own food."

—*Utne Reader*

"Gussow is a reminder of how important passionate people are to all of us, because they share their contagious excitement with the timid. . . . Most of us want to be part of something of larger significance. Gussow's book will light one possible path for many readers to come."

—*Natural Home* magazine

"Joan Gussow is one of those rare authorities for whom the personal and political are always one and the same. Eloquent, funny, wise, she is one of our most important voices in the ever growing Real Food Movement."

—Barbara Damrosch, author of *The Garden Primer*

"[Gussow's] message could be strident but instead is compelling and informative, partly because she maintains a good sense of humor and partly because she walks her tal'

Heath

"Joan Dye Gussow's account of her pursuit of the good life in genuine practical harmony with nature is a delight. It's rare to encounter a book that is at once a serious contribution to its field and a fine lively entertainment. An engaging personal story, stray thoughts on history, a little science, a few gardening instructions, a handful of low-key recipes and some slyly inserted politics—what a good, healthy, enjoyable salad this is!"

—Nach Waxman, Owner, Kitchen Arts & Letters, NYC

"Almost any conference having to do with our food system—processing, organics, security—will likely include Joan Dye Gussow. She comes to food with a global perspective, concerned that our agricultural 'progress'—genetically engineered food, synthetic additives, industrialized production, and artificial price supports—is destroying environments as well as economies around the world."

—*The Valley Table*

"One of the unsung heroes of the environmental movement."

—*New Age*

"Reading *This Organic Life* could be dangerous. It might make us question the tradeoffs that many of us take for granted—how we spend our time, our money, where we buy our food and what that implies about our individual and collective futures. It might make us excited about doing things differently, even make us want to try it."

—*The Times Argus*

"*This Organic Life* is a passionate statement from a woman who cares deeply about the environment, the planet and the way we live. The fact that many of us cannot till our own gardens does not mean that Joan Gussow's message is not directed to us. As individuals, as parents and grandparents, and as citizens, hers is a call to arms, both in our self-interest and in the interest of future generations."

—Stephen Viederman, Needmor Fund

Dr. Gussow has a knack for cutting to the core of complex issues. She regales the reader with wisdom, knowledge, and passion about why we need to care about what—and how—we eat. Through her we come to see gardening as connection, as metaphor, and as practice of ongoing continuity, of the human family at home in the living world.

—Nancy Jack Todd

THIS ORGANIC LIFE

CO-OP AMERICA is a nonprofit organization dedicated to harnessing the strength of consumers, investors, communities, and businesses to build a green economy, where *green* stands for cooperation, social justice, and environmental health.

Through a series of powerful and practical education and outreach programs at Co-op America, we:

1. *Give people the information and inspiration they need to bring their economic choices in line with their values through our green living newsletter* REAL MONEY.

2. *Help green and Fair Trade businesses emerge and thrive. Through the* NATIONAL GREEN PAGES—*the "Yellow Pages for People and the Planet" we are growing the green marketplace.*

3. *Pressure irresponsible corporations to reform egregious social and environmental practices such as sweatshop and child labor, deforestation, and predatory lending. We give consumers and investors the tools to take action through consumer and investor education programs such as our* SWEATSHOP AND FAIR TRADE EDUCATION PROJECT, *our* WOODWISE CONSUMER PROGRAM, *and our* COMMUNITY INVESTING INITIATIVE. *Plus, consumers can research the corporations they purchase from by visiting our corporate research center online, www.responsibleshopper.org.*

4. *Build healthy and sustainable communities. Our journal on sustainability issues, the* CO-OP AMERICA QUARTERLY, *explores the most pressing social and environmental issues facing people and communities around the world.*

Memberships in Co-op America are available to individuals and for businesses that pass our social and environmental responsibility screens. For more information, or to join today, call 1-800-58-GREEN, or visit us online at www.coopamerica.org.

Co-op America
building an economy for people and the planet

THIS ORGANIC LIFE

Confessions of a Suburban Homesteader

JOAN DYE GUSSOW

CHELSEA GREEN PUBLISHING COMPANY

White River Junction, Vermont

Printed in the United States.
First printing, March 2001.
First paperback printing, September 2002.
05 04 03 02   1 2 3 4 5

Library of Congress Cataloging-in-Publication data

Gussow, Joan Dye.
This organic life : confessions of a suburban homesteader / Joan Dye Gussow.
p.   cm.
Includes bibliographical references and index.
ISBN 1-931498-24-5 (alk. paper)
1. Vegetable gardening—New York (State)—Piermont. 2. Organic gardening—New York
(State)—Piermont. 3. Gussow, Joan Dye. 4. Cookery (Vegetables) I. Title.

SB324.3 .G87 2001
635'.0484'0974728—dc21   00-052313

CHELSEA GREEN PUBLISHING COMPANY
P.O. Box 428
White River Junction, VT 05001
(800) 639-4099
www.chelseagreen.com

Contents

RECIPES

PREFACE

MANY YEARS AGO, asked to write a chapter on gardening for a book to be titled *Peace Now or Never*, I decided I would try to use the nature-as-enemy mode of contemporary agriculture as a metaphor for our nation's behavior toward the now-dissolved Soviet Union. As I began writing the essay, which I planned to call "Peas and Peace," I found myself speaking in an unfamiliar voice. Logical thinking came naturally to me. I was a practiced journalist, and seven years as a *Time* magazine researcher had taught me how to collect and lay out facts in a single draft.

"Peas and Peace," however, began not with facts, but with a story about my husband and me interrupting our *al fresco* dinner to warn away from our organic vegetable plot a youth spraying pesticide onto our neighbor's trees. I was attracted by the idea of using the vegetable garden as metaphor, yet several pages into the allegory, I stopped. I could find no way to tell the rest of the story in the same voice, and ended up reverting to my more familiar didactic style. When I offered the chapter draft to my doctoral students for criticism, it was clear that the allegory captured their interest much more than the rest of the chapter.

That original metaphorical effort, intended to introduce a chapter of someone else's never-published book, was later cut in half and published as the prologue and epilogue of a book of my own—

Chicken Little, Tomato Sauce and Agriculture. That book received its finest notice when a farmer I admire read large sections of the prologue approvingly to a meeting of organic farmers. In writing the present volume, therefore, I have taken note of those earlier hints that it was time to try once more for metaphor.

Yet it was nothing so intentional as a belated nod to the power of the metaphorical story—what I have come to think of as writing from my right brain—that stimulated this book. This book began the day I realized that I was not, as planned, going to write a hilarious account of my husband's and my adventures in leaving one house and then gutting and razing a second with only five months to build a third. I had kept a detailed journal of the whole desperate process, convinced that turning it into a book would require little more than careful editing. I was wrong. It seemed a valuable critique that my writer-son fell asleep while reading the first two chapters I constructed from my journal. Some of the house story turns up in this volume, but the actual structures proved incidental to what finally emerged.

This book really began one day when I was on the phone with Seth, my younger son, telling him the story of our gooseberries and the FBI (see chapter 8), and he laughingly responded, "Don't you think you guys are kind of obsessed about growing food?" It was a June day. I went out to the garden, smiling at his phrase floating about in my head, when I realized abruptly that he was right. "It's all about food!" I said out loud to the bees. It was true. Much of what had happened as my husband and I searched for a last resting place short of the grave was a continuation of my effort to live what I preached— that bringing food-growing closer to home might be the only thing that could assure the world enough food forever.

I ran inside and sat down to write. Without any sense of where I was going, I wrote a chapter. That first impassioned effort failed to survive subsequent "aha's," but it contained recipes. I had not planned to write a book with recipes. I didn't really want to write a book with recipes. The origins of many of mine were long lost and I dreaded trying to find their authors. In the end, I did the best I could with credits; the recipes insisted on being here, and they have prevailed. For as I wrote further into the book, I came gradually to understand that nothing could convey as effectively the possibility, the effort, the frustration, and the joy of year-round local eating as the stories and the foods that the garden created as I pursued my decades-long journey to vegetal self-sufficiency.

One last explanation is needed up front—for the fact that some parts of this book are written in the first person singular and others in the first person plural. So long as my husband was alive—which I had carelessly assumed would be as long as I was—I dealt with the garden as if it were ours, so much so that when Alan died, two and a half years after our move, many of our acquaintances asked me what I intended to do about the garden. "Just what I always did," I said, smiling carefully, "plant and tend it."

Alan loved the garden, but ultimately it was mine to plan—and rescue. He was an artist, too leery of being controlled by anyone or anything to accept uncompromising Nature as a mistress. Nature is a difficult co-worker: She won't allow you to postpone things, and she is often ready for you when you aren't ready for her. Alan loved to walk in the garden and comment idly on things that needed doing (hoping, I think, that I'd put them on *my* mental "to do" list). His mind was not cluttered with such details. He observed, nibbled, observed, sniffed, observed, and then produced glorious works of art such as "The Odor of Daphne," or "Three Bees Sleeping on a Sunflower," based on things he sensed, and that I often missed for focussing on a task. Now that he is gone, I have to remind myself to just look sometimes, not critically, not searching for what needs doing, but just to enjoy. For Nature, stern a mistress as she is, also wants to be loved.

TO ALAN
who found us this lovely spot,
and left it too soon

This Organic Life

1

How It All Began

> Might it not be that eating and farming are inseparable concepts that
> belong together on the farm, not two distinct economic activities
> as we have now made them in the United States?
>
> —Wendell Berry, *The Gift of Good Land*

I ARRIVED AT ADULTHOOD without a hint that vegetable production
might become central to my life. I remember the names of some of
the shrubs my garden-loving mother planted around our California
bungalow, but I have no memories of home-grown produce. In pre-
war Southern California, home gardens were mostly places for Outdoor Living. The citrus or avocado trees that graced them seemed
grown as much for decoration as for fruit. I seem to recall an attempt
at lettuce next to our garage during World War II, but a home-grown
carrot would have been more memorable, and I remember nothing of
the sort. So our vegetables, I suspect, came mostly from Ralph's market.

Serious food production began many years later, when my handsome artist husband Alan and I fled Manhattan with our infant son to
our first house, a large, cheap Victorian that "needed work," twenty
miles north of New York City, in a hamlet called Congers. Cash was
desperately short; growing food seemed economically prudent. So,
on a heavily oak-treed half-acre, we took up food production. Our
first garden was a small, irregular patch north of the house, the only
spot where the sun found its way between the tree tops for a part of
each day. We grew the usual: leaf lettuce, green beans, cucumbers,
broccoli, and tomatoes. We even tried Brussels sprouts. And, of
course, zucchini from giant plants that persisted in producing right

3

through the early stages of the borer attack that unfailingly killed them, by which time we had usually eaten more than enough zucchini for the year.

We had a few triumphs in that small garden, including a peach tree that was so productive it eventually broke under its own weight. But a fact about that early garden more lastingly important than its over-bearing peach was that it hooked us on producing food. The year the surrounding trees finally obliterated the sunny patch (the year the Brussels sprouts headed almost directly east instead of up) we knew we had to find some sun.

But where? We searched the yard. Even if we could have afforded to take down a tree, which we couldn't, we would have had to remove two oak trees and a majestic copper beech to keep the garden where it was. We were desperate enough to consider—briefly—turning the garage into a greenhouse and the sunny unpaved driveway into a gar-den. The financial implications brought us to our senses.

In fact, the financial implications finally solved our problem. We couldn't afford the cost of removing any of our giant oaks, so we had to find someone who would do it for free. Alan, goaded by necessity, had an inspiration. Some branches of the oak tree nearest the drive-way were almost touching the telephone wires. Perhaps we could convince the phone company that the tree was a hazard; removing it would open up at least half of our large south lawn to the sun.

Removing a full-grown oak—a tree at least a hundred years old—seemed a wicked thing to do. I was in graduate school by then, be-coming increasingly aware of environmental limits. Trees were not merely beautiful, they took up carbon dioxide and gave off oxygen. Before we could call the phone company, I had to convince myself that an old tree inhaled and exhaled less than an actively growing vegetable garden.

I convinced myself, and we called. A representative of Ma Bell, who was everyone's phone family in those days, came to scout the situation, and agreed to remove the tree once it had lost its leaves in the fall. We were going to have a real garden! The soon-to-be garden was now, however, a 30-by-40-foot swath of lawn. We had removed sod before and had no desire to do it again. We decided to exploit the months until the oak came down by forcing the grass to rot in place.

Through the summer and fall, we piled onto the lawn anything organic that would cover it: chopped leaves, food scraps, woodchips, and, topping it off, old newspapers with salt hay to hold them down. My gardening neighbor Julia, who had watched me hand-weed dandelions and lovingly tend the grass, peered skeptically over the fence, but I had no doubts.

That is, I had no doubts until October when the phone company came to take down the tree and open the land to the sky. Up in a cherry picker went a uniformed woodsman armed with a chainsaw. As he looked over that magnificent oak, I began to feel queasy. The tree's massive silhouette against the southern sky was familiar and comforting. I found myself resenting this insensitive brute who was ready to destroy it. Then he looked down from his perch and shouted, "It's a shame to take this down. It's a beautiful tree. There's nothing wrong with it." And I had to shout back with a show of dumb female resistance—because if I agreed with him we wouldn't have a garden— "Oh, but we're really worried that branches will come down on your wires." Then I fled into the house, overwhelmed with guilt.

The next spring we began to plant—first large seeds that could be poked right into the ground through the layer of stuff on top: Country Gentleman corn, Provider and scarlet runner beans, Big Max pumpkins. Then we dug deep holes through the accumulated litter and rotted sod for the vegetables we set out as plants: tomatoes, peppers, cauliflower, and Brussels sprouts. Later, when we had chopped trenches the length of rows and filled them with fine compost, came the smaller seeds: lettuce, carrots, beets, herbs. Near the street, right next to the oak stump in the leaf litter and sawdust, we also planted Latham red raspberries, because I remembered that raspberries liked rotting wood.

By this time, I was an aging graduate student teaching two huge classes, working on my doctorate in nutrition education, and gaining a certain notoriety for saying that I thought the American food system was using resources unsustainably. I mention this because I was interviewed in the summer of 1974 by a classy trade magazine called *Food Management* and they sent a photographer out to shoot me in my garden planted through the turf. I know it was a spectacular sight; I have pictures. In one, I am standing, tanned and smiling, up to my armpits in a forest of zucchini; in another, lush corn stalks tower two feet over my head. All of it thriving in the mixture of chopped oak leaves, garbage, old newspapers, and worm droppings, which together with the decaying turf and the years of accumulated Scott's lawn food, produced a burst of fertility. The next spring, when we began to actually *dig* the garden, we realized why our home county was called *Rock*land. It would be years before we reached that level of fertility again.

That year, 1975, was a landmark one for us—in the garden and otherwise. Our seed order showed plans for an ambitious planting: beets, broccoli, Brussels sprouts, cabbage, carrots, chicory, cucumbers, fennel, lettuce, okra, onions, peas, spinach, and two kinds of tomatoes—fourteen different kinds of seeds and two bunches of onion plants. My garden map also shows potatoes, so evidently we put in a serious garden. I doubt that I did much gardening that spring, however, since I was completing my dissertation, and in the space of two weeks in May, I took my oral exam and became department chair (not a recommended career path!). I have no recollection of anything other than stress. Alan probably stepped in to take charge of starting the garden, wisely escaping from the house where I was trying to write my thesis.

But the year's more important gardening event took Alan away before the harvest. He had been hired to teach the fall quarter at the University of California, Santa Cruz. I would not have chosen the year of my first academic appointment to have a bi-coastal marriage. But the California interlude made a permanent mark on our gardening life, for the Santa Cruz campus was the center of a remarkable gardening experiment that fascinated both of us—me as a maverick nutritionist, Alan as an artist.

In 1967, a Shakespearean actor turned gardener-mystic named Alan Chadwick had come to the Santa Cruz campus from England, invited by some of the more "advanced" faculty. There, despite the hostility of the more conventional academics, he had been allowed to start gardening on an impossible campus site, a rocky, precipitous hillside overgrown with brush and young trees. With the help of students, he turned the hillside into a breathtakingly beautiful flower-vegetable-fruit-herb garden from which he and the apprentices prepared communal meals.

By the time my Alan got to Santa Cruz, Chadwick had decamped north after a terminal fight with the trustees. But the garden still flourished under the guidance of former apprentices, and the techniques Chadwick taught had been extended to a campus farm that operated on a flatter piece of ground well down the hillside from the garden. Alan fell in love with the productive beauty of the farm. He spent mornings there learning about double-digging and raised beds, and afternoons leading his art classes in sketching vegetables.

The spring following his return, we began attempting to double-dig our two-year-old vegetable garden, which had, until then, survived on the fertility of the former lawn. I say "began" and "attempting" because beneath the upper six inches, the soil was hard red clay. And buried in the red clay were formidable boulders tangled in the massive roots that had once braced the now-felled giant oak.

I won't detail the process of double-digging; it can be found in words and pictures in the incomparable manual, *How to Grow More Vegetables Than You Ever Thought Possible in Less Space Than You Can Imagine*, by former Chadwick apprentice John Jeavons. In outline, however, the process involves removing the top foot of soil from a bed three to five feet wide, using a digging fork to break up the now exposed lower layer, and then replacing the top layer enriched with compost and fertilizer. Because the process adds so much air down to a level of nearly two feet, the soil is lofted, and a finished bed looks like a long, newly dug grave.

Fortunately, Alan and I had no one to bury, because our "grave-digging" was excruciatingly slow. Our red clay soil could have been used to make ashtrays. That "exposed lower layer" had lain there untouched for years and had no intention of giving in to the whims of novice double-diggers. With two of us working at it—levering up to the surface boulders too heavy for either of us to lift—the first 4-by-20-foot bed took two weeks to dig. That year we dug only two. The rest of the garden we turned over and planted in the usual shallow way.

Ultimately, the 30-by-40-foot plot, opened to the sun by the oak's demise, became the site of nine double-dug beds, four feet wide and varied in length to fit the irregular garden perimeter. The soil became deeply soft, filled with tiny pellets of worm droppings that kept it so loose you could plunge your arm in up to the elbow. This was the spot on which we gradually matured into what I suppose one would call year-round gardeners—addicts who were sometimes still harvesting in December and often began again in late January or early February when a brief thaw allowed us to grub parsnips out of the ground.

Although it now seems obvious that vegetable self-reliance is possible in the northeast—after all, the settlers did it with many fewer storage possibilities than we have—it didn't seem that way when we started. Like everyone in our generation, we had been raised on stories of desperate pioneers, struggling to survive. When I made the decision to work toward eating only what we grew, the likelihood that we would ever reach that goal seemed remote. Our mutation from vegetable gardeners to mini-farmers evolved very slowly, over time. We learned as we went.

We tried sweet bell peppers, not very successfully at the beginning, but it was several years before we tried eggplant or sweet potatoes. Our early attempts to grow garlic were pitiful, since we followed instructions in some newspaper gardening column to plant the cloves in spring and usually got back just about what we planted. Then we learned to plant garlic cloves in the fall so they could push their roots down into the soil before it was deeply frozen. We gave up early on spinach. It was a magnet to leaf miners, who left their little white trails under the skin of the fleshy crinkled leaves and reduced the plants to crumpled brown blobs.

Through all these years of gardening, we never laid down a step-by-step path to self-sufficiency, but I did keep garden records. At first I simply kept copies of seed orders; my plot plans and notes from the 1960s focus on the time of bloom of various flowering trees, shrubs, perennials, and bulbs. Through the 1960s and 1970s, our vegetable orders changed little. We added Waltham butternut squash from time to time, a great hairy scrambling vine that defied squash borers and produced so much that half of last year's crop often remained in storage when planting time arrived! More than once we tried okra, green or purple, acorn squash, and pumpkins.

Most of our novel choices in those days were curiosity driven: "Early Purple Head cauliflower sounds interesting," one of us would say. "I wonder if we could grow it." It grew all right. Huge. And made a purple cauliflower atop its giant stalk. We concluded that cauliflower in general wasn't worth the space it occupied. In 1978, a giant "melon" squash from the English seed company Thompson and Morgan climbed all over the arbor at the garden entrance and then leaped a path to the adjoining shed and garage, producing so overwhelmingly that we stopped growing it. One squash could feed more people than we wanted to have to dinner, and anyway, after six months in storage, it *didn't*, as promised, taste like a melon, more like an old squash. Green soybeans were a successful novelty that we never omitted after our first experimental year; they freeze wonderfully and always stay *al dente* when cooked, even after freezing. Twenty-five years later you can find them in some markets as *edamame*.

Our potato-growing started early, with Red Norland, a variety that produces bright red tubers—easy to see, fun to dig. That was the only variety we grew for several years even though they needed to be eaten soon, started sprouting in storage in November, and were useless by January. When we got serious about self-reliance, we learned that other varieties stored better, even through the winter.

As I think back, it seems clear that the first serious sign of our move toward vegetal self-reliance was when we stopped planting everything in the spring. Up to then, we had planted "the garden" all at once as soon as the risk of frost was past. Now we learned that we

could start some things earlier: lettuce, peas, spinach, carrots, potatoes, and then wait until I had finished teaching in mid-May or early
June to have a planting orgy.

For years we battled slugs for our carrot seedlings. Those slender
green shoots emerging from the ground were perfect appetizers. A
grazing slug on early spring patrol could clear a bed in one night. And
the broccoli plants carefully started indoors were usually killed or
crippled by root maggots, whose presence was announced when the
plants' crisp blue-green leaves abruptly wilted in the midday sun of
May.

One summer, it occurred to us that when the carrots and broccoli
were ready to harvest, everything else was too, overwhelming us with
produce. Planted later, carrots could stay in the ground long after the
tomatoes and eggplant had succumbed to the first frost. And carrots
newly emerging in late June or early July would be of much less interest to slugs who had so many other things to enjoy.

As for the broccoli, the flies that laid maggot eggs at the bases of its
stems flew only in early spring. If our garden held no broccoli seedlings to invest their future in, they would go elsewhere. Broccoli
seeded outdoors in early June comes on strong just as the basil and
tomatoes are in full production, which allows for a lovely pasta dish.

PASTA WITH BROCCOLI AND PESTO

Make a 1-cup batch of pesto. In processor or blender purée:
  *1½ cup fresh **basil leaves***
  *1 clove **garlic***
  *2 tablespoons **pine nuts***
Add:
  *2 tablespoons **butter***
  *2 tablespoons **olive oil***
Blend, and remove to small bowl. Stir in:
  *¼-cup mixture of grated **Parmesan and Pecorino Romano cheese***
Set aside.

Core and cut into bite-sized wedges:

*1 large (or 2 to 3 small) red ripe **tomato***

Cut into small flowerettes:

*1 bunch **broccoli***

Trim broccoli stems, cut into bite-sized pieces, and steam until crisp and tender (3 to 5 minutes).

In a saucepan heat:

*3 tablespoons **olive oil***

Add:

*1 clove **garlic**, finely chopped*
the broccoli
*½ teaspoon (or more) **hot red pepper flakes***

Cook over medium heat, stirring gently to warm through. Hold.

Cook in boiling salted water:

*1 pound **rigatoni or other tubular pasta***

Drain, reserving a little boiling water to thin pesto.

When ready to serve, put cooked pasta into a bowl, add one or two tablespoons hot pasta water to pesto, stir until thinned, and pour over pasta. Salt to taste. Add broccoli and tomato, and toss to blend. Serve immediately.

Note: I use a pasta pot that has a steamer basket over it, so I steam the broccoli while the pasta is cooking, and add it to the olive oil/garlic/pepper mix just about the time I drain the pasta.

Over time, our success at extending the season evolved into a decision that we should try growing all our own vegetables and as much of our fruit as we could. I've had trouble, however, remembering just when that choice was made. The closing essay for my 1978 book, *The Feeding Web,* about problems in the food system, concludes with a tip of the pen to the term "relocalization," which I saw as encompassing "many of the changes that look most promising where the food supply is concerned." Research then going on about a largely Vermont-based diet seemed extreme to many people, I said, but "in a time when a snowstorm or truckers' strike can cut off all food from a city the size of Boston, such research is surely at least as potentially useful as that aimed at designing one more packaged cake mix." But words are not deeds, and I talked about the idea of eating locally long before we started seriously trying to do it.

However, my professional commitment to living by what I believe caught up with me. Sometime in the 1980s—after one of my fiery speeches about problems in the food system—I was challenged once too often about what on earth I thought residents of the frozen north were going to eat in the dead of winter. Responding to the (incorrect) assumption that I favored exclusion of all citrus north of the Mason-Dixon line, I learned to point out that midwesterners got their vitamin C by eating cabbage and potatoes long before Europeans "discovered" California or Florida and began growing oranges.

Ultimately, however, theory was not enough. Like Farley Mowat, the Canadian naturalist who consumed field mice to prove that wolves were living on rodents rather than endangered caribou, I realized that I would need to eat locally myself to prove that a human being could do so. I never meant our food growing to be a demonstration that every New Yorker could feed herself entirely from her own land. That would have been naive. The effort was always intended to demonstrate what *could* be grown locally, provided consumers encouraged farmers to grow all the variety they could for their neighborhoods. I wanted to prove that eating locally was feasible, healthy, and even tasty—if northeastern eaters would learn to enjoy living on what nature allowed.

I remember setting myself the goal of writing a very local (Rockland County) cookbook, showing what you could eat in the difficult months, and it was then that I realized that I needed a good harvest calendar. I had a notebook in which I wrote down what was going on in the garden through the year, but it was incomplete and inconsistent enough to be frustrating. I didn't want to compete for the earliest tomato prize, but when *did* our first tomato ripen? How long did the tomato sauce we put away in the freezer last? When did gaps occur in the yearly production and how might they be filled? If we decided to use only produce from the garden, could we do it? When would we be reduced to foods we didn't produce? What could we plant to compensate for that?

I made a card for each vegetable we grew, with the months listed across the top and the years listed down the left side. Then I recorded when we sowed, when we planted out, when we began to harvest, how long the harvest continued, and how long we had crops stored in the cold cellar and the freezer. And gradually we extended our harvest season. We learned to sow early spinach under a floating row cover that kept out leaf miners. When the spinach went to seed in the summer heat, we pulled it out and planted parsnips in the same bed, as a winter crop. When we harvested broccoli heads, we learned to cut the stem very close to its root, just above the first two leaves, so that the sturdy stalk wouldn't send up tiny new shoots from each of fifteen leaf nodes, but just two vigorous new shoots to produce a second crop of broccoli heads late into the fall. We learned to grow enough storage onions from seed to meet our needs all year; and we learned that potatoes can be long keepers as well as short keepers, that they come in early, middle, and late varieties, and that you can readily grow at home not only white, but yellow, red, and blue potatoes that sell for gourmet prices in the stores. Potatoes became a mainstay of our cold-season diet.

Another winter mainstay was kale, a green that can sometimes hold out till spring and can—if forcibly discouraged from expressing its sexuality by alert removal of flowering stalks—produce for a second season. My romance with kale might never have occurred had Alan not been artist-in-residence at the Cape Cod National Seashore one fall. He was given kale—the only thing left in their gardens in October—by his Portuguese neighbors who appreciated his efforts to cook for himself. They taught him to steam kale with the Portuguese sausage *linguisa*. The next year, when we were still in the small shaded north garden at Congers, Alan insisted that we plant kale.

My relationship with kale was decidedly unfriendly at the time, as is reflected in some remarks about a garden I once tried in Maine, which I came across when writing this chapter. To my surprise, that garden contained kale, a memory I had totally suppressed. I wrote "N.G. bitter, blue gray, wasted." That about says it.

But while I didn't *like* kale, I went along with Alan's request that we *plant* it because I judged it morally essential to learn to like this incredibly nutritious vegetable. We planted the seeds in spring, and it did well. But each time that summer, when Alan would suggest we cook some, I would protest, "Oh, it's hardy, and other things will freeze. Let's wait till fall." I really dreaded having to eat it. In September, I gave in; Alan cooked some up in a heavy frying pan with a little *linguisa*—and I loved it.

Later I learned to make wonderful Kale and Potato Soup. This recipe has been sufficiently modified from its original sources that I feel comfortable claiming it.

JOAN'S KALE AND POTATO SOUP

If you are not using canned beans, cook 1 cup **kidney, pinto,** or **brown beans** before beginning soup, and if you're not a vegetarian, boil half a **chorizo** or **kielbasa** with beans for 15 minutes during the cooking.

Steam in a large kettle until wilted and bright green:
   *4 cups finely cut **kale leaves***
Cool and hold.

Heat in a soup pot:
   *3 tablespoons **olive oil***

Add:

> *1 medium **yellow or red onion**, diced*
> *3 to 6 cloves **garlic**, minced*
> *¹/₂ teaspoon **chili flakes***
> *1 to 2 **bay leaves***

Sauté over low heat until onion is soft but not brown.

Add:

> *1 pound **red or yellow potatoes**, cut into ¹/₂-inch cubes*
> *2 teaspoons **nutritional yeast** (optional)*
> *6 cups **water or stock** (bean or bean/chorizo water may be used)*

Bring to a boil, and simmer about 15 minutes or until potatoes are tender.

Roughly crush potatoes against side of pot so most are sort of mashed.

Add:

> *2 cups cooked **beans***
> *shredded **kale**, which has been re-chopped finely after steaming*
> *sliced parboiled **chorizo***

Boil 6 to 8 minutes. Serve.

Tender kale, shredded raw, can also substitute for lettuce on Mexican tostadas, or be stuffed into soft tacos with mashed beans and cheese. Kale is much sweeter after the first frost.

And so, in time, we learned how to produce enough vegetables to last us—with the help of the freezer—through the year. And just about the time we had improved our garden soil enough to feed ourselves from it, we decided it was time to move.

2

A New Place

Something tells me I won't be here long—
I got my suitcase packed
And my trunk's already gone.

—L. C. Williams, "I Won't Be Here Long"

OUR YOUNGER SON TOLD ME—when the move from Congers was underway—that he had always felt our old house didn't suit me. He was right. We had purchased it thirty-six years earlier, in 1958, a young couple with a one-year-old son and a second on the way. As a California native who grew up outdoors when Southern California was near-rural, I literally could not imagine raising children in Manhattan. So we had looked for something outside the city, within commuting distance, and economically feasible. That meant a $7,000 down payment with my profit sharing from Time Inc., and a mortgage we could carry with Alan's minimal income from part-time art teaching. In 1958 that bought us a $19,000 house, a sturdy but shabby three-story Victorian on a half-acre of land. The imposing white elephant (*not* a metaphor) appealed to Alan's notion of how an artist should live; I yielded simply because we could afford it. We had looked at lots of places we couldn't afford; in a community long shunned by real estate agents because it had once been chopped into unbuildable 25-foot lots, we could (just barely) pay for that large enclosed space and the clump of eight lots it sat on.

Alas, however, no money was left over to make its oversized rooms into the home of my dreams. As a conventionally brought up young woman, I had fairly bland ideas of what a "house" ought to look like. Bookcases made of bricks and boards didn't appropriately furnish 15-

by-30-foot rooms with 10 foot high ceilings. But once we had mailed off our $90 monthly mortgage payment, paid for enough electricity to light our way and enough gas to make thirteen uninsulated rooms barely habitable, we had $30 per week on which to live. Commuting to New York to teach, Alan spent half of that on gas, tolls and parking. I spread the remaining $15 over food, clothing, furniture, home decoration, entertainment, and luxuries. So we furnished with scavenged bricks and old boards, plus my Manhattan mother-in-law's castoffs.

I was unusually well equipped for coping, since my inventive engineer father had taught me much of what he knew. When the Great Depression hit three years after my sister was born and months after my first birthday, my parents stopped at two—both daughters. Denied a son, my father had to settle for working with me. He could do anything in the way of construction or reconstruction; I had helped mix cement, roof a patio, and build concrete block walls; I had repaired lamps, made electrical cords for Dad's unsuccessful appliance store, and taken on a number of other "manly" chores.

Alan, by contrast, was raised in a three-son family who hired local youths to put up storm windows. When we were courting, I helped him repair and paint the walls of his first apartment. Unlike most of the men I had met in New York, he was not only not threatened by my skills—he coveted them. They certainly came in handy in our new home.

The land, like the house, challenged the impoverished. The house faced west, tight up against a north-south running street. Two 60-foot swamp maples flanked its entrance. The towering black walnut tree that occupied the shallow backyard competed successfully with anything else I tried to grow there, including lawn. And the rest of the half-acre—made up of large north and south lawns—was shaded by five giant oaks.

The house had been built, in 1898, on a full acre, and subsequently owned by a family whose breadwinner helped landscape the 1939 World's Fair. He brought home living leftovers, giant remnants of which dotted the half acre we had purchased. These included an over-grown border of 100-foot-tall trees on the north, among them a magnificent copper beech, a blue cedar, and a larch. Crowded together along the back of the lot to the south of the house were a collection of native rhododendron and mountain laurel, dumped there by post–World War II owner-renovators who banished to the edges everything that couldn't be mowed. The scale of the existing trees made whatever tiny shrubs I could afford to buy nearly pointless. We once splurged $25 on twenty-five baby rhododendrons to "fill in" under two 100-foot oak trees bracketing the southwest corner. For at least a decade, they struggled against drought and tree roots to look significant. Fifteen years later, they were magnificent.

Frustrated by my inability to achieve visual satisfaction, indoors or out, I made miserable the lives of my nearest and dearest by my constant attempts to do so. I bought 50¢ chairs and $2.00 lamps at the local auction, and then scraped, oiled, steel wooled, caned, polished, upholstered, and rewired to fill one or another gaping hole in the indoor landscape. Then, in the mid-1960s, with my sons in school at least half the day, I found part-time work at home. Given our financial circumstances, the tiny salary seemed inspiring. My relation to the house and grounds was ultimately most improved, however, by the fact that as the 1960s ended, I began graduate school and lacked time to worry about anything else.

Our sons went off to college a few years later, giving me for the first time a room of my own for an office. I earned an advanced degree, became a professor and department chair, and in the late 1980s, as Alan and I approached our seventh decades, our finances finally allowed us to have the mansion elegantly painted outside, to get it mostly fixed up inside, and to hire a cleaning woman once a week.

I should add here, because it makes our later exertions more predictable, that in the early 1980s, we made a dramatic indoor change—almost entirely with our own hands. We moved Alan's third-floor studio downstairs to the living room and moved the living room to the third floor, where we created a beautiful, tent-like space by rip-

ping out the walls and ceilings of Alan's office, his studio, his painting
storage room, and the hallway—and lining every nook we uncovered
with wainscot board. An architect, whom we called in for advice on
what we could pull out without bringing the house down, gave us a
carte blanche for stud removal, but told us later he never believed we
could carry it off. We did, and in the process learned more about
rafters, beams, kneewalls and tin-shingled roofs than we would have
chosen to know.

By this time, one of the swamp maples, the black walnut, and two
of the oaks had come down—the one we removed and another that
fell of its own volition, rotted at heart. The vegetable garden had been
moved to the south lawn, and since plants, like children, finally grow
up and fill out, the landscaping we had added began to take the form
I had long imagined. We now had a house and yard everyone but me
loved: a house that welcomed evergreen roping, wreaths, 18-foot
Christmas trees, and summer suppers on the porch; grounds that
hosted Easter egg hunts and summer solstice camp outs. It was lovely.
But for me, everything about it spelled work. Work I had done, work
it still needed, work forever into the future.

On the south, I had transmuted the vast spaces of inherited grass
into a more complex mix of vegetables, flowers, shrubs, and rock garden. On the north, we left the lawn unmowed to become a meadow—
until Mother Nature revealed that unmowed meadows under oak
trees grow into living illustrations of the old saw about the future of
tiny acorns. Our decision to move was provoked, however, not by a
burgeoning oak grove, but by a wake-up call that came in the mail.

Sometime toward the end of the 1980s, the postman brought a
Christmas letter from a literary couple whose holiday list carried our
name because we had once mail-ordered a book from them. Although
we had never met, their Christmas messages were welcome because
their lives were worth reading about. This particular year had been an
especially difficult one. Both of them had been sick, she with cancer,
he with some sort of heart problem. Conscious of their own mortality,
they were reflecting on how they wished to spend their final years.

They wanted to age, they had decided, in a house sized appropriately for them, in a village where most things were within walking or
biking distance, near a library, with a decent restaurant or two nearby,
and friends all around. All of this made good sense to me. Yet here was
I in a three-story Victorian house that never "fit;" with neighbors I
seldom spoke to, on a half-acre of land that needed endless maintain-
ing, on top of a hill that placed formidable obstacles in the way of
casual walking or biking to a town that had little to offer in the way of
interest when I got there! Our local library was a 10-minute ride away
on a hard-to-exit, hard-to-re-enter, bike-treacherous main road. By
all the criteria on our correspondents' list, our place flunked.

Over the next few months, I urged Alan to reflect on *our* criteria.
His first geographic thought was Santa Cruz, where he had taught
several times, and where, as a visiting faculty family, we had lived in a
townhouse nestled among redwoods on the lovely hilltop campus.
My highly developed aversion to what Southern California had become did not extend to Northern California. The coastline there reminded me of childhood trips to visit my father's cousin on the Russian River. I wasn't certain, however, that I could tolerate moving so
far from friends and children. I suggested nearby Nyack on the
Hudson River as an alternative, and occasionally over the next year or
two Alan and I talked about an ultimate move—never choosing between the two.

Our needs were simple: a smaller, lower-maintenance house—no
more three stories of painted clapboard and leaking roof valleys. I
wanted space for a vegetable garden—no more shrubs, hedges, trees,
or lawns that always needed shaping, shearing, pruning, or mowing.
Alan needed a studio. There was no urgency. We didn't *need* to move.
But when my left knee began clicking as I went downstairs, it focussed
my mind.

Alan liked shopping, so sometime in 1990 he spoke to several
Nyack real estate agents, and one or the other would call from time to
time to tell us about a listing. Thinking back now to those prospective-
home viewing trips, I see that they should have alerted us to an eccen-

tricity in our goals. Neither of us paid much attention to the houses we saw, except to make sure that they were smaller than the one we had! We knew from bloody experience that houses could be changed. But we had to have some sunny land, and we quickly noticed how often small lots in old towns had yards shaded by massive irremovable trees—on other people's property.

Neither of us recognized how odd we must have seemed as house buyers. No sun, no sale. We saw two places that might have worked—if a few trees were cut—but even the preferred one didn't seem like something we'd rush to move to. We could fix it up, we agreed, and rent it out until we were ready to move. By the time we were ready to ask serious questions, it was off the market.

Santa Cruz remained a possibility until Alan's last long appointment there in the spring of 1992. Its foggy summers had already given us pause; in some locations home-grown essentials such as peppers and tomatoes were out of the question. And on that trip we lived off campus, at the edge of "downtown," and realized for the first time that Santa Cruz was a community on wheels, no different in that sense from the rest of California. We decided to stay on the east coast.

As we continued to look in Nyack, fate intervened by moving the woman who cut our hair to a salon in Piermont, a small village south of Nyack on the west bank of the Hudson River. One October day, Alan came home freshly trimmed with the news that he had seen a "For Sale" sign and—ever curious—had asked the real estate agent whose sign it was to take him there. The house sat on the river side of Piermont's main street, he said, and had a boardwalk. He conveyed no particular excitement but thought I should "at least look."

When I did look, a day or two later, nothing about the place we parked in front of matched my vision of a future home. The house was a slab-sided box with gray concrete-like walls and maroon trim. It sat tight to the street, pavement up to its neck, facing west on a very narrow lot that continued invisibly east behind the house, toward the river. At the street, eight feet or so of cracked concrete paving separated the property from an undistinguished brown stucco row house on its north. On the south, a four-foot walkway to the back of the house was separated by an elderly chainlink fence from a gravelled parking area terminating at its far end in two run-down garages. The neighborhood was decidedly . . . shabby.

The interior of the house turned out to be only marginally less depressing. From the entrance you stepped *down* into the first floor—a sign, as we later learned, that the building was old enough to have had the street repeatedly raised in front of it. The stairway that led up from the front door to the main living space tilted noticeably down toward the center of the house. The kitchen had a faux beamed ceiling and a (new) wide-plank floor. Behind it was a shallow living room whose shed roof sloped down to low windows looking over a long narrow yard that ran to a boardwalk edging the Hudson. The windows also gave a wide-angle view of the cold November river and of a motley collection of motorized vehicles—boats, bulldozers, trucks, and a seaplane!—in the yard to the north.

Abutting the property to the south and also ending at a boardwalk on the riverbank was a trapezoidal public plot of grass with a flagpole in its middle: an unimproved park named Parelli after a former village official. Running alongside the rest of the backyard, occupying the hundred-odd feet between the shallow park at the river end and the parking lot on the street, was a wasteland of weeds, rock, trash, telephone poles, old cars, and boats—anything and everything that had been washed up in major storms or discarded by the neighbors as too big for the trash collectors.

We looked quickly at the three tiny second-floor bedrooms, then walked from the living room outdoors onto a rough cantilevered deck from which wooden stairs led down to the yard. Descending the steps, we headed for the river into a bitter November wind. Old chainlink fences (sometimes more than one) and collections of old vines and weed trees edged both property lines. Halfway out, a giant willow leaned across a crushed chainlink fence into the park. As Alan walked ahead, charming the owner, I followed grudgingly, thoroughly chilled, feigning interest to humor them both. Halfway to the river, I turned and looked back . . . and knew I had to live there.

As a person who checks *Consumer Reports* before buying a can opener, I am still at a loss to explain that moment, except to conclude that I fell in love. Did the narrow yard overhung with a giant willow remind me of growing up on a narrow lot in Southern California and playing in sun-baked schoolyards cooled by willow-like pepper trees? I don't know. Later I was to experience the breath-catching sunrises, the moonlight that tracked across the river, the endless sky, but on that first day the weather was wretched.

My infatuation seemed decidedly rash. We were anticipating our second and final house purchase in almost four decades of marriage. Soon after we bought our first one, thirty-five years earlier, I had learned at a Cooperative Extension lawn workshop that a third of all Americans moved every year. We didn't. Buying this property would be the single most expensive undertaking of my entire life, single or married; yet I was prepared to leap blindly. The house appeared to be in seriously bad shape and turned out to be worse; it had a downstairs apartment neither of us had ever seen. I didn't care. I wanted to live on that spot.

Alan did not have to be convinced. He had seen it first, after all, and he was entranced by the river, which he had loved and painted for years. He hardly dared to imagine that one day he might *live* on the Hudson. So we made a bid. When it was accepted—an absurdly high price—my reactions, recorded in letters to friends, were as intemperate as my initial decision.

> . . . The great and glorious Gussow news is that we have just bought a wreck of a house in a wonderful community called Piermont. It has a piece of flat land that runs to the water, just big enough for a giant vegetable garden and little else. It's a block from the center of a tiny community (2,130 people) which is attracting more and more people like us. It was a factory town until 1982, a very "unfashionable" place. The factories went out of business as did most of the shops on the one-block "downtown."

Then the "quaint" main street was discovered by Woody Allen for "The Purple Rose of Cairo." The local joke was that Woody had to upgrade everything to make it look like a Depression-era town. There are good places for walking and, within two blocks, a wonderful food store, a library, and all sorts of marvelous restaurants! Also, we are right next to a long landing out into the Hudson that has mostly non-visible condos at its near end; beyond that is a public park with reeds and water that makes you feel you are somewhere in Maine. And it's all much closer to the city than we are now.

We're totally psyched, though our friends who have seen it find us a bit batty since the house is really a disaster. What I think is hard for them to understand is that we are buying a way of life, not a house. My only regret is that it will probably take us a year-and-a-half minimum to get in, and I wish we had done it ten years ago so I would have more time to live there! I suddenly realize how much of my life I have devoted to being museum-keeper (as my niece put it) in this glorious and impractical house. It's now in perfect shape, but I've lost interest in working so hard to keep the whole place up. Half an acre of oak leaves every fall, etc. I can find much better things to do with my time. . . . We are very fortunate, and we know it.

So we bought the house, after which we set out to learn just what we owned. Although early maps of the town showed only some unidentified structure on the site, both the prior owners and the real estate agent seemed to think our new house dated from the early 1900s, and might once have been an Oddfellows hall. We knew that forty or fifty years earlier, a large Italian family had fit a two-story apartment into the space, and we had seen, through a trapdoor on the second floor, a brown plaster ceiling with a medallion three feet above the ceiling joists of the existing second floor.

So we began to search the deed books, aware of my historian sister's warning that the history of buildings was hard to tease out because most title records described only the lot. We were in luck. Working back through the transactions in the courthouse plat books, we discovered that each deed described the property as beginning "four feet south of the existing building which is Lodge #73 of the Independent Order of the Oddfellows." In 1849, the entries stopped. That seemed to be it. We had bought a 150-year-old Oddfellows hall!

Why did we fail to imagine that 150 years on the edge of a Hudson River floodplain might not be good news for a building? Why did it not occur to us that such proximity to water might have hollowed the bones of the house we had purchased? The answer seems to be that we were blinded by love, and bent now on restoring an antique. So, alas, was our architect, who failed to notice any of the obvious signs that something structural might be seriously amiss.

A few days later, some old friends came to visit and we took them down to see "our" house. The husband tried unsuccessfully to hide his misgivings; his wife, seeing me hopelessly in love, tried to be more positive. Later, when we stood looking at two small downstairs rooms I had barely glanced at that first remarkable day, she stepped away from a partition she was leaning on, bringing the wallpaper with her. A dampness problem? Of course. The owner and my friend both apologized; I waved away their concerns.

My dismissive attention to the first floor was consistent. I first saw the apartment that occupied the river side of the ground floor just before we closed, when the tenant moved out. Would we have backed off if both of us had looked earlier and found mushrooms growing from a vast hole in the floor? Probably not. (There were no mushrooms; only a battered trap door leading to a very wet crawl space.) We planned to gut the house anyway, since Alan needed to carve a large studio from the multitude of first floor rooms. Why worry about the surface? We were going down to the studs, and I couldn't wait to start.

On Thanksgiving Day, we took our older son down to see what we were about to buy. When we asked him afterward what he thought, he tried hard to be tactful. "Well, it's obviously your dream; I don't think

I should comment on your dream." True to form, I smiled at his obvious dismay. He couldn't imagine what it would become, I thought, but he would see.

"What about the inspection?" any intelligent homeowner will now ask. Of course—the inspection. We were innocents, recall, despite having owned a house for nearly forty years. I don't remember that we had an inspector for the Congers purchase, although the bank must surely have insisted. We called the inspector recommended by the real estate agent ("You did what?"). Much later, when the purchasers of our Congers home came with their inspector to look over that house, we learned what we should have done when our prospective home was inspected. But we didn't. Our inspector went down to Piermont—alone.

When his report arrived, it was sobering. Nothing rated higher than "satisfactory." Even in our entranced state, we recognized that to be a dubious recommendation. Trying to be brave, we called him back and urged with all the sincerity we could muster, "Be honest. Are you trying to tell us this house cannot be saved? We're quite prepared to demolish it if necessary." "Absolutely not," he said emphatically. If that was what he meant, he would have said so. So we smiled at each other and decided we could save our Oddfellows hall.

Two days after we agreed to buy, the *New York Times* carried a story on the front page of its metropolitan section about our new community reinventing itself from a run-down mill town. The story was dated December 5, 1992, the day when the storm of the century roared down the Hudson, inundating Piermont's riverfront, tearing up "our" boardwalk, and flooding our soon-to-be home.

Going down to look, we found the back yard under water from the boardwalk to the back door. A scraggy-looking fishpond full of plastic stuff driven in from the not-too-clean Hudson flowed up the yard into the ground floor of the house. Nature had spoken; the house was going to have to be raised. As someone who taught about humanity's impact on the planet, I believed that greenhouse warming was real, which meant sea-level rise in our lifetimes and more frequent unsettled weather—this "hundred-year" storm might well repeat next year! What we were referring to as our final resting place short of the grave had to last at least as long as we did.

The next day, our younger son, who had been wildly enthusiastic since we first mentioned the house, arrived from Michigan to see it. We sloshed with him through the grassy town park, trying to reach the river end of our property without getting wet to the knees. There we climbed onto the storm-broken boardwalk and looked toward the house, surveying a back yard still nine inches deep in water. Seth remained determinedly enthusiastic. He loved the town and assured us it was great. When we walked downtown through giant puddles, he laughingly teased us, "Yeah, Mom, I think you and Dad could hobble this far."

A little over a week later, a much less enthusiastic visitor, an old friend and his new wife who were renovating a house across the river, arrived in Congers for Christmas breakfast. After breakfast, we headed down to Piermont to tour the house. My journal entry describes his reaction:

> CHRISTMAS DAY, 1992—J. is incredibly negative and keeps saying "you're going to have to tear it down." The first few times I say, "Well, we know that's an option, but we hope to save it." He keeps pointing out that the roof is crooked, the floors are crooked, etc., and that all that is a symbol of how bad the structure is and that it can't be saved. Finally, I can't take any more. I'm tense enough about preparing to spend in one gulp more money than I have ever spent in my life, and as we're walking out to our cars I say somewhat more testily than usual, "Would you please cut that out! We've *heard* you. We're willing to take the house down if we have to, but you don't have to keep insisting."

I may have been a bit too harsh. We didn't see them again for a year!

3

Garden and House

I have cut down on many things, but nothing short of total
decrepitude could make me decide to give up the vegetables. . . .
Scarlett O'Hara grubbing for yams evidently made
more of an impression than I realized at the time.

—Eleanor Perenyi, *Green Thoughts*

I'VE OFTEN WONDERED what our future Piermont neighbors told
each other about the new folks on the block. One summer, this older
couple closes a sale on a house; a year later, after months of gutting,
they have nothing but a hole in the ground and a flourishing vegetable garden running almost to the river. The neighbors may have
speculated among themselves, but the only one who commented on
our priorities was the cigar-chewing, loud-mouthed man next door, a
village native. Incensed by our replacing an ugly collection of chainlink with a handsome wooden fence, on what he belatedly decided
was his property, he shouted "What ya out here for anyhow? Why
aren't ya working inside?" Looking at what was then our half-gutted
house, it was a logical question.

The equally logical answer was that we liked gardening more than
gutting. Less easy to explain is why at least a year earlier, even before
we *owned* the Piermont property, we had begun to grow food there
while our garden in Congers was still producing overwhelmingly.

Our agreed-upon closing date, April 15, passed without contact
from the sellers. By the 24th of May, frantic with impatience, we
learned that their lawyer was on vacation and no closing was possible
until mid-June. The season was moving along toward summer. We
needed to clean out the house and get it rebuilt before winter. We
wanted to convert the yard to vegetable beds and do some trial plant-

ing to see how productive the land was. Clearly we couldn't begin gutting the house until the sellers moved out. When they told us we could begin to garden while they were still on site, our impatience over the delayed closing overwhelmed our misgivings.

In late May, Alan drove down to Piermont with plans to dig a bed and plant some leftover tomato and eggplant seedlings. He came home exhausted and exultant. He had gone as far as possible from the house to dig—onto the raised riverbank at what the British call the bottom of the garden, next to the boardwalk, which was still torn up from the storm of the century. It was wonderful down by the water, he said. It felt like Maine. So two days later we took a picnic lunch and a scraggly-looking potted palm down to the river. I made this entry in my journal.

MAY 27—It was a beautiful sunny day and we trooped off looking like migrant workers carrying plants, our giant potted palm, shovels, pruners, etc. When we got to Piermont and unloaded, we walked out to the water and—after I admired Alan's garden bed— we picnicked looking out over the river. There was a wonderful sense, sitting out there, of being in a resort. It's not really private at all, with sights and sounds of boats getting ready to move out of the boat yard on the north, with people walking and sitting on the boardwalk to the south. But after all, you don't have complete privacy at the beach either. Down by the water, space is shared. Farther back, the yard seems very private. Our first Piermont picnic was open-faced salami, onion, pepper, and home-dried tomato sandwiches, sweet potato chips, Coke, and an apple.

And then we set to work. Alan wanted to make sure his new plants had enough water. I wanted to aestheticize—using the sod he had removed for his eggplant and tomatoes to fill the corner of the bulkhead that had washed out in the storm. I began moving sod in a beat-up wheelbarrow we found, while Alan tramped back and forth the 200 feet to the house with a small watering can. Between loads of sod, I picked rocks and old bricks out of the grass—something I had wanted to do since I first saw the place!

We had most of the sod moved when I realized that if we cut back some of the weedy jungle along the south fence, we could put the trimmings in the gaping storm-produced hole I was trying to fill, sod over them, and then cover it all with some compost Alan had dropped there a couple of weeks ago. So I began pruning, eliminating at least one small tree and cutting way back on some other shrubs without opening up the yard too much to the park next door. And Alan moved the trimmings to my landfill! The plan worked fabulously. When we got the whole area almost leveled up, we scraped the compost off of the rough grass onto the new landfill, and put our scruffy potted palm as a kind of marker flag out by the boardwalk. We dug two new holes where the compost had killed the grass, and planted hubbard and butternut squash, which we covered with a bit of dried hay I found by the north fence. A few bricks for edging, a few stakes to indicate where people shouldn't walk. Then I found some leftover black Valentine beans I had brought along, so Alan added fertilizer along the edge of the fill and planted black beans. What an improvement! A lovely, lovely day that vented some of our pent-up energy directed toward the house.

As I read this entry, even I am amused at the elation with which we sixty-plusers were pruning someone else's shrubs, repairing someone else's bulkhead, and cleaning up the bottom of the garden at a house owned and occupied by relative strangers. At the time, it seemed not merely exhilarating, but reasonable. There was the fact that we had leftover plants—tomatoes and eggplant—that would go to waste if they weren't used at Piermont. And we needed to start gardening, we told ourselves, to find out how hard it would be to feed ourselves off this land. Assuming we'd be out of Congers by the following summer, the soil at Piermont would be the only soil we owned. We had to find out what it could produce.

As it turned out, the soil on the riverbank was pretty awful. We didn't know then that the raised bank had been added only a few years earlier, following the hundred-year storm immediately preceding the hundred-year storm we were cleaning up after, so the soil was mostly river sand and fill. The tomato fruits had black-bottom rot caused by water stress, but the plants themselves were a revelation:

The foliage grew so thick that the tomatoes were almost invisible, and the leaves—stimulated by the big sky, the intense sun, and moisture and reflections from the river—were not the light, bright green we were familiar with, but a deep, forest green. The tomatoes and eggplants gloried in the light as much as I did; I was grateful I hadn't known plants could look like that until I had a gardening spot sunny enough to produce such vigor. The black-bottomed plum tomatoes, of course, didn't go to waste. With their bottoms cut off, they could be dried, and, reconstituted by brief heating in a mix of wine and balsamic vinegars, they took part in many Piermont picnics.

Our near-illicit gardening was not limited to tomatoes and eggplant, nor, after our initial hesitant start, was it confined to the riverbank. We knew from experience that sweet potatoes could grow anywhere, so the day after our first Piermont picnic, we picked a section of lawn back a bit from the riverbank. No one had mowed the grass since the winter storm. Organic matter! While Alan powermowed the high grass using a grass catcher, I laid thick layers of the *New York Times* over the doomed section of lawn, and topped them off with bag after bag of grass clippings. Before we went home to Congers, I pushed a soil thermometer through the mat. A few days later, when the thermometer registered 70 degrees Fahrenheit, we chopped slits through the thick paper, and pushed the rooted cuttings into the unyielding turf. They would dig their own way into the unturned soil, feeding on the rotting sod.

We had grown sweet potatoes for many years by the time we planted them at Piermont. Some outside stimulus must have encouraged us to try growing what seems like a southern crop, and I imagine it was the article on sweet potatoes that is still in my files, torn from an old copy of *Organic Gardening*. Sweet potatoes are planted as slips or cuttings, which you can grow yourself from one or more of last year's crop of sweets. We didn't know that when we began, so we bought our first slips—for Georgia Jet, Jewel, Vardaman, and Puerto Rico—from Fred's Plant Farm in Dresden, Tennessee. Cuttings root easily in water, and once planted about fifteen inches apart, each sends out roots underground. At some point—sometimes at several points—these roots swell into fleshy bulges of often grand proportions. We must have been remarkably successful with sweet potatoes even as beginners, because we have a very happy picture of me taken in the 1970s, standing behind a wheelbarrow filled with "the crop." I am smilingly holding a sweet potato plant from which dangle fifteen enormous bulges.

It took us a while, however, to learn how to store these giant gifts through the winter. Right after sweet potatoes are dug, they need to cure for a week or so in a warm and humid place. We learned to put them in boxes near a pan of water and a self-regulating heater set to 80 degrees, with everything covered with a sheet. After a week of curing, the sweets will last until—even *through*—the following summer. But they have to be stored at around 60 degrees, as we learned from unfortunate experience. If you store them where it's cool and damp, as you do white potatoes, they shrink and turn black and that's the end of sweet potatoes for the year.

That first year in Piermont, we dug over fifty pounds of sweets out of the former lawn, but when we rinsed off the soil, much of what looked like dirt didn't disappear. The sweet potatoes were riddled with holes produced by what turned out to be wireworms. I had never met a wireworm until they made their way through our sweet potatoes, but the first time I saw one, I knew what it had to be. They are shaped like skinny worms but made up of multiple segments of shiny yellow-brown armor. When you pick them up (which you need to do if you hope to get rid of them), they writhe like living wires. So you crack them in half with your thumbnail. Unfortunately, you usually find them only *after* they have bored their way through your root crop, often several times, leaving black entrance and exit holes connected by long tunnels lined with grit.

We'd never had sweet potato damage before and had no notion of how to deal with wireworms. Since we grow things we intend to eat, we never think of using pesticides, and none of our organic gardening books provided an answer. So we tried the help table at an organic farming conference that fall. The young man on duty said, "I *hate* wireworms!"—a sentiment I shared. But he offered no further advice.

The following year, we planted our slips in beds where we had forced the turf to rot out by laying garden-bed-sized strips of old carpeting. That second crop was only marginally less damaged. In successive years, however, we gradually won the battle. Since wireworms live and eat for several years, every little one we thumbnailed was one fewer to tunnel through next year's sweet potatoes. Even more helpful was the information that turned up in one of our garden books: Wireworms thrive in wet soil where there has been turf. We had soggy soil and lots of former lawn! The third year, we planted in a bed where the soil was lighter from having been thoroughly dug over for two previous years. The crop was almost undamaged.

Now, I am not unaware that I veered off into sweet potatoes just as Alan and I were beginning to garden at the new house—before we owned it. Nor am I unmindful of the fact that I began this chapter with a teaser about a hole in the ground with a fully planted vegetable garden out back. To cut to the chase as I probably ought to—we had to tear the old house down—leaves out the long-awaited closing at the end of June and the July 4 party that followed where we sat on our own boardwalk with friends and family, ate junk food, and, against a full orange moon, watched fireworks shoot up from the village pier. To shorten the story leaves out the long hot summer Alan and I spent ecstatically gutting our new purchase, taking off and out what turned out to be by weight at the dumping station twelve tons of plaster and lath. It leaves out the ceiling-razing party we held in October, when we invited friends and their children to come sit on the joists of the old brown ceiling the Oddfellows had built and smash down the heavy brown plaster and filthy lath installed 150 years earlier. Those children, who came down looking like demented raccoons when they removed their dust masks, will never be the same.

To rush to the deconstruction leaves out the slow recognition that followed the ceiling removal: The Oddfellows were not the builders, but the first remuddlers. Once everything was out, you could see that the new ceiling cut across windows—now invisible from the out-side—that once let light into a third floor.

Moving straight to the demolition would also leave out the discov-ery I made one June evening—just before we learned the building was doomed—when I went down alone to Piermont to see how the final (professional) gutting was proceeding. As I came in from the river side, I noticed that the first floor was covered with piles of dusty hay. The workmen removing the downstairs ceiling had discovered salt hay insulation between the ceiling joists, salt hay cut from the Pier-mont Marsh, which had probably been there for two centuries, since the building was first constructed! I picked up the dusty, centuries-old piles of hay and carried them outdoors. That summer, our first full-sized Piermont garden, riverside of a demolished building, was mulched with ancient hay.

All these adventures were preliminaries to the morning when—with the space completely liberated from its centuries of occupa-tion—the architect invited in an engineer to see whether the struc-ture would tolerate being jacked up above the high-water mark. The engineer drove his penknife up to its hilt in one of the posts. We were not raising the building, as it turned out, but razing it—the only joke worth making about the whole thing. Let my journal carry the story.

> JUNE 20—Today was the day when, having completed the plans
> for the house, and having gotten all the clearances from the
> Planning Board and the Zoning Board of Appeals and the Corps
> of Engineers, and having had the final interior demolition done so
> construction could begin . . . we learned that the whole structure
> has to come down because there is significant dry rot in the main
> structural members!

The day began well since the intense heat has broken and the humidity has dropped. So we did a few chores before heading down to meet the architect and a structural engineer at Piermont. Cleanup was supposed to be finished today and raising to begin on Wednesday. I must say that my own reaction to looking at the naked structure upstairs has been less optimistic than everyone else's, and I have had some uneasiness imagining this rather fragile looking building raised four feet in the air. Little more than tarpaper and stucco appeared to be holding it together, and they were talking about taking off the stucco before they raised it. We got there before J. [the architect], but the two carpenters were upstairs. We began working a bit in the back yard, and then the ceiling fell in, figuratively, of course.

I was working in the yard and Alan came out and said J. had arrived with the engineer and we should be there as they walked around. They went in upstairs and the engineer immediately looked serious. He kept shaking his head. He noticed that three massive girders that once tied together the outside walls at about the 9-foot level had been cut out and it gradually became clear that a lot of "renovation" had been done on this building even before the 1920s.

Although the order in which this all emerged is not clear, everyone seemed eventually to agree on the explanation that this was once a post-and-beam building, perhaps a barn, three stories—which explains both the clearstory windows and the remains of frames of three windows that go above and below the present rafters in both the front and back walls! The post-and-beam structure was held together side to side by massive girders in the front wall, the back wall, and on each in-between post (three of them) and the third floor was above those girders. When the Oddfellows founded their lodge in 1846, and decided they wanted a dramatic high-ceilinged meeting hall, they apparently cut out the girders in order to combine the second and third floors (the ends are still pegged into the posts) and set them over the existing roof plate.

Then they plastered the whole thing over with all the fancy plaster we found when we demolished the lower ceiling. Essentially, they made a three-story building into a two-story one and in the process did a lot of structural damage. That decision, and the fact that the original barn had been built on what was a floodplain, meant that, once gutted, the structure was not only unstable, but rotted. It's not at all clear what is holding the north and south walls together, for example, except the (quite rotted) girders at the front and back.

That's the structure a local family built their own house into in the 1920s. Meanwhile, time passed, one of the sons inherited the house and the posts began to rot, so he cut off one of the posts downstairs on the south side with the intention, apparently, of propping it up. But he never propped, so the whole building is sagging on the south side. And, as we walk around rationalizing that if we had to we could still pull it all back together with new girder equivalents, the structural engineer goes around sticking his knife into the posts. Everything seems OK to me until I see that his knife has gone in up to the handle on the middle post on the north wall. (Downstairs that post turns out to be rotted half-way up.) Everyone seems stunned. I am probably least stunned of anyone—perhaps even relieved—since I think I had suspected all this for a long time, and certainly since the upstairs space was emptied out. I did not share the guys' enthusiasm for that "glorious" space, which looked pretty hacked up when you could actually examine it.

At some point the chief carpenter arrives and as he is coming upstairs, I say, "Bad news." "What?" "We've got no building." "Bummer . . . " All the guys get involved in discussing details, how it once fit together, etc. Meanwhile, I am depressed and probably angry and really want to hit something or someone, so I walk over to the front and look out to the river, in order to remember why we're here. Could anyone have told us the truth before everything stood revealed? Probably not. Should we have known? Should our architect have known? I think so. I think he should have asked to see the interior of an outside wall to get a sense of the construction long before this. Perhaps if he had not been so caught up with the idea of restoring an Oddfellows' hall he would have learned more quickly. Meanwhile, the guys go on murmuring politely, stolidly, unemotionally—the conversation even moves to the meaning in English of names. The carpenter's name had some meaning. Then the architect said his name meant *shining sword* in German, but he thought it was probably a bit dulled at the moment. My sense of humor (and probably my sense of anger) overcame me and I couldn't resist suggesting that he "fall on it," a joke that didn't go over very well!

But in the end, it was me who tried to cheer everyone up by saying that we were going from having a restored Oddfellows hall to having just an odd-fellows hall. We can call it "Gussows' Folly," I suggest. "Who are these people who have carefully gutted this house only to tear the whole thing down in the end?"

Clearly I was upset. So why did I ramble on earlier about wireworm damage and give such short shrift to dry rot? It's hard to convey the comfort it was to be creating an edible landscape in this blessed spot, as we made our way through the chaos of destruction and reconstruction that followed our discovery.

It would be misleading to deny that I was angry to learn that we had spent some part of our remaining hours on earth gutting a house that would soon be torn to the ground. But I wasn't as upset as I should have been. We had both loved the work; and "Gardening in Hudson Light" (as Alan titled the pastels he did around that time) was literally enchanting for both of us. Moreover, I think we had it right symbolically. Vegetable gardens, as this book is intended to say, are much more important than houses in the overall scheme of things. Agriculture is the foundation of civilization. Houses come and go, but soil must be cherished if food is to be grown for us to eat.

So if I expressed more concern about whether we could grow sweet potatoes without wireworm holes than about whether we had to tear down our house, it is because the house represented nothing but time, money, work, and disappointment, while sweet potatoes—and the garden as a whole—had come to symbolize long-term survival.

Writing about surviving on sweet potatoes reminded me of a funny article titled "Humans as Walking Legumes" that once ran in a nutrition journal (an infrequent source of humor). The author was speculating on how it was possible for a particular group of South Sea Island natives to live, as they seemed to, almost entirely on sweet potatoes, one of only a few vegetable types nearly devoid of protein. The author speculated that this group of humans was somehow behaving like beans and peas, which can manufacture their own protein from nitrogen in the air.

The natives weren't fixing their own nitrogen, of course, and we don't either. But like the South Sea Islanders, we have to be willing to eat the crops we grow frequently—to make up for the well-travelled foods we don't use. So we look for new ways to use them. I doubt that I would ever have tried what has become one of my favorite sweet potato recipes if I hadn't been looking for a new taste.

GRILLED ANDOUILLE SAUSAGE AND SWEET POTATO SALAD

Steam until just about tender (10 to 20 minutes depending on how fresh they are):

3 pounds quartered **sweet potatoes** *(peel if you want to)*

Drain and set aside to cool.

Preheat grill or broiler, and cook, turning frequently, until well browned:

½ pound (or less) **andouille sausage (kielbasa** *or* **chorizo** *may be substituted)*

Remove from grill, quarter, and slice ¼-inch thick.

In a medium bowl, whisk together until well blended:

*3 tablespoons grainy **mustard***
*3 tablespoons extra-virgin **olive oil***
*¹/₃ cup **balsamic vinegar***
*pinch **sugar***

Cut sweet potatoes into ¹/₂-inch cubes, and put in large mixing bowl. Pour dressing over them and add:

*sausage, **salt and pepper** to taste*
*1 large **red onion**, chopped*

Mix well but gently so sweet potatoes hold their shape. Sprinkle with:

*¹/₂ cup chopped **parsley***

Serve warm or cooled. A splendid dish, fit for company. Also keeps well.

I said earlier that you can grow your own sweet potato slips, but we spent several years planting wilted-looking sprouts that had weathered the U.S. mail before we decided to produce our own. It's theoretically easy. Sometime in early spring, just stick three tooth-picks halfway up (or halfway down) a sweet potato and put its bottom in a glass of water, with its top held out of the water by the toothpicks. I used to grow little avocado trees from big avocado seeds this way during my California youth. Roots come out the bottom of sweet potatoes and lots of sprouts come out the top and sides. When the sprouts are big enough, you break them off and put them in a glass of water, where they grow roots with surprising eagerness.

I call this task *theoretically* easy, because it turns out that sprouting reliably is as challenging as any part of the enterprise. In my experi-ence, some sweet potatoes just won't sprout. After a week or so in water, the bottom will get a little fuzzy-looking—which begins to suggest mold—but no roots will appear. Several such experiences taught me to choose sweet potatoes that had tiny sprouts at the top and put them feet-down in the water; sometimes I still got nothing but incipient decay.

One year, I got frustrated and turned the reluctant sweet potato upside down so the embryo sprouts (not roots) were in the water and the rotting bottom stuck up in the air. The little sprouts enlarged, turned up toward the sun, and rooted like crazy. I've never had better shoots. Indeed, they developed so fast that I had to pre-plant them in a box of dirt before the garden soil got up to 70 degrees when they could be planted out where they belonged. Obviously, I had been much too conventional in assuming that sweets had an assigned top and bottom. Clearly they don't. Now, whenever roots don't appear within a week, I turn my sweet potatoes upside down.

Since my earlier sprouting was not successful with all varieties, we gradually dropped off to a single unidentified variety that will produce 100-plus pounds in a 3-by-15 foot bed. Our potatoes are red-brown-skinned and deep-yellow-fleshed and taste great, so I'm not prepared to worry about what they're called, since they bake beautifully. And here's my second-favorite sweet potato recipe.

CURRIED SWEET POTATO LATKES

In a large bowl mix together:
  *1/2 cup **all-purpose flour***
  *2 teaspoons **sugar***
  *1 teaspoon **brown sugar***
  *1 teaspoon **baking powder***
  *1/2 teaspoon **cayenne powder***
  *2 teaspoons **curry powder***
  *1 teaspoon **cumin***
  ***salt** and freshly ground **pepper**, to taste*
Add:
  *2 large **eggs**, beaten*
  *1/2 cup (or less) of **milk** (just enough to make a stiff batter)*
  *1 pound **sweet potatoes**, peeled and coarsely grated*

If batter is too stiff, add a little more milk, and drop by spoonfuls into a preheated frying pan with ¼ inch of **peanut oil**. Flatten with back of spatula. Cook on each side until golden, and drain on paper towels. Makes about 16 pancakes. *Delicious!* They also keep well.

A final sweet potato note: Sweet potatoes grow vigorously! After several years of being unable to walk down the paths that bordered the sweet potato bed without crushing gorgeous reddish-green vines, I've simply conceded that sweet potatoes need to ramble. I now plant them between beds dedicated to crops that will be harvested by mid- or late summer, garlic and onions for example, or that can hold their own without my intervention, such as teepees of pinto or scarlet runner beans. In the latter case, I just let the crops slug it out until the beans are dry and ready to harvest and the sweets are ready to dig. And in the meantime, I stop walking down those paths as autumn approaches. I now dig the sweets gradually, starting in September when company comes and I can offer them sweet potatoes dug out of the ground while they watch. Sweet potatoes, like their fellow vegetables, taste wonderful when they're fresh and I'm happy to have help consuming them, since I seem unable not to grow too many. And while the roots are waiting to be dug, the shiny purplish leaves of the not-yet-harvested plants lend their beauty to the garden.

4

A Riverside Garden

> Removing the weeds, putting fresh soil about the bean stems,
> and encouraging this weed which I had sown, making the yellow soil
> express its summer thought in bean leaves and blossoms rather than
> in wormwood and piper and millet grass, making the earth say beans
> instead of grass—this was my daily work.
>
> —Henry David Thoreau, *Walden*

IT WAS THE GARDEN that saved our marriage. Without the solace of the garden, I doubt that my beloved and I could have made it in tandem through the endless filthy work of gutting that aged and rotting structure, much less the chaos of demolition and reconstruction. Creating the vegetable garden in that glorious Hudson light was what sustained me between the June day when we first took possession and the June day almost a year later when we learned that we had bought not a house but an "encumbered lot." So, having lost myself in sweet potatoes to lead you to the structure's ultimate demise, I need to back up and talk about the garden Alan and I created as we deconstructed the house.

I threw my heart into the garden from the moment we took possession, and, as we struggled with the architect we had hoped would help us remodel, more than one person told us that all the couples who engaged Frank Lloyd Wright had separated before their house was completed. I'm certain that's true—but I doubt that any of them had a vegetable garden to hide in while the process was unravelling!

Looking back, I can see that my gardening passion, like Alan's enthusiasm for gutting, diverted me from confronting the terminal state of the house. Our persistent struggle to save the wretched structure we had bought, despite early warnings from the inspection and heads-up threats from the sodden downstairs floor, was at least partly explained by the fact that we had fallen deeply in love with gardening in Piermont as if we lived there. We hoped to postpone as long as possible being displaced by construction. Between the end of June when we finally took possession of the old beast, and December, when heating it would have been flamboyantly wasteful, we spent long days living in and gardening out of our unfurnished house by the river; we even camped there several times.

Three times we spent a weekend. Once, instead of going to the end of Long Island, we went to Piermont for our annual August retreat; absent ocean swimming, the possibilities for enjoyment seemed no less on our bank of the Hudson than on a different, more distant shore. We had a card table, some camping pots and dishes, and a place to hang clothes. We slept in the upstairs living room facing the river, on a bed Alan improvised from two folding cots and several sleeping bags. From there, morning after morning, we watched the sun rise over the east shore of the Hudson, an experience that fully compensated for the discomfort of the bed and discouraged critical mindedness regarding the wretched shelter from which we looked out.

OCTOBER 2—When I wake up, I look over and see Alan sleeping with his head tilted up against the pillow, his eyes squinted, and a beatific smile on his face. He looks really happy! He says dawn was really rosy fingered; but even now it is a soft pink. Lovely. We light the fire he laid last night and Alan says he just loves being here. How lovely. He so seldom expresses unalloyed pleasure. We heat the coffee left over from yesterday, and warm a blueberry bran muffin he has brought from home and take it out to the boardwalk to start the day. Heavy dewfall.

Caretaking our only somewhat sordid kitchen, bedroom, and bath suite as we began gutting the remainder bonded us to the old wreck, even after the ceiling-razing party had coated the entire space around our haven with ancient black grit. Picnic breakfasts and lunches and sometimes dinners on the boardwalk were pure pleasure, as was eating out in the restaurants that tourism had brought to Piermont. But better than anything for me was the gardening. While we "lived" there I could plant and weed and dig in the sunlight off the river, and dream about our Hudson shoreline home from dawn to after dusk.

Alan found gutting deeply satisfying. I, on the other hand, preferred gardening, and approached the land with a sureness that came from almost four decades of frustration in Congers. What had to be done here seemed so easy by comparison. Almost from the moment I laid eyes on that narrow strip of land running to the water, I had known that running to the water was exactly what this garden had to do. But the space we inherited expressed other intentions.

This is what we saw when we committed to buying the property: a skinny rectangle 36 feet wide and 160 feet deep stripped by winter of everything but weedy grass, interrupted from one side or the other by boulder-bordered beds, and sloping up as it approached the river to a raised riverbank that occupied the 25 feet adjacent to the boardwalk. When the tide was low, we had a beach; when the tide was high, as we later learned, the Hudson rose up the bulkhead that braced the end of the property to within a foot of the boardwalk; when a northeaster's raging winds and low barometric pressure pushed the water even higher, the river sent waves crashing *over* the boardwalk—and even tore it up. Which was why, when we visited our newly purchased home with our younger son Seth toward the end of December 1992, the boardwalk *was* torn up, rocks had been washed out of the bulkhead, and most of the yard was underwater. The crumpling of the boardwalk was our first lesson in the vulnerability of river-front dwellers. There were to be others.

By the time the house was vacated, at the end of the following June, the boardwalk was intact (although the friends who helped repair it even before the closing warned that they would return to destroy it if the sale fell through). The beat-up chainlink fences that edged both long sides of the property were now embedded in a wild tangle of honeysuckle, Virginia creeper, and mulberry, and the massive leaning willow midway down the south fence had leafed out and was shading the middle third of the yard. Back near the house, a 50-foot-high silver maple threw shade over the deck and over a mix of evergreens and hosta tangled in invading ivy. Along the south fence-line, between the silver maple and the willow, the yard was shaded by a row of weed trees, self-sown red maples.

Up near the house, a picnic table set on a platform of 16-inch square pavers occupied the north side; on the south, a broken-down brick fireplace sat at the property line, surrounded on three sides by a pavement of assorted blue-stone slabs, one old millstone, and one carefully cut flat granite rock that revealed itself, when we later turned it over, to be an incised but obviously unused tombstone. As the land headed toward the river, it was intersected first by a bed of mixed evergreen plants on the right, then, on the left, by a raised plot with some roses and other perennial plants. Then came the dominating willow on the right, and finally, again on the left, our already planted sweet potatoes sprawled, facing down a bed of daisies. Behind them, up on the riverbank, was Alan's flourishing patch of tomatoes and eggplant.

Our earliest efforts were mostly devoted to clearing out over-grown ivy and pruning back shrubs. Late in August, we began our five-day vacation there. Despite being astrologically resistant, even I found it auspicious that the day of our first awakening in Piermont was the second convergence of Venus and Neptune in what was billed by the local paper as a rare triple-convergence year. Surely a positive omen. By this time, I was impatient to open up the vista from the house to the Hudson. By the end of our third day, I had talked Alan into helping me move and reset—or chop down—a dozen or so shrubs that blocked the way of anyone trying to head straight for the river.

I had settled on the general layout: I would bring together the assortment of evergreens scattered around the yard into a mass in the area up near the house that would be permanently shaded by the maple. The willow, and probably the weedy self-sown red maples along the fenceline, would be cut to allow sun into the rest of the yard.

A central grass path wide enough to accommodate our garden cart would run from the house to the riverbank, and raised beds of vegetables separated by grass paths would branch out from the path on either side. The riverbank would have a minimal patch of grass for sitting, and shrubs, grasses, and flowers edging the boardwalk and both property lines.

The vegetable beds would be 36 inches wide. Our beds in Congers had spanned 48, but I was getting older, and leaping across or straddling a 4-foot bed had been a bit of a stretch even when I was younger, so we settled on 3-foot beds with 2-foot paths between them. We found what we hoped was the center line of the property (the fence lines were pretty thick with undergrowth), and measured 2½ feet out on either side to mark a 5-foot path. Then, starting just back from the low evergreens that marked the edge of the riverbank, we laid out alternating 3-foot beds and 2-foot paths, coming back well past the middle of the yard to the edge of the shadow of the great maple that shaded the porch. The morning of our second Piermont sleep-over, we measured the path without laying out the beds. We breakfasted afterward at the diner and discovered, exultantly, that we were going to have lots of space.

> SEPTEMBER 25—If we do 3-foot beds and 2-foot paths, there will be room for twenty 15-foot-long beds on each side of the path!!! Wow! Who said we weren't going to have a spectacular garden?
>
> I think we're both relieved because somehow with all the stuff that's in our present half-acre, we couldn't figure how we could have all we wanted in Piermont . . . But even if we take out lots of these designated beds for a shed, for blueberries, raspberries, currants, kiwi, gooseberries, apple, pear, plum trees, there's still almost as much actual bed space as in our entire current garden—including paths!

We marked out the future beds and, leaving a 2-foot grass path next to each, we covered most of them with 3-foot-wide strips of old carpeting salvaged from the house. Then we numbered the beds on a garden plan, starting at the river end, "a" on the left, "b" on the right, running from 1a and b to 20a and b. We dug very few beds that fall; the grass under the carpeting would rot out through the winter, leaving the sod's fertility in place when we did our spring dig. We did put in garlic, however, where the sod was already gone and the soil turned over from harvesting the sweet potatoes. That first Piermont double-dig was revelatory. Except for turning up concrete and macadam chunks, apparently once thrown in as fill, the ground was rock-free and delicious. "This is a very different soil than Congers," I wrote happily in my journal, "much less clay!" The spot once occupied by the sweet potatoes became beds 2a and 3a and, as the first full moon after the first frost began to wane, we planted garlic there.

By the time we began serious planting in the spring, we knew that we would not be living in our renovated house that summer. We still believed that we were preparing to remodel, but approval of our plans by all the folks who needed to approve them had taken too long and we were not yet ready to begin reconstruction. So we would plant in Congers as well as in Piermont. We readied the Piermont beds gradually for planting. First the strips of carpeting came off to join the collection of trash in the dumpster; then we covered the beds with newspaper and compost that would rot out and could be chopped in when the time came to plant.

Meanwhile, spring pushed the grass into growth, and Alan was getting bored by the seemingly endless necessity of mowing the paths between the beds. Two days before workmen came in to do the final gutting, he came up with an inspired alternative. We were removing from near the house anything that might be smashed if machinery had to be brought in. That included not only slabs of bluestone, the millstone, and the gravestone, but the patio pavers incised to look like brick. Inspiration struck: With a row of bricks on either side, the patio pavers would be wide enough to cover the 2-foot paths—though we had only enough to cover nine. Alan laid the pavers over plastic to keep down the grass between them, and I laid the brick edging. Since the pavers added one inch to the height of the paths, we began what was only the first of many bed raisings, adding compost from the community composting facility to our own compost to raise the soil to the level of the brick edges.

And so, almost unintentionally, the basic structure of the garden was laid down. Beds of vegetables separated by brick paths (we bought more pavers to finish both sides of the center path) with the only grass running down the center path.

Eventually, the beds planted in vegetables were reduced to eleven on each side and the remainder given over to blueberries and raspberries, a permanent asparagus bed, a compost bin, and other necessities. I have always thought vegetables were beautiful; I believe I would grow them even if they didn't produce anything to eat. And despite the protestations of my friends that I was not a "formal" person, I found it deeply satisfying to see the formal brick paths edging lush beds of potatoes, tomatoes, eggplant, and peppers, or a springy mix of kale, collards, and flamboyant ruby chard, or beds given over to blocks of spinach, carrots, beets, and mesclun. This was the garden that was revealed when the house came down a year after we took possession. By the time the demolition of the house opened our back yard to the wondering neighborhood, there was something out there worth looking at.

But long before the garden had begun to show its promise, when it consisted of little more than shabby strips of carpet separating weedy strips of lawn, we had two chores to complete: The chainlink fences that ran the length of the property lines had to be torn out and replaced, and the willow had to be cut down to give us a long stretch of sunny land. I also wanted to act on my private vision of flowers planted along the boardwalk and waving against the water.

Until the old fences were wrenched out and the new ones installed, nothing could be planted in their vicinity. We wanted to replace the fence on the north as soon as possible, but we planned to wait until November or December, when the ground was firmer, to clean up the side that adjoined the park and the trash-filled parking area. That would clear the way for digging the beds to the edges of the property in spring. Our north-side neighbor, whom we had come to know as Barry, made sure things did not go according to plan.

In October, we let Barry know that we wanted to replace the tangles of chainlink fence and foliage between our properties with a stockade fence. He announced himself ready and willing, and two afternoons later the drama began. First an assortment of family members carted off the extra fences leaning against Barry's side of the main fence, after which the chainlink itself was loosed from its posts and cut free of its top rail. Barry's son-in-law started the backhoe, which had a chain wrapped around its bucket arm, and the fun began.

> OCTOBER 18 — The chain is wrapped around the posts and they are pulled out like plugs in a sink. Amazing. It all happens like nothing. There is a double fence all along—one buried a foot or so in the ground, the other probably buried 3 feet with the added dirt on Barry's side. It does not pull out! The backhoe strains and strains, but no luck. . . . So while Barry goes along the deeply buried fence . . . cutting the chainlink with a bolt cutter, someone begins using a blowtorch to cut the posts that can't be pulled.

The job which had seemed enormous in anticipation was finished off the next day, and as I began to clean up the rocks and macadam along the property line, Alan began the much more serious task of digging postholes along the line where the old fence had been. That task proved much harder than we had thought, in more ways than we could have imagined.

> October 24—We're out of the house before 8:00, heading down to Piermont to set up one or two sections before Sunday breakfast. Ahem. Three hours later, we have discovered all the different measurements that can be wrong. Since the measurements were done from west to east along the property line, and holes dug exactly 8 feet apart on center, we have ended up at the dock a little

short of the end. But that's OK. So we set up the post and then try to figure out what is "level" in relationship to a very chewed up hole. The hole seems lower than the ground directly west to the next hole, so we prop up a section of fence, figure out where it should come out at the top of the post, prop up the fence to that height, set in the next post—and think we have it solved, until we realize that the fence section that is supposed to come to the center of the post doesn't get that far. The second post is set too far west. Then, when we measure from the next hole, it isn't eight feet! So we start over, remeasuring from hole three to hole two. By this time we have set both post one and post two. Post one is really set, post two will have to be taken up, all the rocks and gravel removed, and the hole dug farther east. Otherwise the entire fence will be moved west and all holes will need redigging! So out come the rocks and gravel etc., and out comes the crowbar to be pounded into the hole to break out the macadam that blocks putting the pole in the right place.

I have failed to mention yet that the riverbank sat slightly off kilter from the rest of our land. At the point where the land began to rise to the riverbank, the property line angled toward the north and continued thirty feet in that direction to the river. There, the property ended at a bulkhead continuous with Barry's bulkhead on the north. On the south, it dropped three feet to the beach in front of Parelli Park. It looked on the surveyor's map as if someone had simply shoved the last thirty feet of the property slightly north. So when the old fence was pulled up, we began setting the new fence along the same bent line.

Sometime during this initial pole setting, Barry came stomping out into his yard bellowing that we were putting our fence on his property. To our protest that we were only putting the posts where the old fence was, he roared in reply that the old fence was *temporary* (despite being set in concrete!). He seemed only half-serious, and his protest seemed absurd, so we didn't take him seriously, and kept working.

Eventually, we got the hole redug, got the pole set in at the right easterly distance, got the posts straight both north to south and east to west, got the fence roughly level, drilled the holes and put in the bolts. One section up and only three hours in the doing! Phew. We clean up the area, clean up ourselves, load our stuff into our Piermont basket, and head for the diner. It's 11:30. Boy have we earned breakfast.

By the end of the next day, we had managed to finish three fence sections, and went home to a message from the architect to the effect that he had a good bid on raising the house to get it out of the flood-plain and that he was sure that we could save it.

. . . he said he saw no reason for not going right ahead, that we did not have to wait till spring to begin building, since contractors liked to have winter work. What was now going to take the most time was getting all the approvals from the Zoning Board of Appeals, from the State Department of Environmental Conservation, and from the Army Corps of Engineers! Well, we're really going to have a house after all. I think, until now, I was afraid someone would come along and say, "Tear it down. There's nothing else to do." Hooray!

Three days later, Alan and I began setting fence posts again, and all hell broke loose. We had four posts in solidly, and were moving onto the next section, when Barry came storming out bellowing, "I'm going to take it down." Then he went crazy: Damn new people move in and try to tell him what's what; the fence was on his property and it looked awful from his deck; we should come up and see how the line cut off his dock; he didn't want his daughters to have trouble getting the property straightened out. He would listen to nothing.

OCTOBER 28—At some point he even had the nerve to say he was sure we had work to do in the house, so what were we doing outside anyway? The space between Barry's house and ours is filled with a pile of lath 7 feet high from the ceiling razing and he dares to suggest we're not working on the house?!!!

It would have been funny if it weren't so disturbing. Barry had been born there; we hadn't. He knew how to yell; Alan hadn't yelled since infancy. Needless to say, we were both pretty upset, so we packed it up and went home. The next few weeks were painfully pointless. We tried a polite, carefully written letter and received no response. I kept writing logical scenarios in my journal, explaining to myself how obviously we were in the right. We were willing to be reasonable, even to move the fence if we had to, but we needed more than Barry's word for where the property line ought to be, something on paper, some sort of survey.

We went to the previous owners for clarification and to a relative of Barry's who was a lawyer for advice. We learned that all the properties, Barry's, ours, and the park to our south, had formerly ended as riverbank at least 25 feet back from the present bulkhead and had been illegally filled in by Barry in the late 1980s. Our riverbank angled because Barry had constructed the bulkhead at right angles to the river's slanting edge. We had no title insurance on that land and most of Barry's land was probably uninsurable, filled in illegally over the years. On the tax map, his lot was 75 feet deep and ours was 200-plus, but the lots ended side by side at the edge of the Hudson. We shouldn't worry, the previous owner told us. "Well," Alan wrote after that conversation, "I will worry."

But words and reactive silence did not suffice for long, and the men moved on to more atavistic behaviors. In early November, Alan discovered that Barry had planted a tall rod along our boardwalk, 37 inches in from the fence, as a silent assertion of where he thought the new fence should be. Twelve days of no progress later, Alan broke, and from then on I added his occasional outpourings to my journal.

NOVEMBER 12—*At some deep level I have been profoundly troubled by the confrontation with Barry. The shouting, the assertions, the willful placement of a very tall metal rod where Barry thinks the property line should be—all these events, coupled with lack of resolution of the dispute, has played havoc with my emotions. Bolstered by Joan, who said, "Why don't you just take it out?" I decided that today I had to act.*

So this afternoon, armed with the quit claim deed, the other deed, and Rahnefeld's survey, I went down to Piermont. Taking the poaching spade and the sledgehammer, I went out to the boardwalk and began to remove the rocks and soil around the pole that Barry had planted. And remove rocks I did, rocks and more rocks and more rocks. They began to pile up on all sides. Deeper and deeper, wider and wider. "Unbelievable," I muttered. "He must have been crazy."

Four feet down, surrounded by piles of rock, Alan finally got the pole out, filled in the hole, and then began to worry about what Barry would do when he found his manhood gone. A week later, with the fence still in limbo, I went down to Piermont and removed Barry's weaker assertion of "his" property line, a string tied to a child's plastic toy letter and wrapped around a small stick planted in the same spot. Alan thought we had won. I doubted it.

So when a workman appeared in Barry's yard a few days later and offered to finish off our fence for a reasonable price, we hired him on the spot. We might have won, but the unsettling confrontations with Barry had wiped out whatever enthusiasm we had for the task. Two days later, Nikki began where we had left off and had all but two of the sections installed when Barry struck again.

NOVEMBER 21—Barry comes storming out shouting that we are on his property, and will have to take down the fence. This time, instead of backing off, or trying to distract him, Alan shouted back, saying we would both lose if this went to court. Barry talked, Alan talked, both went over onto his property . . . and gradually, Alan followed Barry up to his apartment.

As I was to learn, the resolution they worked out reflected Barry's conviction that in Piermont he could do anything he wanted. Nothing had yet convinced him otherwise! They came back down to the river and told me what they had agreed: We would straighten out the property line adjoining Barry's property, if Barry would straighten out the property line on the south; in other words, Barry would build a new bulkhead that didn't bend north. When Barry said he would do it for $1,000, it was my turn to rage. We had bought the property including the part he claimed he owned; we had a survey showing we owned it; we had paid Barry to take the old fence down even though he had talked at the beginning about helping pay for it; now he wanted us to pay for the bulkhead! Not only that, the whole thing was illegal.

Alan and Barry climbed down to the beach and began figuring out where the new bulkhead would have to run to be straight. I was fuming at the air. When they came back up, Alan tried to reassure me that Barry wouldn't get us into trouble. "Oh, sure," I scoffed. "And what's it going to cost?"

"I told Barry we'd pay for the two loads of rock." "How much are they?" "Eighty dollars each." That's more like it—at least for now—$160 total. Barry insists that we won't get in trouble, that it will happen fast, even if it has to happen at night! We agree to go ahead.

That night, both of us were in a state of disarray. I felt manipulated; Alan had once more used his charm to get in deeper than he planned. Now he was worried that if Barry went ahead before the Village was granted permission for the remodelling, our survey would be incorrect, which would look pretty suspicious. So he telephoned our architect, who told him to go ahead, quickly, and have a new survey done before we took our plan to the zoning board.

Rain and cold kept us in until Thanksgiving, when we took visiting friends from California down to see Piermont while the turkey was cooking. The bulkhead was built! Barry had finished the crib and filled it with large rocks. All that was needed was planting soil and we would have a triangular bed at the edge of the water. When was all of this done? How long did it take? No real answers were forthcoming, but it was clear that it was done quickly (and certainly without any special permission). It looked terrific.

The fence could now be finished, with the first three sections moved to the line that Barry had marked with his pole, and when he was asked to look at the new bulkhead, the surveyor merely asked somewhat quizzically, "What's going on down there?" The question was hard to answer—in watery Piermont, property lines are sometimes surprisingly fluid, but the Gussow property now ran straight to the water and we had five feet of new waterfront.

As for the fence along the south property line, we had no heart for it that winter. By the time we began seriously digging and planting the vegetable beds in the spring, we had decided to leave the chainlink in place and wire the new stockade fence to it. We didn't need another property-line dispute and the fierce winter storms had showed us that without the support of something buried immovably in the ground, the fences we had so painstakingly installed would blow down. And although Barry's bark was fierce, he ended up saving our common fence by strapping it to metal posts set in concrete on his side. We couldn't easily live with him, but we couldn't live without him either.

Now for the willow. From the moment we settled on buying the house, the willow was doomed because it shaded much of what was to be the vegetable garden. It also seemed dangerous, leaning so heavily against the fence that separated us from the park that it had bent the 1½-inch steel pipe that topped the fence into an arc. We put off its demise until folks had moved indoors for winter, partly because we weren't certain what tree removal would do to our reputation in the village and partly because we had lots of other things on our mind. Then we called an arborist and got sticker shock—more than $1,000 just for cutting the tree and taking away its massive trunk.

Alan and Barry were dickering over payment for the bulkhead—

for which Barry extracted multiples of $160 since Alan avoided con-frontation if possible—when Alan remarked that we had been quoted a very high estimate for taking the tree down. Barry was now certain he had a sucker on the hook, so he made an offer he hoped Alan couldn't refuse. However, Alan had learned. He low-balled the esti-mate, Barry underbid Alan's imaginary figure, and we said yes.

Neither of us was there to see the great willow come down. Barry hired a crew of casual laborers and took it down before noon the next day, and when I got there in the early afternoon, four men were cut-ting up the giant carcass. Alan arrived later, went out to see the tree, and then came in and sat looking out the window. Later he wrote for my journal:

> DECEMBER 16—*The yard looked bigger, open, wider, lighter. It didn't look gap-toothed, just open. From the inside the property seemed wider. We are, of course, more open to the public (although at this time of year, there is very little "public"). The stump remains about four feet above the ground. And in the corner of the lot are huge pieces of willow, looking as if a truck loaded with giant wheels of Parmesan cheese had turned over and spilled its contents.*

The next day, Barry came with a chipper and reduced the willow branches to a giant pile of chips, which he dumped back near the maple tree. A good location; four rainy days later, that area was flooded, and I spent the afternoon of the shortest day of the year pulling mounds of wood chips into the lowest spots. This began what was to be a constant theme of our garden: raising it against floods. As it grew dark, we strung Christmas tree lights around one of the small evergreens, and went home to Congers.

After six months of ownership, we had a gutted house, a straight-ened fence, and no willow. Serious gardening could begin. In six more months, we would learn that the house had to be torn down. But by then we would have potatoes and green onions planted, the pepper and tomato plants set, and the corn would be up with its companion beans and squash (the Three Sisters, as the Native Americans called this combination). Rosemary would grow at either side of the tombstone that sat at the end of bed 6a. And one early June day as we were leaving, we picked about a dozen absolutely huge strawberries from strawberry plants left by the previous owners.

Using sand hauled up from the riverbank and garbagepailsful of town compost that Alan had brought in, we levelled the space at the inner edge of the boardwalk. There we planted what we could find to plant—day lilies and sage, rosemary and a tiny Russian sage seedling all brought from Congers—and sowed all the open spaces with thyme, dill, coriander, and wildflower seed. Everything flourished. On many mornings, we sat with friends at a small card table on the boardwalk among poppies and bachelor buttons, looking out across the wide river toward the hills on the other side and eating breakfasts of homegrown onions and tomatoes, pâté, goat cheese, and Havarti cheese with dill on bagels and pumpernickel. Then on June 20, we learned that the house had to come down. Alan's reflections:

> JUNE 21 — *The longest day, and with wetness and grey skies, a day to match my mood. The house in Piermont will come down. End/beginning. The end is where we start from. To make an end is to make a beginning. We have loved this funny place, slept there, picnicked there, entertained friends there, had a lobster supper there, had a party to take down the ceiling above the ceiling. We made a home there even as we disassembled the place, keeping bathrooms, the kitchen, the front room with glass and fireplace, alive. . . . So after almost a year, with the acceleration of the last ten days, the house stood revealed, wounded, fragile, unrestorable, even perhaps dangerous. I lightly had said (often) that we would buy the place even if the house had to be torn down, never really thinking what that meant. Now it is a fact. We will have this open space, this long open space from the road to the river, and we will be making our home there.*

> JUNE 27 — We hear a weather forecast that suggests rain all afternoon, so I prevail upon Alan to go down to have breakfast on

the pier. He prevails upon me to go early without breakfast and come home for pancakes. We do that. We have early coffee on the boardwalk, then I get to work really weeding the riverbank lawn and all the vegetable beds. Things have really grown—especially the weeds! Alan helps with the weeding, then mows the lawn. No one is working on the house today. Demolition begins tomorrow.

JUNE 28—I think we have been going through a period of mourning—for the building on which we had pinned such hopes, for last summer when we spent such a glorious time in the existing space, for the hopes of this summer which will now be limited to the garden (still glorious), but no enclosed space except perhaps a port-o-potty! The garden is really planted and needs only weeding. There isn't a lot to do unless there is no rain and we have to water. But the last few days have been full of big thunderstorms, so the problem now is weeds, which are coming up like Topsy. The first burst of bloom on the riverbank is fading—the bachelor's buttons and poppies have a lot of seed heads and dead flowers, which obscure the glory of the blossoms, and the picnic table area back by the maple is beginning to look seedy with stuff. I am going to clean it up the next time I am down.

We had started this garden behind a house we never meant to tear down, intending it to flourish not behind a hole in the ground, but behind a venerable structure being restored. But through July, August, and September, the garden we had planted in April, May, and June was visible to passersby, who, for the first time since the post-and-beam barn was built there perhaps two hundred years earlier, could look out from the road across the garden to the river. Then our house began to go up, and the garden was ours again.

5

Building It

In building a house, one digs a hole only to fill it with concrete. . . .
Houses can fall. Against this possibility we set them in concrete.
—Richard Manning, *A Good House: Building a Life on the Land*

DURING THE BREATHLESS, sleepless, raging seven months between the moment we learned we had lost our new house and the day we finally managed to vacate our old one, construction details devoured our lives, but a single idea dominated our thoughts: "Stay vigilant." The discovery that the house was to be demolished marked the beginning of two months of unsteady backward progress. The day after we got the bad news, the demolition commenced, some wires shorted out, and the fire department had to hose the poor wreck down. Next we got to watch the fortune we had just invested be dismantled and carted away in dumpsters.

Then came the hot day in early August when the last rotted beams of the old barn had been removed, the rubble that passed for a foundation dug out, and a power shovel brought in to excavate *our* foundation. The operator began to dig, then stopped. Though nothing solid had supported our old barn, the infrastructure of some unidentified earlier building had been laid to last. Two days with a jackhammer were needed to clear out enough rubble to let the digging continue. We should have been grateful, I suppose, that no archaeologist was on site, or it might have taken months. As it was, Alan and I went around collecting what the workmen *had* turned up: old canning jars with screw-on zinc lids lined with white glass. I was thrilled; the Italian family that had built the first house into the Oddfellows hall had left us something in which to store food. Better yet, in removing the floor, the workmen found a wooden bocce ball. Forty years earlier, Alan and I had courted in a small north Italian restaurant below Washington Square with a bocce court in its back room. We were sure it was a good omen. We were wrong.

Eight days later, after several extended pauses, the pit where our house was to stand was finished. The workers had been instructed to stop when they hit the water table—very high since the Hudson was at our doorstep so to speak. Now they were to stake out the footing. A week later—it was now past the middle of August—the hole was still empty. Alan and I had been busy, shopping for doors, windows, medicine cabinets, sink cabinets, vanities, floor coverings, showers, toilets, lights . . .

> AUGUST 12 — What a sweat. I *hate* this. My desire for perfection fights dreadfully with my hatred of shopping. I want to get the best for the money and something that will not make me regret my choice later (since of course I feel the need to have JUST what I want), but I despise having to spend so much time thinking about *things*.

I had also gone to Manhattan to move the contents of my office, the powers-that-were having chosen this moment to displace me universally; and Nature had provided several days of rain, including one $3^{1}/_{2}$-inch downpour in as many hours. The good news was that the rain drained rapidly out of the pit. The bad news was that it was still just a pit.

Then, late one afternoon while we were working in the garden, some Portuguese workmen arrived. Their foreman, just back from Portugal, exclaimed about the beauty of our garden and the river view. Then he sent his workers into the excavation to outline the footing with yellow string. "A pencil drawing in a wet space," as Alan later wrote. We were on our way!

AUGUST 23 — In late afternoon, we go to Piermont to see what has happened on the foundation, and arrive just as one of the workmen is leaving. I go into the garden. The workman and Alan get into a conversation in which Alan can't figure out what he is saying. They come over to me to see if I can make it out, and suddenly Alan realizes he's saying they need the building inspector before they can pour cement.

As Alan began wandering around looking at the forms for the footing, I headed back to the garden. Minutes later Alan let out a cry of alarm. "What's wrong?" I yelled, running toward the excavation. "The forms are backward," he said. And they were. The outline of the south-side entry porch was on the north; Alan's studio, meant to face the street, faced the river.

The crew, we learned, couldn't read English; on the plan, they had "read" the road in front of the house as the river in the back. Here is Alan's account:

> AUGUST 23—*How careful do you have to be? I have the crew boss get out the plans and I show him that things have to be turned around. The rest of the crew arrives after a break and starts digging for the correct footings. I try to alert J. by phone, only to discover that all the telephones are out (after a fire at the NYNEX substation) and I can only call in Piermont, but not out to Nyack.*
>
> *This is the first action to actually build the house . . . not to demolish, not to excavate, but to actually start the building process—August 22, 1994, a year and two months after we have taken title!*

And less than five months before we were supposed to vacate Congers.

Meanwhile, we still owned the Victorian mansion, and our potential buyers had asked for a water test. A water test? Giving up our delicious Congers well water was one of the few negatives about moving to Piermont.

AUGUST 25—I am at the moment filling the bathtub with water, since the man who came to get the *E. coli* out of our well (stay tuned) says we won't have water for twenty-four hours! Ah, yes, another day in the life of the Gussows.

Alan began his day by calling J. to say, "No front door. No oculus at $1,000, and what the hell did you mean about saying the deck is at ground level; on the original plans it wasn't and you never told us you were going to change it." He said we really didn't care about the oculus and that if J. wanted it for architectural reasons, he could donate it to the house. J. laughed tensely.

Meanwhile, I worked indoors and, just as I was going outside to join Alan (who was digging a hole to find out whether we had two or three courses of concrete block in the foundation of the shed, because—in order to sell this place—we have to file a posthoc plan of the shed for which we never filed a building plan!), R. [the purchaser] called. They had the report back on our water and it has *E. coli* in it and is "undrinkable." We had better switch to bottled water. Oh, right!

R. gave me the name of the company that had done the inspection. I went out to tell Alan who was now mowing the back lawn. He agreed that I had better call M., the health commissioner [a friend], to find out what came next. . . . I did and left a message. Then I went outside, leaving the fax machine on, to begin the balling and burlapping as scheduled—well, sort of as scheduled. Amazingly, that task went well. We balled and burlapped four lavenders, one giant potentilla and two small ones. It was now almost 2 P.M. and no raspberries had been pruned, but we had done at least one thing on my list.

When we came in for a quick lunch, there was a fax that said we needed to call Barmore to have the water treated. There was another fax from J., some pictures of round windows of various sizes and prices. He had circled the most expensive one and written a note saying, "please call." No information about quality, anything. Absolutely typical. This is something he wants, and it's got to be taken care of right away!

We, however, felt the more urgent task was to take care of the water, though it seemed hardly credible that it could be bad, since I was drinking about a quart of milk a day made from that water plus extra glasses of water plain. Alan called Barmore and learned that if we could uncover the wellhead it would cost only $75 to get the water cleaned up. We got out the plans for the house and located the wellhead. Then we went out back and measured the right distance and Alan began digging. He hit something hard and said, "This must be the wrong place." And I said, "No, it's probably the wellhead." And it was. So Alan went back in to call Barmore and—first lucky event of the day—the workman was just leaving in his truck and would be over in 10 minutes!

And he was. He pried off the concrete slab above the well and had some conversation with Alan including asking whether or not we could do without water for twenty-four hours. Well, we have company coming tomorrow, etc., but we can. Finally the workman put on big rubber boots and climbed down in. . . . I tried to get some other work done (ha-ha) and then Alan said I should come out and get instructions from the Barmore man on what we were to do. The well had now been filled with chlorine. We were to run every outlet in the house—toilets, washing machine, all faucets, showerheads, etc.—until every single one stank of chlorine. Then we were to use nothing but the toilet for twenty-four hours. Then we were to take the hose out into the street and run the water until it no longer smelled of chlorine. After that we were to run out the chlorine in the house, after which could use the water again.

Well, so much for dinner tonight. Plans have not worked out well today. Alan had taken a quick shower just before the water went bad and we had run a lot of water into the bathtub (which we now had to put into bottles so we could drain the tub and get the chlorine running through it). Somehow I had managed to avoid getting dirty in the outdoor work. So we went in and started running water.

When every room smelled the way swimming pools used to smell, we changed clothes and went to our favorite Mexican restaurant for dinner. After dinner we headed across to Piermont just to check things out. No work on the foundation. Apparently they can't pour until the building inspector has checked. And since the building inspector has had a heart attack, they have an ad hoc building inspector. So . . .

Walking back from the garden, we notice J. standing by the house site with another man who turns out to be the temporary building inspector. He is inspecting, things are OK, and it looks as if they will pour tomorrow!!!

And the next afternoon, when we headed down to Piermont to take our company out to dinner—the water system being still unpurged—the parking lot was full of cement trucks. They were pouring the footing! A whole crew of men was stomping around in the pit, filling the forms with heavy wet cement. At their invitation, Alan tossed in a coin for luck. We needed it.

It was now September, only four months from January 1, when we were supposed to vacate Congers. But the forms for the foundation were at last in place and in our delight one evening we picked a lot of scorchingly hot Scotch Bonnet peppers from our flourishing houseless garden and took them out to a Jamaican restaurant at the other end of the county. The suspicious owner found it hard to believe we were trying to give, not sell, the perfect red and yellow bonnets. We reassured him by buying and devouring a plate of his jerk chicken to celebrate. Had life been more intact, we would have made our own.

CHICKEN WITH JERK SAUCE (BAJAN FRIED CHICKEN)

For:

2 fryer chickens

Put in the blender:

¼ cup fresh thyme leaves

¼ cup fresh marjoram leaves

¼ cup fresh sage leaves

2 large garlic cloves, peeled and chopped coarsely

2 to 3 Scotch Bonnet peppers, carefully seeded while wearing rubber or plastic gloves

2 tablespoons corn oil

juice of one lime

Process to a fairly smooth paste.

Then chop into fine mince and blend into pepper mix:

6 scallions including green part

Add:

1 teaspoon paprika

½ teaspoon ground cloves

salt and pepper, to taste

Stir together.

Quarter chickens, remove skin, and make small slits in flesh.

Using plastic gloves, rub seasoning into and over the chicken. Let sit in refrigerator for one or two days. Grill under hot boiler, turning often, until juices run clear. Or, dip the seasoned chicken into a mixture of 1 egg and 1 cup buttermilk, roll in breadcrumbs and fry.

Very, very spicy, but delicious!

The very next day, we signed the contract to sell the Congers house. The ceremony injected into a generally sober period a small interval of hope and levity.

SEPTEMBER 2 — There is then a long argument about the time of closing. The closing is scheduled for January 2, but standard contract language says something about a reasonable postponement. The buyers want the closing to be no later than January 15. Lenny talks about the problems of setting a firm date, saying that the state in its wisdom has decided that contracts should read so as to leave people leeway for unforeseen events. "The Gussows are building their house with every intention of being in it by the end of the year, but what if Hurricane Joan came up the river and wiped them out?" So R. asks whether Lenny has ever written a contract with a firm closing date. Aha! He fell into the trap. Lenny proceeds to explain that he has, and it hasn't turned out well. "There was this one man who lived in the South and had to make a trip North for the closing so he wanted it set on a particular date, absolutely fixed. And then he couldn't get to his own closing—had an auto accident on the way up." So I turned to R. and said laughing, "You see, R. If you insist on a date, you'll die."

That same day, the foundation was poured. The smell of cement was terrific, and on subsequent days we went down a couple of times to hop around on the sturdy walls. A week after the pouring, we went down to find the forms removed, and a backhoe lifting gravel over the naked foundation wall to dump on the future basement floor. I went out to the riverbank to weed. Once again, Alan went up to watch the work. Once again he came running back with an anguished shout. Our new foundation was breached. The backhoe and driver had left, but two big cracks ran right through the thick concrete wall. As we learned when the crew returned, the backhoe operator had "tripped" his machine on the base of the old outdoor fireplace that had cooked our July 4 franks, and crashed into our new house!

The foundation was fixed with pins, epoxy, and a new section, the basement floor was poured and leveled, and by mid-September the framing finally began on a house that we had to move into by January. The smell in the air was no longer of concrete. The air was filled with the scent of new wood and with the curses of the framer that the foundation was "a load of junk"—his technical term for seriously off-level. He took two weeks to level it, enraging the head carpenter who was marching to a different schedule, but delighting every workman who came after him and experienced the perfection of the framing.

The day the plywood for the first floor went down, Alan and I took pictures of each other standing in our respective workplaces, I in my office, he in his studio. Weeks later, a visiting writer who had come to talk about eating locally stood on the framed terrace, looked out at our glorious garden and the river and said, "You know it's perfect, don't you?" And of course we did—but it needed to be habitable as well.

And because architects and carpenters and masons and window suppliers and stucco appliers and terrace finishers all want to be paid for completing some task, I could write by mid-November:

NOVEMBER 19—It was a joy to see the house in the early light. The big doors are in with the fixed windows on either side, and the columns are finished so that the terrace begins to look as it will from the back of the house. It is really quite astonishingly beautiful. It looks established, like it has been there a long time. It has nothing new-looking about it. We kept looking up at the house and sort of marvelling at what we had created. I can't imagine anything that would have been as lovely as the rosy and pale yellow stucco.

And because plumbers and electricians and drywall installers and tapers and painters and floor layers and kitchen-cabinet designers and appliance dealers also have families to support, the house eventually got built. But not by January 2.

We signed the closing papers on our Congers house (after a second successful water test) in early January with miles yet to go, and received an extension to the end of the month. On January 27, we moved into a seriously incomplete house almost literally over the twitching body of a very angry head carpenter who was nailing up door moldings under the feet of the movers. One coat of primer paint covered all the walls; nothing covered several plywood floors awaiting tile or carpeting; the stair railing was a 2-by-4, and there was nothing in the way of working plumbing downstairs except our toilet and shower. But we had come at last to live with our garden.

Going back over the journal for these painful months, I am struck by the degree to which throwing our energies into the patch of earth on which these disasters repeatedly occurred compensated for the horrors that attended the deconstruction and reconstruction of our home-to-be. "I needed to see the garden coming along," I wrote on July 1, after hours of weeding, trimming, and planting, "in light of the house coming down." The day after Independence Day, a real comedown from the prior year's celebration, I recorded my thoughts.

> JULY 5 — I suddenly realized this morning that it must seem weird that there is this beautiful productive vegetable garden with no house! Who are the people who have put in this elaborate garden without having a house? Funny. The garden did look beautiful. Everything seems to be growing wildly. . . . We are now completely open to the street. We have no shelter at all, and everyone passing on the street can look out and see the garden.

Visiting friends were driven down to Piermont, not to look at the site, where little was happening, but at the garden, where much was happening. When demolition had been completed and no excavation had yet begun, I wrote:

> JULY 21—*Nothing* is happening on the house. The garden is hard to keep up with when we're not there. And everything is growing so hectically that it's almost a burden. But we go down in the late afternoon when it cools off and do some weeding and harvesting,

including our first tomato. I think we could get tomatoes really early here.

And as we struggled with the architect over closets and bathrooms, over window sizes and placements, over ceiling heights and deck heights, over roofing and downspouts and house colors, and so on and on and on, the garden was unfailingly cooperative. The sun and rain and soil produced a sometimes overwhelming bounty.

AUGUST 5 — Quick trip down to see whether the excavation is finished. It seems to have stopped, but is not finished. Thank God for the garden, which makes the whole thing seem worthwhile.

The day the footing was finally laid out in string, Alan harvested an entire bucket of tomatoes, peppers, eggplants, soldier beans, habanero peppers, and a head of broccoli, products of our busy spring of digging and planting. Meanwhile, I finished uprooting the last large patch of crabgrass, which I had been obsessively weeding out of the small oblong of seedy lawn on the riverbank. It seemed to be the only problem I had a chance of bringing under control.

Here's Alan—always better at relaxing than I was—on a day when I had to work in New York.

AUGUST 2 1—*I went to Piermont with the lawn mower in the car. The grass continues to grow, not with typical mid-summer slowness, but with rapid springlike surges. I harvest tomatoes (throwing away many that are rotting), and pick more eggplant and peppers, including yellow Scotch Bonnets. Their color is wonderfully variable this year. After cutting and harvesting, I take a few moments and sit, with great ease, in my Adirondack chair on the boardwalk and breathe the salty air and feel truly at home. The garden is beautiful. Joan has created a flowering high garden and the special grasses are getting their seed heads. While there is always work to do, weeding, picking, cleaning up, this is a moment to pause, and I feel wonderful.*

We picked soybeans, pinto beans, black beans, brown beans, and soldier beans, and back in Congers we shelled the dry beans and popped the green soybeans out of their shells for freezing, after a 3-minute boil. And the day before the well was sanitized with chlorine, Alan put broccoli, tomato sauce, and cut-up peppers into the freezer.

During these stressful days, the garden and the food it produced were vital to our sanity, as became obvious when the garden was invaded. The evening we drained our chlorine-filled water system into the street in Congers, we went down late to Piermont for a last look.

AUGUST 25 — Things looked fine except someone had pulled four young carrots!!! We put some fencing in front of the carrots and I wrote on a piece of paper Alan found in the car, "If you want a carrot please wait until they are big enough to eat, and then *ask* us. The Gussows." For extra discouragement, we ran a wire across the yard out by the boardwalk about a foot off the ground. It will at least let someone know we have noticed.

It was the end of August and we still had nothing but a footing and forms for a foundation in place. When the carrot thief was detected four days later, I was grimly serious. We were sitting on the boardwalk, when our neighbor Barry came over to chide us gruffly about the mistakes he insisted we were building into our foundation. In a few minutes, Alan, Barry, and I walked toward the street to look at the site, with me slowing down to check on the vegetable beds as I came. When I caught up with them at the excavation, I noticed that Barry had a small perfect carrot in his hand.

AUGUST 29 — "You're the one who's been taking our carrots!" I say accusingly. "Did you see me take it?" he shouts. "Of course not," I say, "but there's no other place you could get a carrot between the boardwalk and here, so of course you did. You can't do that. That's our food." "That's your problem," he responds in a typical non sequitur. "Damn it, Barry," I shout, "We grow carrots to eat in the winter. We don't even pick them now. You can't just take anything you like from the garden." "That's your problem," he repeats. "No," I respond, "It's your problem. It's not funny. Just cut it out."

But he didn't. A few days later he turned up in our yard again, this time with a nephew who had grown up in our now-demolished house.

SEPTEMBER 3 — While Alan and Joe are talking, Barry walks over to the onion bed, pulls a red onion, and wipes it off on his sleeve. I react like I was burned. "Barry, don't you dare take that." He looks straight at me and begins to pinch the root off, and I leap across the bed and grab it away from him. "Damn it, Barry, this is our food. We grow onions for the winter. When we run out we don't buy them. You're taking food out of our mouths. You can't just take what you want."

He trails off down the yard with Joe and Alan to look at the house, and when they come back I am pulling the rest of the onions. He stands there and I start in again. "I really resent having to pull these onions, Barry. They're not ready to be pulled and I have to do it." "Why?" he asks. "Because I can't trust you. I have to take them home because I can't trust you not to take them. . . . This is my work. I make money teaching and giving speeches about food and growing it. It's not a game with us. It's not funny." And finally, they leave.

Of course I bought onions when our crop ran out, but I had lost my sense of humor. The old house was gone, the new house was slow aborning, and producing our food from the garden was my sanity.

My journal for the period captures a Roadrunner-like madness: two frantic characters zipping back and forth the twelve miles from Congers to Piermont, stopping, starting, crying, yelling, sowing, fighting, sorting, tossing, packing, picking, roasting, eating, freezing,

digging, weeding, and letting all that productive labor and the pleasures of the waterfront compensate for the painfully slow forward
progress on the house that was to front this wonderful garden. We
planted our parsnips in Piermont in mid-summer, knowing that we
would be living there to harvest them in January. In mid-September,
as the carpenter finished leveling the foundation, I spent the day in
the Congers yard, which looked abandoned, cleaning up the vegetable garden, transplanting lettuce seedlings, and harvesting. In the
evening, I made two quarts of Tomatillo Enchilada Sauce, even as I
was cooking kale and potato soup.

TOMATILLO ENCHILADA SAUCE

If you are using fresh tomatillos, prepare them beforehand by
removing their papery husks, rinsing them, and then *gently* (so
they will not burst) simmering them for about 10 minutes in
enough water to cover. Drain and briefly chop in food processor.

Combine in processor:
  *2½ pounds (about 8 cups) drained **tomatillos***
  *2 roasted **Anaheim peppers** with seeds removed*
  *2 large **tomatoes**, broiled until skin is charred*
  *4 cloves **garlic***
  *1 teaspoon **cumin***
  *1 teaspoon **salt***
Heat in a large frying pan:
  *4 tablespoons **peanut or other oil***
Add sauce and cook for about 5 minutes.

Use to make enchiladas, or freeze in ice trays and turn out the
cubes of sauce into a plastic bag for winter storage.

SEPTEMBER 20—We began the day by roasting peppers and eggplant to try to reduce the produce litter, and I froze the tomatillo enchilada sauce I made last night. Then I suggested to Alan that we could make pita bread sandwiches and take a quick trip to Piermont to see what progress had been made yesterday—I assumed the framing of the walls would have begun.

The framing of the walls had not, of course, begun.

SEPTEMBER 21—When I came home, Alan had put up green chili, tomato, and tomatillo salsa, and finished cleaning his paintings out of the hall—by thoroughly trashing his studio. In the evening, he froze *corno di toro* peppers and I made a list of things we might offer the auctioneer.

SEPTEMBER 27—Terrible, rainy day. No work on the house, obviously. But having just come back from Piermont, I need to reflect on the astonishing change of mood that place created. Nothing more has been done. The rain prevented work today, and prevented us from being out in the garden. But the place (was it the changing weather? There was a stiff wind off the water and the sky kept changing, going silver and gray) just made me elated. When we got back into the car, we drove out the pier to look at the wild weather and I realized that my mood was totally changed. I have been depressed for days—partly the weather, I think, but it's not only that. I simply *love* it in Piermont. I feel so wonderful when I'm there. It's just elating to be where you can connect so intimately with the weather every day. In this big house, we know if it's raining or gloomy, and sometimes at night, when I get up to pee, I can see the moon so I know whether or not it's full. But there, you are aware of every nuance, every changing cloud, you feel the weather all the time, and it's wonderful, sometimes even frightening as it almost was today with the wind driving heavy

waves against the pier. We are going to live there, and I'm going
to love it.

Earlier in the summer, a friend who was studying landscape suggested an explanation for the deep affinity I felt for this spot. She had
encountered in the writing of a scholar named Jay Appleton the idea
that two qualities in the landscape were particularly reassuring to
relatively helpless mammals such as humans: refuge and prospect.
Refuge for hiding out, prospect for watching out—for enemies and
food. Congers had no prospect. We never sat out on our lawn, only on
the porch, and then only "in season." I had enclosed that porch
view—with a grapevine and evergreens close to the house and with
shrubs around the edges of the property—to protect us from the corner traffic. But Piermont offered both refuge (note our reluctance to
lose the shelter of the old house) and the prospect of the river from
the terrace and from the boardwalk. It was not merely foolhardiness,
but mammalian longing that made us buy a house we had to demolish!

In late October, we made compost at Piermont, combining the
abundant foliage of the sweet potatoes with oak leaves brought down
from Congers. Through the fall, we harvested almost daily salads
from the cold frame. We dug carrots, planted saffron crocus and rhubarb, and gave tomatillos and serrano peppers to one of the carpenters who liked to make hot sauce.

And finally, one day in early November, we came back from a
meeting in the city to a house that had for the first time a locked door.
"We unlocked our own door," I wrote, "and changed clothes in our
new house," feeling wonderful that we could once more find shelter
in the place we had so happily found refuge before the demolition
began. And then we went out to clean up the corn, tomato, pepper,
and eggplant beds, and to harvest kale and parsley and dry beans. The
day before the stucco went on, we came home with "tons" of parsley
and had Pizzaiola Pasta for dinner with a salad from the cold frame.
The produce just kept coming in.

Pizzaiola Pasta

Put into processor:

1½ cup fresh **parsley leaves** *and small stems*
3 cloves **garlic** *(or more)*

Purée.

Add:

¼ cup (or less) **olive oil**
½ to 1 teaspoon **red wine vinegar**
½ can (1 ounce) **anchovy fillets** *with oil*
½ teaspoon **red pepper flakes**

Process until blended.

Serve over:

1 pound **spaghetti**, *boiled and drained.*

Delicious!

And even as the house began to take shape, and its beauty became obvious, we couldn't live there, but we could plant.

NOVEMBER 19—Well, it's garlic-planting time—since the first full moon after the first frost is now on the wane. . . . I sorted garlic cloves, taking sixty big ones to plant, along with 6 shallots and a bag of potato onions from the cold cellar. I then dug leeks and scallions. We loaded everything into the car and went down to Piermont, planning to plant the scallions and leeks against the north fence.

Back home I made a hominy stew with the last of our tiny green beans.

DECEMBER 1 — When [the architect] called this morning, I asked
when we were likely to be through, and he said, as if that were
always the predicted date, "Oh, we'll make it by the end of January." I said, "The *end* of January? You said the first of January." He
acknowledged that he had. I realized with a thump today that one
of the things bothering me was the sense I had that we had been
displaced from our home. We used to be able to go down there
whenever we wanted, work on the house, walk out to the boardwalk, have lunch, etc. But for months now, it has not been our
place. It is filled with other people and there is almost no time we
can go down there and feel that it is in any sense ours. Since we
are very much detaching from Congers, we are sort of in limbo.

In early December we picked a salad from the cold frame and
came back home to the warmth of Congers to eat it. It would be
almost two months before "back home" would mean Piermont.

6

Giving Things Up

> The things most worth wanting are not available everywhere all the time.
>
> —Alice Waters

BY THE TIME WE MOVED in January, the Piermont garden was frozen solid, but while the house was under construction, we regularly offered the workmen beautiful produce, and told them to ask for anything they wanted. One week in October, when the garden was offering up carrots, tomatoes, peppers, scallions, leeks, eggplant, and an assortment of greens eager to be picked, I went to the community market to pick up a loaf of bread and found one of our workmen buying fresh asparagus. "Where on earth are they growing asparagus *this* season?" I asked in a tone of near outrage. He smiled benignly and said, "Oh, sometimes I just *feel* like asparagus." I had to restrain myself from snapping back, "In *October*?" although my mind was spitting out names like Guatemala and Columbia.

It was not his fault, of course, for he, like all the rest of us, had been well taught that "feeling like it" ought to be our guiding principle where food is concerned, and that anything we might feel like should be available all the time. Since food manufacturers expend enormous sums to make us "just feel like" the things they want to sell, it seems that eating locally, as I have been urging, would be drastically limiting.

The apparent perversity of my relocalization goal became starkly clear to me years ago, when Alan and I were visiting my mother in California. Going out to shop for a picnic, we ended up in one of

those vast Southern California supermarkets where you are intended
to lose the day. Every variety of fresh fruit known to God was laid out
there, whole, cut up, and combined for effortless fruit salads. Vegetables were presented with equal inventiveness; ditto cakes, pies,
breads, pastries, salad bars; in addition there was canned, boxed, frozen, chilled, and bagged infinitude. The bakery was on the premises,
as were other kitchens making fresh tacos and Chinese egg rolls.

This sort of food intemperance has since spread from California
eastward. But it was unusual then, and I went reeling out into the
blazing heat of the parking lot with my little grocery bag, wailing to
Alan, "Good grief! If that's what's meant by 'choice,' how can local
food compete?!" Hoping to inform my thinking on that daunting
question, I began conducting workshops to explore the limits of local
eating.

I would open these with a little rap about the 5-calorie strawberry
flown to New York from California at a cost of 435 fossil-fuel calories
as an example of the unsustainability of our present food system.
Then I would ask the attendees which locally unproducible foods
they would find hardest to give up, and list their answers on a black-
board. The contents and lengths of these lists varied a lot depending
on where we were geographically and on whether a lot of local growers were in attendance. Farmers are most likely to know what *could* be
produced locally if anyone wanted it.

I've done these workshops mostly in the Northeast, and in this
part of the country the usual suspects appear right away. First come all
the crops Europe set up its colonies to produce in the tropics: coffee,
tea, cocoa, sugar, bananas. Then come pineapples and citrus fruits. In
the Northeast, people are also concerned about losing grains, especially rice.

After everyone's contributions have been posted (and the lists are
often surprisingly short), I ask whether any foods are up there by
mistake. Non-gardeners often name things that growers know are
easy to produce almost anywhere at some time during the year. So
someone will call out, "I grow eggplant." And someone else will

shout, "You can take broccoli off the list." In this way, crops that are grown in the region are removed from the list of ungrowables, as are some foods that are not normally produced in the vicinity but could be, such as sweet potatoes, which, as I remarked earlier, most people think of as a southern crop.

In these workshops, we don't presume that we need to have available fresh all year whatever can be locally produced. Most people interested in organic farming are well aware that when cold weather comes, canned tomatoes or frozen broccoli can add variety to the standard winter vegetables. We don't talk either about convenience foods, since the attendees are usually people who like fresh food, still know how to cook it from scratch, and want to.

I had my most provocative experience with losing a food from the list of not-locally-producibles during an organic farming meeting in Vermont. Some of the best organic farmers around were in that workshop, people who knew so much more than I did that I just stood back and let things happen. What happened was that someone listed artichokes as a vegetable they didn't want to give up.

Almost all the artichokes Americans eat are grown in California, around Castroville, a town on California's Monterey coast that bills itself as "the artichoke capital of the world." A field of artichokes is a beautiful sight because they look like giant thistle plants with the artichokes thrusting out at the top as giant buds. I said "like" giant thistle plants because, although they share the vast flowering family *Acteraceae* with thistles, artichokes are no more closely related to thistles than radishes are to broccoli. On the other hand, I said "as giant buds" because, of course, they are giant buds. Left unpicked, artichoke buds become oversized thistle-like flowers. In the United States, artichokes are grown on a commercial scale almost exclusively in California because they are a tender perennial. That means they come up in succeeding years where the climate is mild, but really cold weather will kill them.

But at the Vermont workshop, one of the participants shouted, "You can take artichokes off the list—I grow them." In icy Vermont?

It turned out that Alan LePage, who like his grandfather before him farms in Barre, Vermont, grows artichokes (different from the California variety as it turns out) from seed each year; his prowess is acknowledged in my Fedco seed catalogue next to the picture of the Imperial Star Globe Artichoke. Later that winter, Alan LePage sent me some artichoke seeds, which I planted the following spring—too late. The seedlings weren't big enough when I set them out in the garden, and although I grew some handsome plants, they produced no artichokes.

The next year, however, I started the seeds early and set out some lusty young artichoke plants in May. They grew into enormous rosettes of spiky gray-green leaves (the catalogue said to space them three feet apart, but mine demanded more room than that) and in the fall I got artichokes! A big one for each plant and then, when the central bud had been cut off, a lot of little side buds of the kind they sell for a dollar a bag in Castroville. These are the kind you can eat whole because they haven't developed that bristly center appropriately named "the choke." Gourmets find artichokes grown from seed more watery and less flavorful than the California ones grown from cuttings, but I suspect the *idea* of having a homegrown artichoke in New York overcame my taste discrimination.

Artichokes are a pretty specialized food, even in California, so I'll resist the temptation to put my favorite recipe here. I'd like to say, however, that if you eat artichokes, you need to overcome whatever saturated fat fear my nutrition colleagues have implanted, and serve them with butter; not margarine, but melted butter (okay, warm olive oil if you're really worried about saturated fats). Artichokes are too insistent to tolerate synthetics.

Moreover, I can't comfortably recommend margarine, since the only thing in the world I'm really famous for is a remark I once made to a reporter from the *New York Times*. I said that I ate butter rather than margarine because I trusted the cows more than the chemists, a comment that has turned up on British menus, in books of quotations, and even as the slogan at the head of an October page on a 1997 weekly planner—always attributed to me. I'm not embarrassed. I really do trust the cows more, and more-recent discoveries regarding the hazards of trans-fatty acids in margarine have made my incautious remark to *The New York Times* seem prescient.

What the artichoke story illustrates most dramatically, however, is that many food plants that could be grown widely around the country are not produced on a commercial scale simply because they can't compete with produce grown in California with subsidized water and transportation. In a recent book, *The Fruits of Natural Advantage*, which describes the development of California's fruit monopoly, Steven Stoll captures the illusions that drove the state's boosters. So convinced were its orchardists and their supporters of the "natural advantage" of California's climate that when a promoter went east in 1886 to see why freight-loads of fruit were not getting through in good shape, he was stunned to discover Michigan producing prodigious quantities of exquisite peaches:

> Before entering Michigan the writer was filled with the traditional California conceit, and honestly believed in common with thousands of fellow-Californians that there is no other spot in the land so highly favored for fruit, and especially peach culture, as California.

"Providence did not intend giving California exclusive control of all fruits," he admitted. "Our Eastern brethren have been permitted to share some of our privileges." So informed, California growers set out to compete as hard as they could by aggressive and cooperative marketing, with results that are visible in supermarkets everywhere.

It is, alas, not merely competition from California that daunts local growers. Because food trade is global now, farmers must also compete with products grown on other continents where land is cheaper and labor poorly paid. Consequently, foods shipped to where you live include not only "out of season" produce but things you ought to be able to buy from someone just around the corner. At a workshop I conducted in Mississippi, a woman once burst out angrily that the only catfish she could buy in her market were from Brazil instead of from the fish farms just up the delta.

Some years ago, one of my students did a dissertation exploring the dietary implications of trying to eat a local diet in her home state of Montana. Given its generally frigid climate and less than optimal soil resources, we figured that if Montana could grow its own, most other states could too. She learned that before World War II, when Montana grew a great variety of fruits and vegetables as well as the beef and wheat that now dominate its agricultural production, the state produced almost 70 percent of its own food. By 1985, she calculated, 66 percent of the state's food came from outside its borders. In fact, the more recent figures were misleading because most of the beef and wheat had to be shipped out of state to be slaughtered or ground and then reimported. So the reasons why so much of our food does not come from nearby often have little to do with climate.

In much of the continental United States, of course, and certainly in regions where the ground freezes in winter, some tropical plants just can't be grown. Would eating locally mean we had to give them up? Perhaps not; trade in some of these foods might be managed in a fair and earth-friendly fashion. But most fresh fruits and vegetables probably aren't among them. The high water content of these foods (88 percent of a peach is water) and their tendency to rot if they get warm, means that we are, in effect, burning lots of petroleum to ship cold water around. Because the value of unfettered global trade is unquestioned and petroleum is artificially cheap, these sorts of costs are not being examined. So when the only tomatoes my local supermarket offers are air-shipped from Holland—in August, when local tomato vines are heavy with fruit—I'm supposed to ignore the energy cost of chilling, packaging, air-shipping, and trucking those flawless-looking objects to my neighborhood.

One can begin the process of going local, then, by cleaning up obvious absurdities like these, after which we might behave as responsibly as we presently know how by trying to buy fresh foods produced, say, within a day's leisurely drive of our homes. The distance is entirely arbitrary. But then, so was the decision made by others long ago that we ought to have produce from all around the world. The driving-distance goal is at least designed to maintain a living countryside.

I once conceived the radical idea that we could meet our winter yearning for summer produce by using local foods in summer and fall while California and Florida renewed their stressed fields by planting clover, vetch, and other cover crops in the heat of summer. When winter came, California and Florida farmers could plow in the greenery and plant peppers and tomatoes and other warm weather produce to ship to us while our fields were frozen.

I'm not at all certain that such a trade off is botanically possible, even if it were politically feasible. But before I had a chance to explore the idea, a friend and colleague had a student calculate the very considerable cost to the environment—just counting the greenhouse gases produced—to ship fresh tomatoes to New Jersey year-round. That was a reminder that sending fresh produce junketing around the country is simply too wasteful an activity to make it part of any ultimate solution. Tomatoes, for example, are even more watery than peaches. Keeping all that water cool as it moves north from Florida or east from California is helping warm the planet. So it seems preferable, especially where tomatoes and other fragile fruits are concerned, to limit our consumption of fresh ones to the four or five months when they can be grown locally, and enjoy them dried, canned, or frozen during the rest of the year.

A second step we can take to move toward sustainability would be to limit our consumption of "exotics"—not necessarily to a single orange in the Christmas stocking, though that is a good image. It's unlikely that everyone outside the citrus belt would need to give up citrus even if we had a rational food supply. But I'm convinced that drinking freshly squeezed orange juice every morning in my part of the country is a bad idea. Using precious energy to ship oranges north from Florida or Brazil, east from California, or west from Israel or Spain is a careless use of a finite resource. One advantage of beginning to think of certain foods as especially precious is that you use them in a different way. You don't slug down a glass of freshly squeezed orange juice in Iowa as if it could be ladled out of a local lake.

The list of exotics includes, alas, bananas. I have always loved bananas and I still do, although an extended fling with home-grown bananas in Hawaii has cooled my ardor for the blandness of the lumpen Cavendish that is grown for the U.S. market. Still, familiarity sometimes wins, and I do eat bananas at other people's houses. But bananas fill me with ambiguity, and sometimes even rage. Like this very brief story that appeared recently in the *New York Times'* "Metropolitan Diary":

> Dear Diary: Consider the street banana. Grown in a tropical paradise amid chattering birds and baby monkeys at play, it has traveled thousands of miles over land and sea. On trucks, boats, and trains it has ridden, handled by scores of people; yet its skin is unblemished, its fruit still sweet. You give the man a quarter. He gives you a banana. No change. No receipt. No bag. A transaction direct from the agora. A journey through space and time.

That little story demonstrates a desperate ignorance about how food is produced at the millennium, and at what cost. For this stroller's banana was undoubtedly grown not in a tropical paradise but in a banana tree desert from which chattering birds and baby monkeys were long ago banished to protect the ripening fruit from our competitors. Blissfully oblivious to the real conditions under which her banana was grown, she is equally blithe about those thousands of miles her banana has travelled, "on trucks, boats, and trains" that spewed into the air combustion products that are helping warm the planet right where she's standing. Bananas may well continue to be part of even the most conscientious diets, I suppose, but one ought, at least, to strive for consciousness in buying one.

Bananas grown organically and fair-traded so their producers can earn enough to live on are now available to the affluent. But transport remains an environmental problem, and my own solution has been to try for a substitute. A number of years ago, I learned that a tree native to the Northeast, called the paw-paw, yields fruit that is supposed to taste something like a banana. The paw-paw is the only tropical fruit tree to survive the ice age in the northern hemisphere, and our ancestors used the fruit extensively, even drying it for winter.

My banana-substitution project has been a determined and—as it turned out—long-term effort, since the paw-paw has a taproot that doesn't like to be disturbed. The first two times Alan and I ordered one from a nursery while we were still in Congers, the frail slip that made it through the mail and into the ground never broke bud at all. We were about to give up when I saw a note in the Seed Exchange column of *Gardening* magazine offering paw-paw seeds gathered in the wild. I sent my stamped, self-addressed envelope to the address listed, and back in a lumpy package came six or seven black seeds, giant flattened ovals not unlike wildly overgrown watermelon seeds.

By this time we were in Piermont, gutting a house we didn't know was to be torn down. Where to plant a tree that hates to be moved when you don't even know where you'll want a tree? Not anywhere near the 75 feet of garden beds already planted in vegetables. Not down the middle of the lot where I had a 5-foot path running to the river. And so, I split the difference halfway from the house to the river, tucking three or four seeds deep into the soil bordering the fence on either side of the property. I would train these trees, which the books said aspired to be big, to hug a fence.

I had no idea whether any of the seeds would come up and in the coming months my mind was elsewhere. No one had yet told me that you couldn't grow a paw-paw from seed. Through the summer, I checked from time to time to see what had come up, and of course nothing had. In late August, I checked again; once again, nothing. Then, in mid-September, cleaning up the yard, I noticed, one—no, two—no, four identical little tree seedlings among the other weeds against the north fence, each bearing at its tip two tiny drooping leaves that reminded me of nothing so much as the avocado tree we used to have in our California backyard. "Alan," I yelled, "I think I've got a paw-paw."

And through the year of ground raising and yard shifting and flooding and chaos that accompanied our final landing in Piermont, the seedlings got taller, put on heft, and grew long, oval, avocado-like leaves. When the yard began to take shape and it became obvious that the 2-foot-high adolescents had to be moved, I was worried about disturbing their roots, but it couldn't be helped. I gave two away, one to a farmer-professor, one to a local landscaper-friend, and both apparently survived. Then I transplanted one so it could be espaliered at the end of my raspberry frame and moved another so I could train it onto the north fence ("They can reach a mature height of 60 feet." "Not on my property they can't!"). Both of mine lived, and five years after their emergence, the largest put out odd dark brown blooms that spoke of the tropics, but no fruit—yet.

I'm actually a little anxious about the fruit. I've learned more about paw-paws since I began my journey toward a banana-free life and understand that the quality of the fruit they produce can vary wildly. At a Midwest organic farming conference, I actually had a chance to taste a paw-paw. It was not, I hoped, in prime condition, since I didn't like it much. Moreover, since those big black seeds fill the fruit, it seems as if it's going to be as easy to get fruit out of a paw-paw as blood out of a turnip! Nevertheless, in the tropical-fruit-import replacement campaign, put me down as "trying."

Exotics such as coffee, tea, chocolate, and spices are in some ways easier to deal with than fruits and vegetables. They are durable, don't need to be kept cold, and—because they're dry—are comparatively light, so they cost much less to ship than succulent produce does. Some of these products can now be purchased from fair trading companies that buy directly from growers with whom, as their name implies, they trade fairly by paying more than the going price. But the environmental costs of processing and transporting these foods still needs to be considered in any rational planning for sustainability, as do possible alternative uses for the land on which these crops presently grow.

Locally grown herbs can be used in place of the often elaborately processed leaves of *Thea sinensis* that most people now drink as tea. Ordinary tea is in the camellia family, and could be grown in the United States, in places such as California and the South where camellias flourish, but the cost of labor for picking and processing would likely be prohibitive. (According to my 1912 Century dictionary, even then "the cost of labor has so far prevented its economic success.") Herb teas that can be simply dried and packaged should be economically more feasible to produce locally.

Coffee and chocolate could be given up. But it's not clear that they would need to be, even by the most committed proponent of local diets. These luxuries certainly ought not to be grown as they so often are today, on land needed for the production of edible staples. If they are grown (sustainably) as a trade good after local food needs have been met, and if they are priced to cover the true costs (including environmental) of their production and processing, it may be possible to keep them as luxuries in our diets if we choose to.

Many herbs and spices, such as mint and other herbal teas mentioned above, can be produced locally in parts of the country where they presently are not. In *Future Food*, a remarkably far-sighted book published in 1976, Colin Tudge first made the point that seasonings derived from tropical plants—vanilla beans, cinnamon bark, and nutmeg seeds, for example—are among the most acceptable foods to be used as trade goods. Like coffee, tea, and chocolate, they are dry, durable, easily transportable, and used in very small quantities. "All countries should move toward self-reliance in food; partly for political safety," Tudge writes,

> . . . and partly because one important way to save energy would be to stop shifting food around the world. But self-reliance merely

means producing one's own basic foods, so that the people do not starve, even in a blockade. It does not mean an end to all trade, and the tropical spices in particular—which require little land, are cheap to transport, and yet are valuable—should be used and made available worldwide, with the profit going to the producer countries. . . . Tomorrow's food should be spicy, and where there's spice there's flavor.

It seems worth mentioning here that saffron, the world's most luxurious spice, can be produced domestically. Those threads that season Spanish rice are stamens of a crocus that blooms in the fall in much of the country. I grew enough *Crocus sativus* in Congers to give me a jarful of red-golden threads. Although the current garden's tendency to go underwater has so far daunted similar efforts in Piermont, I am planting some fresh crocus bulbs in a high spot this year, hoping for the best. This most expensive of spices centers the most welcome of flowers, pale purple crocuses that come just as you think the garden is about to shut down for the year. If you're careful, you can pull off the little stamens without destroying the beauty of the flower. What better way is there to spend a few minutes each fall morning than crouched over some fragile purple crocus, thinking about a local *Arroz con Pollo*.

ARROZ CON POLLO
(CHICKEN WITH PEAS AND SAFFRON RICE)

Cut into serving pieces:
 one 2¹/₂- to 3-pound chicken
Wash and pat dry.

Heat in a heavy 3 to 4 quart casserole:
 *1 tablespoon **corn or safflower oil***
Add:
 *¹/₄ pound **salt pork**, finely cubed*

Fry slowly until cubes are brown. Drain on a paper towel.

Add chicken, and brown quickly over medium-high heat, turning often. Remove to platter.

Pour off all but 1 to 2 teaspoons fat from casserole.

Add:
   *1 cup **onions**, finely chopped*
   *1 large clove **garlic**, finely chopped*
Cook to soften but not brown.

Stir in:
   *1 tablespoon **paprika***
   *1 cup **tomatoes** (fresh, canned, or frozen), finely chopped*
Bring to a fast boil over medium heat, stirring until most of the liquid evaporates.

Return chicken and salt pork to casserole. Add:
   *1 1/2 cups **short-grain brown rice***
   *1 cup **fresh or frozen peas***
   *3 cups boiling **water or light chicken stock***
   *1/8 teaspoon **saffron threads**, crushed*
   ***salt**, to taste*

Bring to boil quickly, then cover tightly, reduce heat, and allow to simmer for 30 minutes or until rice has absorbed the liquid and the chicken is tender. Let stand for 5 to 10 minutes before serving.

Arroz con pollo means rice and chicken. And chicken brings up the issue of local lifestock. If you're anxious to know whether people with passionate commitments like mine eat animal products and how on earth they justify it if they do, skip to chapter 11, where you will find the answer carefully embedded in story and eco-lore. The simpler question of how animals and their products fit into local diets is different issue. If we consumed them at a reasonable level (a big "if"), most meat and dairy products could be produced locally and sustainably. As even the most casual thought will reveal, cattle and chickens now flourish—or have flourished—from Maine to Florida and from Texas to North Dakota. To be raised sustainably, cattle and sheep need grazing land. In my region, New England, we now have what is seen as a plague of deer, making full use of the browse in fields (and backyards) where the fields used to be kept in pasture for grazing cattle. Local sheep can be managed on unfarmable hills with, among other devices, sheepdogs, some of whom believe themselves to be sheep, and use their unsheeplike barks, claws, and teeth to keep predators at bay.

The custom of making butter and cheese, including sheep cheese, has been revived in New England with the creation of a market not only among gourmets, but also among people who want to buy food from animals raised without hormones, antibiotics, and growth promoters. Hogs and poultry can be raised on pasture that they enrich as they grow. Hogs can also use clean human garbage, crop and dairy leftovers, and some wet mud in summer. Chickens can exploit weeds and bugs. So raising some animals locally is no problem. Slaughtering and processing them is. Sanitary laws that, as Wendell Berry has noted, help replace the dirt in your food with poisons, have encouraged giantism in the food system, thereby eliminating small-scale processors. Reviving local processing plants needs to be a priority if we hope to have local meat.

Among my colleagues is a group of chefs committed to supporting local food producers. As I was leaving a workshop where we had been talking about the meaning of "local," a much-admired Manhattan chef came up and said to me, "I know what you mean, Joan. I get my prosciutto locally." I laughed, thinking he was teasing me and meant he bought from a local supplier. "No," he insisted seriously, "my butcher makes it for me on West 12th Street." Create a market for the local, and surprising things turn up there.

That *Arroz con Pollo* I was making with my saffron also contains rice, no problem for the folks in California and some parts of the South, but not normally a local food for the rest of us. One of the farmers at my Vermont workshop insisted that we could grow rice there if we wanted to, but rice is just one of the grains that raise a different issue where localness is concerned. The American Midwest has been one of the great grain-growing regions of the world, supplying much of the world's exportable surplus. Indeed, U.S. farmers produce so much more grain than we can use domestically that finding export markets is urgent. So the nation has never needed to import grains. That doesn't mean they aren't imported, of course, since the "market" dictates that many of the same products will be imported and exported to someone's advantage. Unfortunately, growing grain as we do it leads to topsoil loss, so our level of export cannot be maintained without seriously running down our natural inheritance.

Whether the Midwest should be, absent the pull of export, the source of grains for the rest of the nation is an open question. Shipping grain around the country from the Midwest raises transportation issues again, but different ones. Railroads move foods more energy-efficiently than trucks, and unlike vegetables and fruits, grain is shipped unrefrigerated. It's also dry and therefore high in calories per pound—in equal weights, cornmeal has sixteen times more calories than tomatoes. What is shipped is predominantly wheat, corn, and soybeans, most of which could readily be grown in many parts of the country—my own state of New York, for example. But more thought needs to be given to the question of whether such a shift to the local makes ecological sense where grains are concerned.

The problem with the focus on these three crops is that organic farmers need to plant a greater variety of crops to keep their fields in good tilth. We need to create markets for other grains—oats and millet, for example—that farmers could produce in various parts of

the country, providing us with more varied local diets. And then
there's buckwheat. For small gardeners like me, buckwheat, not tech-
nically a grain, is best known as a very fast-growing cover crop—
something one grows to harvest sunlight, keep the ground covered,
and turn into the soil before the next crop to add organic matter and
nutrients.

Analyzing the nutritional adequacy of a diet made up year-round
largely of products produced or producible in the Northeast, a colleague and I discovered that Penn Yan, New York, is home to Birkett
Mills, the world's largest producer of buckwheat products. We wondered if a northeast diet should put more emphasis on buckwheat, a
food most familiar in its cracked form as kasha. Trying to expand
possibilities, we used buckwheat groats instead of rice in a surprisingly good risotto, doubtless capable of improvement in the hands of
a gifted chef.

BUTTERNUT SQUASH AND BUCKWHEAT RISOTTO

Bring to a low simmer:
> *3½ to 4 cups **chicken stock***

Meanwhile, sauté until slightly browned:
> *1 tablespoon **olive oil***
> *2 ounces or less finely minced **Italian salami**, or **pancetta***

Add:
> *½ cup finely chopped **onion***
> *2 large cloves **garlic**, minced*

Lower heat, and sauté until onion is tender but not brown.

Add:
> *1½ cups **whole buckwheat groats***

Stir a minute or so, then add:
> *½ cup **dry white wine***

Cook, stirring, until wine is absorbed.

Add:

> 3 cups **butternut squash**, *cut in* 1/2-*inch cubes*
>
> 2 teaspoons **sugar**
>
> 1 1/2 cups **simmering stock**

Stir, cover, and cook about 5 minutes.

· Add:

> 1/2 *tablespoon chopped fresh* **sage leaves**

Add remaining stock about 1/2 cup at a time, stirring constantly for about 15 minutes until squash is tender and groats are cooked. Season to taste with **salt** and **pepper**. Serve with **Parmesan cheese** on the side.

Aware that buckwheat-based soba noodles are a delicacy in Japanese cuisine, we used them as a substitute for pasta in another dish. Alas, the only soba noodles we could find were imported from Japan—hardly a boon to localism—and were significantly more expensive than wheat-based noodles. It seems unlikely that the ability to make buckwheat noodles is genetically or geographically determined. And since the high price of imported noodles seems to reflect a demand, surely we could support noodle factories in our state. We could have much wider local food choices in every region if food makers would turn from inventing new flavors of soft drinks to amplifying our notion of what the lands we live on could provide—if asked.

7

Put It in the Cellar

> I *am* worried about the decline of farming communities of all kinds,
> because I think that among the practical consequences of that decline
> will sooner or later be hunger.
>
> —Wendell Berry, *The Gift of Good Land*

BEFORE WE HIRED AN ARCHITECT to help us plan what was still just a renovation, we had pretty much determined the layout of our future home. It was a row house, after all, 25 feet wide and 60 feet deep including its deck. It faced west, toward the street with a view toward sunrise on the river side. We wanted a big room, kitchen/dining/living room, facing the water upstairs, with Alan's office and a guest bedroom behind facing the street. Alan's studio would be a large room facing the street downstairs (he didn't work from nature in the studio), with our bedroom and my office facing the water and the rising sun. Since so many of our choices were settled, one of our earliest questions to the first architect we hired was whether we could have a cold cellar on the same floor as the kitchen.

We had a fine cold cellar in Congers. Because our old Victorian's basement lovingly reflected every bay and angle of the upstairs, we had available an alcove 15 feet wide and 8 feet deep that angled off from the rest of the cellar and had a small window where the stone foundation joined the timbers. Along each of the 8-foot walls was rough shelving, which we had cleaned off and painted. We walled the alcove off from the rest of the basement, insulated our wall, put in a door, and used the cool space to store produce through the winter.

Mostly we stored potatoes (in boxes on the shelves) and onions (hanging in net bags). Once we dug all our carrots before a hard freeze and stored them down there in sand. We stored our sweet potatoes there too, until we discovered that sweet potatoes shrivel up and turn black in the damp cold, after which we put them in a back bedroom. The other cold-cellar staple from December to March was a bushel box of incredibly sweet and juicy grapefruit that my mother always sent for Christmas. Those grapefruit taught me that even militantly local eating ought to allow for treats. And once my sister sent us a box of kiwi that lasted so long in the cold cellar it seemed the perfect transition fruit, so we planted two kiwi vines for the future.

We learned from this experience that a cold cellar was essential to our winter eating. And while our Congers cold cellar occupied the ideal and obvious place—the cellar—I had been finding it increasingly inconvenient to scramble down one steep railless flight of steps and run to the back of the basement every time I wanted a potato or an onion for dinner. Moreover, the kitchen/dining/living room of the new house was to be on the second floor, facing the river, and the entrance to the cellar stairs was to be somewhere in the back reaches of Alan's first-floor studio, which faced the street. Any basement cold cellar in Piermont would be *two* flights down and a long hike. I wanted a cold cellar I could walk into from the kitchen.

I'm afraid the first architect gave himself away when he disdainfully raised his eyebrows and said that perhaps we could store vegetables under benches out on the porch. But they'd freeze, I said, not even mentioning that I would too when I went out to get them. He seemed unmoved by that (as by most of the other things we asked for). When we had to tell him he wouldn't work out, he said, "Well, at least I made clear what *I* wanted." And he had.

The second architect, J., seemed more responsive, and helped us design a pantry/cold cellar near the kitchen. It was to be a long, narrow space divided into two shorter rooms with the entrance from the kitchen into a small pantry area that would hold our small upright freezer. Through an insulated door beyond that would be a "cold" room, which was to be connected to the basement and the outdoors by vents and fully insulated from the rest of the house. We hoped that a fan would pull cold air up from the basement to the floor of the cold cellar through a pipe, and warm air would flow out the other vent near the ceiling.

Luckily we were on site the day the plumber began installing the *heating pipes* indicated on the architect's plans, and were thus able to prevent our cold room from being toasty. We failed to notice until it was too late, however, that he had left out the floor vent through which cold air was to be sucked up from the basement into the cold room. "Not too bad," we thought at first, when we moved in at the frigid end of January. "We'll just open up the 1-by-2-foot vent at the top of the north wall and cold air will force its way in, exactly as it does when you've accidentally left the window open a crack." No such luck. The builders had done a magnificent job of sealing the room. No air flowed in or out. The stored food probably generated enough metabolic heat to rise and push the cold air out, and the room stayed comfortably warm, even with the vent fully uncovered. Our potatoes, the mainstay of our winter diet, were sprouting much more quickly than we had planned; our self-provisioning goal was falling victim to heat.

Six months after we moved in, a former student came to visit with her husband who was, fortuitously, a refrigeration engineer. He looked over our cold-cellar problem and seemed to have a perfect solution, at least for the frigid months when we had the most produce to store. He would put a little refrigerator fan up in the vent to draw in cold air, with an attached thermostat that would turn the fan off when it had pulled in enough outside air to drop the temperature to 35 degrees Fahrenheit. He took some measurements, went back home, and in a month or so, our solution came in the mail. We installed it. Problem solved.

Solved, that is, until the morning I went in and saw that the temperature on the thermometer had fallen to 21 degrees and the fan was still running. The fan is now set on a timer that turns it on for a few hours during the middle of the night, and again just before dawn, usually the coldest of the twenty-four hours. That way, if we don't open the door too much, the temperature stays pretty cool, but nothing freezes. It isn't as steady a cold as we used to have in the Congers basement, but it keeps the good-storing potatoes until late April. And the onions do fine.

So the winter storage problem seemed to be solved; now all we needed was a yearly supply of onions and potatoes to store. And that turned out to be a more persistent challenge. I reported several chapters back that one of our earliest views of this now productive mini-farm was of a long strip of grass—under water. Days after we signed the purchase agreement, the entire community was hit by a northeaster that produced a "hundred-year flood." Of course, hundred-year floods are not what they used to be, given our penchant to exhale greenhouse gases every time we drive to the store. Hundred-year floods, torrential rains, tornadoes, and other expressions of Nature's disapproval of our careless affluence are becoming more common. So, we discovered, were floods in our backyard. And floods had not been factored into our plan for self-reliance.

We had grown onions and potatoes for years by the time we moved to Piermont, and were confident of our ability to produce them consistently. Indeed, the point at which we began to grow storage onions and more than one kind of potato represented a major step in our move toward self-supply. There's probably no rational reason to grow onions for yourself, of course. You can buy a bag of perfectly good onions pretty cheap, and home-grown onions don't have any obvious taste superiority. As for loyalty to local produce, New York State has the perfect muck soils for commercial onion growing and produces $40 million-worth a year, so, at least in theory, we could easily buy locally if we didn't grow our own.

We began growing onions, as I recall, because we saw a picture in a seed catalogue for a "Vidalia-type" onion that would grow in our climate. By now, most serious eaters have probably met Vidalia onions—the state of Georgia surely hopes you have. For over two decades, farmers there have been shipping boxes of their big, sweet, yellow granex hybrids out to the rest of us in late spring to sell as a gourmet item at gourmet prices. In ordinary storage, Vidalias don't keep long, so they have been a specialty item available for only a short time after harvest. I recently read, however, that Vedalias are now held under controlled atmosphere storage, so they've become one more thing available eight or nine months a year. Too bad.

The special quality of Vidalias comes from the South Georgia sandy loam in which they grow and the climate of the region. We first discovered Vidalias when Alan and I went south so he could give a talk about art, and someone brought us a box of onions as a departure present. It seemed an odd gift at the time, even for us, but the gift came with instructions from the giver to core the onion, put a bullion cube in the center, and bake until done. I never did the bullion cube trick, but we soon discovered that we were the owners of a box of onions so sweet that Alan would peel them to eat out of hand like an apple.

We couldn't afford to pay gourmet prices for an item as basic as an onion, so when the seed catalogue promised we could grow Vidalia-type onions right at home, we fell for the offer. Onions have rather complicated cultural requirements that gardeners can't do much about. Because they are sensitive to changing day-length, growing big onions in the North requires that you start with plants—either plants shipped up from the South or plants grown under lights indoors.

We tried ordering plants one year, but they came in bundles of 250, a quantity that required more space than we wanted to give over to onions, as well as producing more onions than we needed. So I found myself responsible for adding indoor onion-starting to my spring responsibilities. I was already successfully growing tomato, pepper, and eggplant seedlings under lights in the cellar; it seemed simple enough to add onions. It wasn't. The frail little grassy stems that emerge, bent double, with with their black seed cases nodding at their tips, are shockingly vulnerable to keeling over, and I was unsuc-cessful at eliminating the *Pythium* fungus that caused their collapse. Nevertheless, we managed to grow some Vidalia approximations, and patterns of work once started in a vegetable garden tend to per-sist, so I kept growing onion seedlings indoors despite the problems.

Then, one year, we got a seed catalogue from a fourteen-year-old gardener in upstate New York who was starting his own seed company. Noel asserted that his seeds would produce full-grown onions when started outdoors in spring. And they did—yellow and red onion seedlings, without the weakling babies having to be coddled indoors. Grown indoors or out, onion seedlings must be planted outdoors—a tedious and back-stressing job—into very fertile soil, and kept well watered. We garden by many of the guidelines of John Jeavons, who suggests planting on the diagonal, so we plant the onion seedlings in a diamond pattern about 4 inches apart. As they grow, onions begin to look something like daffodils except that as the bulb (red, yellow, or white) enlarges, it pushes its shoulders out of the ground, and of course there's no yellow flower! As the days begin to shorten, the bulb foliage begins to keel over, just the way daffodil foliage does when the bulbs have finished blooming.

When about half of the onion tops have fallen over spontaneously, you knock the others over so that they close off at the neck and dry out. You want the neck to seal up so the bulbs don't rot in storage. A few days later, the roots will have let go their hold on the soil and the onions will come easily out of the ground. They should be pulled and laid out to dry briefly in the sun right where they grew. At least that's the theory. The first year we lived in Piermont, July gave us long dry days and I pulled our red and yellow onions and laid them out on the hay mulch for a few days. After that, I brought them into the shed and put them in a single layer on screens to cure. The crop was our best ever—over one hundred pounds.

Storage onions can also be grown from tiny little onion bulbs called sets. We first learned about sets when our Maine gardening neighbor gave us a handful and told us that if we pushed them into the ground up to their necks, they would produce scallions. They did. At the time, we had no idea that if we let them grow to full size, they would mature into standard storage onions.

In our hundred-pound onion year, we had more onion seedlings in our cold frame than we could plant out, and the extras left crowded in the seedbed went on to produce tiny onions—our own onion sets. We had so many that I counted out what we would need for the following year—about one hundred—and we washed the remaining red pearl onions, glossed their skins with olive oil, and roasted them whole in the oven with rosemary and a little salt .

Our hundred-plus pounds of onions, produced on 45 square feet, celebrated our new home's first year, and convinced us that we had found horticultural nirvana. That winter, secure in our stored harvest of onions, potatoes, and sweets, all of which had produced obscenely well, we commented several times to each other that "next year" we ought to locate a soup kitchen to which we could regularly bring our future excesses. Fortunately we postponed picking up the phone. Humility comes quickly when Nature is your mistress; and the next growing year was very different.

A gorgeous summer and early autumn were followed by record rainstorms in late fall and early winter. During the long, cold winter that followed, record snowstorms piled up record snowdrifts that left the already low ground saturated when they thawed. The spring was late, characterized by what the *New York Times* called "bone-chilling arctic air." In early March, the cold set all-time records, but we had tough onion sets to plant, not fragile seedlings. Around the fifteenth of the month, despite the cold, I pushed the frost-proof onion sets into the soil at the front of the bed where the garlic had spent the winter. I doubt that I would have had the stamina to crouch in the freezing air and put out seedlings.

Then, four days past the Ides of March, came the flood.

MARCH 19—We had a high tide and flood warning on the radio this morning as we often do, and thought little about it. We've had those before, and it usually means that the water is pretty high at the boardwalk, period. But this evening a strong northeaster started blowing up in the evening, and at 8:45 we walked downtown through the rain to Village Hall to watch the opening of the voting machines. When the counting was over, we walked back home and stepped in the back gate. Water had already filled the center path and 3-foot waves were breaking over the boardwalk!!! High tide wasn't due for another hour, so we were in for it! (Ironically, Alan had bought a tide table for the area on Monday, without which we wouldn't have known how much to worry.) We went to bed with the rain lashing the house, and I told Alan that even if this was the price we had to pay, I was glad we lived on the river. I thought I'd have trouble sleeping, but I didn't. And then in the morning . . .

MARCH 20—I got up and looked out the bedroom window. The entire yard was under water! Close to the house, the 3-by-6-foot cold frame covered with a heavy glass storm window had floated from across the yard. The sunfish that had been stored 100 feet out by the river had sailed up to the house and lodged itself across the path. The two concrete urns, a foot-and-a-half high, were underwater up to their rims. Even from the house, 150 feet away, you could see that the boardwalk and its environs were covered with piles of tumbled driftwood. After sloshing out there through nearly a foot of river water we could see that the planking at the south end of the boardwalk had been ripped off. Worse, 3 feet of the bulkhead had been destroyed, its rock fill scattered on the beach, and the shrubs that grew there uprooted and tossed in the yard. The soil on the garden side of the boardwalk was gone (there goes all that sand and compost we carried in!), along with the plants it held. When the tide surged in again at 10 A.M. we could look down and see the Hudson lapping around the rocks on the inside of the boardwalk!

Further back in the yard, the water was so high that none of the garden beds was visible, and the salt hay we used to mulch the beds had floated off in rafts and lodged itself around the yard wherever there was a plant tall enough to catch it. Indestructible plastic litter had been deposited everywhere—lumps of styrofoam, tampon inserters, condoms, bits of toys and balloons, snap-on plastic bottle caps, pop-it beads. There wasn't much we could do until the water receded, but Alan went out to the boardwalk and began throwing back in what the river had given us. As the water receded, I began clearing up from the house out—logs, poles, and other large chunks of wood in one place; plastic crap in another. I managed to uncover some azaleas up near the house, and to rake out the excess wood chips that had covered them as the water receded. At some point, when the soil in the cold frame emerged above the flood, we carried the frame itself back where it belonged and set it in place—the spinach that was just coming up there was muddy but alive. We had only bare feet or water-filled clogs to walk in and it was cold as blazes, so we went in and let the water go down.

The raised bank at the river edge had been built to prevent the river from simply sweeping in and out of the yard. It was partially successful. Now when the river raged, it didn't sweep in. It came roaring over the boardwalk, filled the yard, and was unable to run back out. It did soak in, but slowly.

It took three days for the beds to reappear, the brick paths that separated them covered with slippery mud. In the bed where the onion sets had been planted, the sprouting green tops of neighboring fall-planted garlic emerged from the waters first, and the onion sets when they reappeared were tipped crazily. It was ten days before the clover path down the center of the property was dry enough not to squish underfoot. None of this did the plants any good. But it was only the beginning.

Twice more before June the path was flooded, not by the river, but by torrential rains coming in bursts. The beds, which sat higher than the path, were never entirely covered again, but they were saturated for a long time. The temperature veered crazily from high to low. That July was the coolest ever recorded.

The onions seemed to be growing normally, but many of them sent up flower stalks, which I broke off, assuming that they would rob the plants of energy. Sometime that spring, I read that onion sets were not as desirable as onion seedlings for making storage onions because they often flowered, making hard, thick necks that didn't cure well. Too true. Half the onion tops defied me when I tried to knock them down. They were too stiff. And when I tried to force them, they broke, leaving open stems vulnerable to rot.

We got half the crop into the shed to cure. When the remainder finally let loose from the soil and we pulled them to dry, I trusted the weatherman who said no rain would come until the next afternoon. We woke up to find our "drying onions" sopping wet, so we brought them into Alan's studio sink and cleaned off the half-rotted outer leaves.

Onions may not like soggy soil, but smaller organisms flourish in the damp. I peeled off the onions' damaged outer layers, trying to see whether I could get to a sound heart, trying to convince the crop to cure despite the 100 percent humidity of our unexpectedly cool August days. We harvested 37 pounds of onions, but despite my best efforts, some of them cured with soft spots where mold had gotten underneath the outer layers and would work its way through the whole onion if we didn't stop it. So we had to cut up many onions and freeze the good parts—or cook them. All of which accounts for the fact that a year and a half after we arrived in Piermont, I found myself one morning cutting up a half-rotten onion to salvage, and realized that a year earlier I would have thrown the whole thing away.

And it was not only the onions that suffered that year. The potatoes joined them. Potatoes should be dug when their tops die down, but I dug them earlier because I sensed that something was going wrong down there. The crops were small, and in one of the beds a third of the potatoes collapsed in my hand, rotted and smelly. It turned out to have been a banner year for wireworms, who liked the densely packed, soaking wet soil our floods produced and who spent the spring eating their way through the potatoes. Although our potato crop is usually saved for winter, that fall I made potato dishes every other day in order not to waste the wormy ones. (If I cut through the potato exactly where the surface holes are and find out just where the tunnels go, I can sometimes salvage almost a whole potato.) I told a friend who called as I was engaged in this enterprise that I was deciding which of the vegetables I had salvaged during the day to put into dinner that night.

POTATO FRITTATA

Preheat oven to 375°F.

Steam until almost tender (about 12 minutes):
  *1 pound **low starch potatoes**, sliced into 1/4-inch slices*
Meanwhile, sauté:
  *2 tablespoons **olive oil***
  *1 large red or yellow **onion**, sliced*
  *1 medium **bell pepper** (preferably red), stemmed, seeded, and sliced*
Cook until tender (10 minutes), stirring frequently.

Add:
  *1 small **roasted Anaheim, ancho, or other hot pepper** (optional)*
  *1 large clove **garlic**, minced (1 teaspoon plus)*
Cook one minute.

Now remove potatoes from steamer, add them to the sauté pan, and season with:
  *1 teaspoon **salt***
  ***pepper**, to taste*
Sauté mix, stirring gently, for 5 to 8 more minutes.

Pour over vegetables:
  *6 large **eggs**, beaten with*
  *1/4 cup mix of minced **parsley or similar herbs (chervil, celery leaf)***

Return pan to stovetop for 3 to 5 minutes, tilting and shaking pan to let eggs settle.

Put pan in oven, and bake until eggs are just set (10 minutes). *Do not overcook.*

The onion/potato crop salvage operation was not driven by parsimony, though I had excellent training in that. There surely was a time when, if I'd known how to grow so much of our food, the money saved would have made a difference. But we're comfortable now, we live in a village where the store is a block away, and can go to the Community Market to buy potatoes and onions if ours fail us. The anxiety produced by our root vegetable shortfall therefore seemed unwarranted. That's when I realized that several years earlier, without really knowing we had stepped over a line, we had achieved the goal I had been heading toward for years. We had reached the point where we simply never bought a vegetable. We found ourselves eating—and trying to feed guests—entirely on what we grew (aside from animal products and grains).

The crops in our first year in our new home were sufficiently oversized that we could use our own potatoes freely for dinner parties, invent dishes to use up sweet potatoes, and eat onions with abandon all winter.

Mashed Potatoes for Twelve
(with enough left over for Mashed Potato Cakes)

Peel and remove eyes from:
   *5 pounds yellow Finn or other good **mashing potatoes***
Cut into 1½- to 2-inch chunks, cover with water, and bring to a boil.

Reduce heat and simmer for ½ hour or until tender.

Remove from heat and drain. Mash potatoes with a potato masher, and remove to bowl of electric mixer (or remove to large bowl and use hand-held beater).

Add:
>   2 teaspoons **garlic powder** (*I know, but it's the only thing I use it for—time saving when I'm cooking a big meal!*)
>   4 tablespoons **butter**

When butter has melted add:
>   ½ cup **milk**, to start (*I use skim*)
>   **salt**, to taste

Now begin beating the potatoes at high speed, adding milk as needed. They should be soft and fluffy like well-beaten egg whites, but not wet. With luck, you'll have some left over.

Mashed Potato Cakes

To make four mashed potato cakes, mix:
>   *about 2 cupfuls* **mashed potato**
>   *1* **egg** (*optional, the potatoes will hold together without an egg*)

Mold a small handful into a patty smaller than a quarter-pounder. Heat a black iron frying pan very, very hot, lightly spray with oil, add the potato cakes, and turn down the heat. When one side is brown and crispy and you can easily slip a spatula under it, turn up the heat for 30 seconds, turn the cake over, and let the other side brown. Scrumptious.

The purpose of trying to grow our own potatoes and onions was never just to feed us; our effort was intended to demonstrate possibilities, and to remind us. We engaged in this self-reliance experiment to show that seasonal, local eating can be feasible, even in the Northeast—if you are willing to take what nature dishes out. Going to the market to fill in seemed an admission that self-reliance in our area wasn't really possible. We didn't want to give up so easily.

Since our own shortfall was weather-related, it seemed unlikely that we could make up for our own losses by buying local produce. If we were having trouble growing onions, the upstate onion growers would surely be sharing our problem. As for the potato farmers, a close cousin of the potato blight organism that set off the Irish famine had turned up in the Northeast a year or two earlier. Wet weather of the sort of that damaged our potato crop surely encouraged the blight to spread.

Despite our own ruined crops, we knew the market would give no indication to local shoppers that the weather had mistreated their farmers. There would still be plenty of onions and potatoes in the stores, from all over the country—and the world—and they would be cheap. As rich folks at the end of a chain that brings us food from around the globe, we consumers have been insulated from the costs of nature's vagaries. But the farmers have not, and we keep assuming they will continue to take the kinds of chances Alan and I were taking for ourselves. It's hard, even for us, to understand what farmers go through because we've never been dependent for our livelihood on bringing in the crops.

The lesson I take away from the realization that our crops will sometimes be drowned is not that those of us who live in the colder states can't be relatively self-reliant; we can. And although Alan and I would have been wise to choose higher ground, I've seen no sensible agricultural scenario that suggests anything can be done to insulate food production from the vagaries of nature. If we wish to feed ourselves from our own regions, and allow others to do the same, we will need to try to adjust our choices and our appetites to what Nature will provide in a given year. We need to accept the fact that in some years we won't have all the potatoes and onions we want. On the other hand, we will sometimes have more raspberries than we can eat, and the crops that succeed will be both safe and tasty.

Our land's vulnerability to flooding has sensitized all my friends to bad weather. They call and ask if we're okay here. "Did the garden flood?" We can improve the odds, of course; we set our new house two feet higher than the old one since we feared the rising waters caused by greenhouse warming. And path by path, bed by bed, we are raising the garden. Having learned belatedly that much of the water that floods us when the river rises is running in from Barry's land to the north, we have built a raised berm of sandbags to try (so far unsuccessfully) to hold back his runoff. By steadily building up the soil in our raised beds, we are working toward a time when our excess water will finally flow in his direction. In a heavy rain now, very often only the center path goes under; the garden is beautiful and productive most of the time. I hope to live long enough to see it rise above even river surges.

8

Gooseberries and the FBI

In physical perfectness of form and texture and color, there is nothing
in all the world that exceeds a well-grown fruit.

—Liberty Hyde Bailey, *The Holy Earth*

SINCE MAN (OR WOMAN) does not live by vegetables alone, one of our
goals over the years was to produce our own fruit. Thus it was that
when we finally sold the great Victorian house that held thirty-six
years of my life, the only things I regretted leaving were the vegetable
garden with its deeply mellow soil and some of the perennial fruit-
bearers that had put their roots down around the yard. The new soil
could and would be improved, but if we wanted a crop of fruit in our
first year in the new house, the perennials would need to be moved in
early spring, almost a year before we intended to transplant ourselves.
We wanted to make a fresh start with raspberries—the canes tend to
get infected with virus after a time—and the grapes were immovable.
So, we learned, was our hardy kiwi. The morning we went out to dig
it up and traced one sturdy root to a spot twenty feet north of the
trunk, we decided to leave it where it was. As it turned out, the
younger of our two apricot trees, a highbush cranberry, and two small
hybrid blueberries that never produced much anyway got moved in
spring, just before we began what we assumed was to be the renovation of our Oddfellows hall.

Two obstacles prevented a spring transplanting of the towering
blueberry bushes that remained. First, it was not at all certain that
these giants could be wrenched from the ground. Second, we didn't
want to lose a single year of the tremendous crop of fruit they reliably

produced. To get any berries, we had to net the bushes and check the nets regularly for trapped blue jays and other fruit lovers, since ravenous birds had proved capable of penetrating the most formidable defenses. Modern science had given us bird-proof netting, but vigilance was also essential. When the berries began to ripen in June, we wouldn't be living in Piermont; at this point, we didn't even have planning board approval for renovation of the house there. Excluding birds from blueberries was no task for absentee owners.

So the big blueberry bushes stayed put through the summer of 1994—the summer we learned that the battered house we intended to renovate had to be razed. In July, we tore down the house. In August, we dug and poured the footing and laid out and poured the foundation. In September, we began to build, from scratch. By October, when the framing for the new house was just going up, we had committed to being out of the old house by January. Our lives had become sufficiently dominated by the combined tasks of general contracting the new house and accumulation-reduction at the old one that plants should have been the furthest thing from our minds.

Nevertheless, when the blueberries lost their leaves in late October, Alan managed to drag two of the largest and most fruitful of them to Piermont. The remainder stayed in Congers, as did twenty-odd gooseberry bushes that grew in the fertile but shady spot where our first vegetable garden had been. So when the sales contract was drawn up, we wrote into it a clause guaranteeing us the right to come back the following spring and remove a number of plants, including several gooseberry bushes.

Gooseberries have always had special meaning for me. When I was a child, our guests at every Christmas dinner were a family from my parents' homestate of Iowa, a mother with two unmarried daughters who had descended on Mom years earlier with an introduction from a remote cousin. The daughters were not much younger than my mother and, though both were childless, they were confident that they knew better than my mother how children ought to be raised. My sister and I were required to endure in silence their frequent cri-

tiques of our manners. What made the holiday dinner tolerable was
that the mother of the family always arrived bearing German anise
picture cookies and gooseberry pie.

Nothing I know of tastes anything like gooseberry pie. My first
Christmas away from home, in 1950, with my whole family across the
continent in California, I tried all over Manhattan to get fresh gooseberries. Finally, in the German section, I got two cans of gooseberries
for a price which was, then, about 20 percent of a week's salary. Well
worth it. My recipe calls for fresh ones.

GOOSEBERRY PIE

Preheat oven to 450° F.

Pick over and wash:
>   *1 quart* **gooseberries***, discarding soft ones and removing stems
>   and tails.*

Combine:
>   *³/4 cup* **sugar**
>   *4 ¹/2 tablespoon* **flour**
>   *¹/8 teaspoons* **salt**

Sprinkle mixture over berries, stirring to distribute.

Turn berries into:
>   *8-inch* **pie crust***, unbaked*

Dot top with:
>   *2 tablespoons* **butter**

Roll pastry for top crust, and cut a design for steam vents. Brush
edge of pastry with water. Lay pastry over pie. Press edge together; trim. Let rest 10 minutes, and flute the edge. Bake in a
450° oven for 15 minutes or until crust is delicately browned.
Then reduce heat to 325° and continue baking 20 to 30 minutes,
or until berries are tender.

Note that I give no instructions for pie crust. Do what you want. Whenever I threatened to make a pie, my sons ran out of the kitchen screaming, "Watch out! Mom's making a pie crust!" It remains a trying experience.

As I copied down this recipe, I remembered why people don't use gooseberries. You have to have a strong taste-memory for the end result to be willing to sit around stemming and tailing them. And because the best kind of gooseberries for pie are green and sour to bland, you can't snack as you go, as you can while taking the little green caps off strawberries. The end product is worth the work, though, and you can always clean gooseberries while listening to *All Things Considered* on National Public Radio.

But back to the gooseberries in our house contract. The first months after Alan and I finally landed in Piermont were incredibly hectic; the house we had moved into was unfinished for months. The first night we slept there, only the bathroom shower had running water. Getting a drink in the middle of the night meant holding a glass to the shower head and turning on the faucet very, very carefully.

And in the garden, that spring was D-day. The year's crops had to be planted or we wouldn't eat. So we didn't pull off the gooseberry transfer that spring as our contract specified. By the following spring, we were a year more organized. The new garden was productive beyond our wildest dreams, and we had picked the perfect spot for the gooseberries. That's when we got the call from the FBI. A soft-spoken agent indicated that he wanted to come with a comrade from the IRS to ask us a few questions—nothing personal, he assured us. They were there in an hour. They loved our new house and garden, and when they finally turned to business, we learned that someone involved with the purchase of our former home was under investigation in a drug-money laundering scheme.

When the agents left, we congratulated ourselves for not having taken back the mortgage and promptly forgot the gooseberries. By the time we remembered, we decided it was probably too late to move them. But Alan was undaunted. Having convinced himself that the whole gooseberry crop was hanging in our old yard unpicked, he called the FBI agent. Did the new owners know that we had been contacted about the investigation? Was there any reason we couldn't go pick gooseberries? No reason at all, the FBI agent said.

When I told our younger son what we were thinking of doing, his response was, "Don't you think you guys are kind of obsessed about growing food?" Which is how I came to realize the extent to which production of our own food had become fundamental—some might say *obsessive*—in our lives. As it turned out, a friend saved us from absurdity by insisting that she had more gooseberries than she could pick, so we went over to her house and helped her out. We made gooseberry chutney from most of the fruit and froze some for a winter gooseberry pie.

The time has come for an admission: The kinds of plants I have been talking about—little fruits that grow on canes or bushes like blueberries, currants, gooseberries, and raspberries—account for most of our fruit successes. We also do well with strawberries, the standard kind as well as alpine strawberries that produce continuously in the summer, even in the shade. Under the right circumstances, they seed themselves and make new little plants, but since they don't run all over the place as standard strawberries do, they make a nice decorative border or manageable ground cover. Alpine strawberries also make incomparable strawberry jam when you can pick enough of them at one time.

PERFECT STRAWBERRY JAM

Wash, drain, and hull:
  4 cups **strawberries**
Put them into a kettle, and cover with:
  5 cups **sugar**
Let stand 3 hours.

Slowly bring to a boil over a low fire, and boil for 8 minutes.

Then add:

    *¹/₂ cup **lemon juice***

Boil for just 2 minutes longer.

Cool and skim. Put in jelly glasses topped with paraffin or seal in
¹/₂-pint jars.

What's especially nice about this recipe is that it's guilt free. When
you make jam or jelly using a thermometer or the slip-off-the-
edge-of-the-spoon test to see when it's done, you can feel pretty
awful if it doesn't jell perfectly, assuming it's your fault. This
recipe does away with all that. It's eight minutes and another two;
then put it in the little jars and seal it up. If it's runny, it's the
recipe's fault, and the jam is still absolutely delicious. This recipe
can also be used for ordinary strawberries, but it's much better
with wild or alpine strawberries.

Our experience with vines is mixed. We had intermittent success
with grapes. We used to get ten or twelve bunches of seedless green
grapes each year from two vines that overran our Congers porch and
garage. But grape vines require a lot of management to produce.
When I began to identify plant foods that we used a lot of but didn't
grow, I hit on raisins. I knew we couldn't grow enough grapes to
satisfy our raisin demand, but I had used dried currants in place of
raisins sometimes and thought they would be a good substitute. We
did well growing currants and I knew—or thought I knew—that
dried currants were dried currants. We had a red currant bush, so I
picked some and dried them. They were a mass of rock-hard seeds: an
utter failure as a raisin substitute. I have since learned that dried currants are really dried grapes of a special kind that don't grow where
we live. One more failure. A friend suggested dried cranberries as a

reasonable substitute, and I've lately discovered that we may be able to grow cranberries. It seems worth a try.

Another vine is kiwi. Since my sister's gift kiwi had lasted so long in our cold cellar, the fruit seemed a marvelous addition to the difficult season. So we put in two hardy kiwi ("Now you can grow right in your own home garden the exotic kiwi . . ."). In seven years, they grew lustily, but bore only leaves. The two of them (they need to mate) probably didn't get enough sun, but we never knew for sure. We weren't really sorry to have to leave them at Congers as we did.

We've done much less well with fruit that grows on trees. On my shelf of favorite books is a volume called *Green Thoughts* by an author named Eleanor Perenyi. It contains the kindest words I ever read in a gardening book. After discussing the fruit trees she currently has, she goes on:

> Others have come and gone: a nectarine, planted too deeply which caused it to turn into a standard—as dwarfs will if you fail to keep the basal graft above ground; an ever-nonbearing pear; another apricot, destroyed by borers; also two varieties of hazelnut, carefully chosen to cross-pollinate, which they never did. This year's harvest was a small bowl of peaches and enough quinces (somewhat damaged by the curculio worm) to make four jars of exquisite jelly.

Growing fruit, Ms. Perenyi reassures me, is best left to professionals. Nevertheless, in pursuit of self-reliance, we try to do it ourselves.

We too have lost stone-fruit trees (in our case, two peaches) to borers. We too have had a never-bearing pear. We had an apricot at Congers for years, the remaining one of a pair whose mate was—like Ms. Perenyi's—killed by borers. Each cold-hardy apricot needed the other's pollen and when we ordered them, we ordered both Moongold and Sungold. The one that didn't succumb to borers survived, grew up, and produced nothing except an absolutely spectacular show of pale pink blossoms every spring whose scent would send you dreaming. As it aged, it lost a major branch, and early one spring we decided to get rid of it and plant something that produced food. First we'd let it bloom, I thought, and then cut it down. It was so misshapen that I did major surgery while it was dormant, cutting off an out-of-scale branch almost the size of the trunk, and pruning it back to a reasonable size. When I got through, it looked good enough to save.

Then I remembered; it wasn't bearing because its mate was dead. We should order a mate. But was the survivor Moongold or Sungold? Since we didn't know, we decided to order both and have three apricot trees. While the order was en route, I accidentally found a little sketch showing that the apricot in our yard—by this time in dazzling bloom again—was Moongold. (A good reason for keeping garden records!) We called the nursery. No, they hadn't sent the trees out, they would be happy to send only Sungold.

One spring day before Sungold arrived, I was standing next to Moongold talking over the fence with my neighbor Julia. I looked idly at the tree. It was *covered* with tiny green apricots. In previous years, these infant apricots soon would have covered the ground. These didn't. They held on and grew and grew and grew and in a couple of months every branch was drooping under the weight of hundreds of soft, golden fruits. Passersby would stop to look at the shining tree. "What *is* that?" "Oh, that's our apricot," we said, feigning modesty. We made dried apricots, apricot jam, apricot compote.

Trying to explain to myself how a tree that needed to exchange pollen with a friend had self-fertilized so successfully while its intended mate was in the mail, I decided I had scared it into producing. Once I started sawing off those big branches, it figured it must produce or die. Someone later told me apricots like to be severely pruned. Okay, and I'd like to report that pruning always works. It doesn't. I've never again forced an apricot to bear that abundantly. I think it knew I was serious.

In Congers, we had a Northern Spy apple tree that produced gnarled little worm-filled fruits only a mother could love, covered with some kind of dark green disease. We don't spray. But the apples were so delicious that we often competed with the yellow jackets to pick up the fruit that fell from the tree and salvaged whatever good flesh we could to make applesauce. So we're not self-sufficient in apples. We *are*, however, local.

Less than half a dozen farmers are left in our county on the edge of New York City—their property is so valuable as potential suburban lots that it's hard to imagine any of them will hold on for another generation. But several of them grow apples along with a few other crops and we try to buy our apples from them during the extended season that controlled atmosphere storage has allowed, even though they spray pesticides. I'd rather they didn't use pesticides, but more than anything I want them to stay in business, because if we lose all our local farmers we'll have to depend completely on apples and other foods shipped from far away. To date, rich folks like us have been able to do this because transportation—that is, gasoline—is so cheap. All the forecasts about future petroleum availability assure us that this will not continue. So we need to keep local farmers in business.

My repeated fruit failures have certainly made me sympathetic to people who grow fruit for a living, especially those who try to do so without chemicals. Little in the supermarket is designed to make us think about the producers who go on year after year growing those succulent peaches, those flawless bunches of cherries, or those slightly gritty golden pears. Although many people claim to be unhappy with the way farming has been industrialized, they don't make a connection between their demand for stone fruit in mid-winter and the global food chain that brings them cheap food from wherever in the world farmers can be paid the least to grow it.

Most people pretty much accept whatever the system provides, no matter that the regionless, seasonless fruit flown into the market is often tasteless, even in season. One reason for trying to grow fruit yourself if you're lucky enough to have land—or for getting to know the farmers who grow it for you—is that most of us need regular reminders of what is really going on out there where it all gets grown and picked and shipped. Sometimes those reminders arrive unbidden.

In the summer of 1996, there was one of those poisoned food scares. This time, the initial panic involved raspberries and strawberries shipped from various parts of the world. The raspberries came from Guatemala and there were theories but no certainties about how they got infected with *Cyclospora* and made 1,463 people sick. The advice in the newspaper was to wash the produce well, preferably with soap and water. I don't know when you last had a raspberry, but the ones I eat are so meltingly soft that they would *dissolve* in soap and water.

Fragile as they are, raspberries seem like an obligatorily local food; you wouldn't want to eat them after they had travelled from Guatemala. It ought to seem risky to eat a raspberry from a country whose water you wouldn't feel safe drinking, and I consider it a privilege to grow my own.

We have grown raspberries ever since the oak came down and left us with a big pile of sawdust and oak litter. Exactly on July 1 every year, our Congers raspberry patch began providing us with a full month of unutterable bliss. Our older son asked us one year in surprise, after his fifteenth morning of raspberries, "Do you think it's possible to get tired of raspberries?" I'm sure it is, but not in a month. We used to freeze raspberries, thinking that we could somehow recreate in winter the raspberry ecstasy of July. And it's true that frozen raspberries whipped in the food processor with Ben and Jerry's vanilla ice cream is a captivating dessert. But over time, we lost interest in trying to recapture fresh summer flavors out of season, and now most of our extra spring raspberries go into syrup for winter pancakes, a recipe I'm going to print here because it's an old one that's hard to find. This one is from a book I inherited from my brother-in-law's aunt, the twentieth edition of *The Settlement Cookbook*, which came out in 1934. I'll write it just as the author presents it. Afterward I'll tell you how I really do it.

RASPBERRY SYRUP

2½ pints **raspberry juice**
2 pounds **sugar**
1 pint **water**

Mash berries well and strain through jelly bag. Place sugar in preserving kettle, add water, place over fire, and stir until dissolved, then boil until clear, and skim. Let syrup boil again until soft ball is formed in cold water, then slowly add the fruit juice. Boil again. Skim and pour into hot sterilized jars and seal.

Black raspberries and currant syrup or cherries, currants, and raspberries are also good.

I don't crush the fruit or put the juice through a jelly bag. I use whole fruit. And for the math-impaired, a pint is roughly a pound, so that's 2 cups of water and 4 cups of sugar. Sugar must have been less refined when the first edition of *The Settlement Cookbook* came out, because nothing needs to be skimmed off my sugar syrup. After the sugar has dissolved and the syrup has cooked to 135° on a candy thermometer (I haven't mastered soft balls in water), I throw in the fruit, bring it to a boil again, and it's done. You could add some seasoning, but I like it plain. It keeps forever in the refrigerator (or you can could it and store it anywhere) and is wonderful on yogurt, ice cream, pancakes, anything.

Raspberries are so crushable that you can't pick a bucketful of ripe ones without reducing the ones on the bottom to juice, so if we didn't grow them, we would look for a local grower. When we moved to Piermont, we had to start fresh with raspberries, and decided to try something new. Years ago, when our spring-summer crop of raspberries was so heavy that they more than sated my raspberry lust, I went to a September celebration of local food in Manhattan and noticed boxes of dusty purple raspberries. I remarked to the farmer in charge that I didn't grow fall raspberries because I harvested enough in the summer to last me for the year. Having them in the fall didn't even seem appropriate, I added. He looked at me rather pityingly and said "I don't think spring raspberries can compare in taste with Heritage." And in the arrogance of ignorance, I figured he was a snob.

But when we moved to Piermont, I remembered his remark and thought it might be interesting to try variety. So we ordered three each of three kinds of raspberries: two spring varieties, and the fall Heritage. In their second spring, the early raspberries were splendid, and when they were finished, I was satisfied that we had grown just enough.

Now, spring raspberries actually ripen in early summer—mid-June through July usually. And berries continue to ripen for about a month, during which time you pick them urgently and frequently by the bowlful, freeze any you choose to freeze, and make syrup from the rest. By August, when you say good-bye until the next year, you don't really mind, because by that time the tomatoes and peppers and eggplant and all the other fruits of the garden are overwhelming you, and you don't need to have raspberries falling reproachfully off their canes.

Meanwhile, the fall raspberries are biding their time, waiting until the garden has passed what Alan once captured in a pastel as "August Madness in the Garden." Late in August, the first fall raspberries begin to ripen. "Nice," I think as I pick a few when I go past to do other garden chores. Visiting children are even more enthusiastic. As September passes and October comes and goes, the raspberries keep coming. The last of the spring-summer raspberries are rushed into overripeness by July heat, and by the time the final stragglers have purpled, there is too much else to do in the garden to worry about them. But fall raspberries are much more reasonably productive— they don't all ripen at once but keep on coming. Whenever I go fall berry picking, I have to move slowly, since the bees are still competing with me for the territory, still looking for flowers to fertilize just when the shortening of the days might begin to depress you.

And they keep on coming. A week after Halloween this year, I went out and picked raspberries to put on morning cereal, an act that seems nothing short of erotic in November. I have remarked to friends more than once over the years that I am often trapped between personal happiness and existential grief. I mourn for the rapid decline of the natural world—to which I am deeply bound. At the same time, I experience irrepressible joy in tending to and eating from that part of the natural world to which I have bound myself.

What all that has to do with raspberries is simply this: The survival of raspberries in our part of the country in mid-November is most likely a serious sign that our exhalations of carbon dioxide really are warming the planet. Springs, the scientists tell us, are generally getting earlier and autumns are coming later. The look of my garden, at a time when little more than kale should remain to announce that edibles once occupied this place, confirms that fact for me.

But we were faced with no such complex emotions in our first two years in Piermont. Since we didn't get raspberry canes planted right away, we ate no raspberries at all the first year. The new canes we planted in the spring of the second year weren't supposed to be allowed to fruit until they got established, so we agreed to let each plant carry just two raspberries to maturity. Each of us had our share in early July. They were a promise of bliss to come. The bowls of raspberries in the third year were worth the wait, a reminder that you don't need even the things you're fondest of all the time.

Our consolation prize those first no-raspberry years was a crop of pears that we rescued from an abandoned tree next door. The owner of the property on which the pear tree grew apparently believed that one day his land would be worth millions, since from its backside it looks over the community organic garden to the Hudson River. In the meantime, however, half the lot was used for parking the cars of his tenants across the street; the other half held two old garages on the verge of collapse. In the midst of this decay sat a magnificent pear tree almost fifty feet high. For the first two years in Piermont, we kept the space around the tree mowed so that when its enormous crop of pears plummeted to the ground behind the cars, they were visible to us. Each morning in the late fall we went out and rescued the mostly intact ones, some of which we cut to dry for winter snacks and some of which we made into incredibly good pear chutney.

JOAN'S PEAR CHUTNEY KOSENKO

Mix together:
*4 cups **pears** cut in 1-inch dice*
*1 cup **light raisins***
*1 cup **cider vinegar***
*³/₄ cup **sugar***
*¹/₈ teaspoon **salt***
*¹/₂ teaspoon each **ginger**, **cinnamon**, **allspice***
*¹/₄ teaspoon ground **cloves***
*2 fresh green or dried red **chilies**, chopped*
*1 medium **onion**, chopped*

Bring to a boil and cook, stirring occasionally, for 30 minutes. Spoon into hot sterilized jars. *Delicious!*

The trash-strewn lot was subsequently cleaned up, the cars behind the garages towed, the garages emptied out and painted, and the short-cut that used to bypass the pear moved so that it passes right under the towering tree. What used to be unnoticed has been made visible. The pear tree still produces, but lots of other people notice the pears and knock them down for harvest. I'm struggling to control my conviction that they all really belong to me, and fortunately, I'm the only one who bothers with the damaged ones that crash from fifty feet up onto the gravel lot; they make great chutney when you cut out the damaged parts. So one lesson of my next-door pears is that if you can find a bag of slightly overage brown-around-the-edges fruit that a local farmer is selling for a reduced price, they'll do just fine for chutney.

I've put off until almost last one of the easiest fruits, one that we've grown off and on for years, a sprawling annual variously called Cape gooseberry, husk cherry, poha, or ground cherry. It has a lot of names because it seems to grow in the wild almost everywhere in the world. Ground cherries don't look or taste like cherries; when you harvest them, they look like small versions of seed pods we used to call Chinese lanterns. With their husks off, they look like tiny unripe tomatoes and taste like a mix of tropical fruits. I first tasted them years ago when I went wild-food hunting with my young sons and recognized the plants from the drawing in Euell Gibbons's *Stalking the Wild Asparagus*. Subsequently, ground cherries turned up in one of our seed catalogues and we grew them for a while at Congers.

The plant is low and sprawling and bears its fruit in little papery husks that start out green and turn pale yellow before the fruits drop softly to the ground. You gather them when they have fallen, and since you never find them all, they sow themselves and sprout the next year as volunteers—that is, plants where you didn't plan to have them. Once gathered, the fruits keep indefinitely as long as you let them stay in their little husks.

Really. Indefinitely. We had some in a shallow basket when we did our final packing to move to Piermont; the basket ended up on top of a box with some kitchen stuff. When we unpacked, the basket—covered with an envelope containing some seeds—was put aside. One day in February, when I had reached that point in the unpacking, I lifted the envelope, and there were the little husks. I popped them open, expecting the fruits to have dried up, but there they were, a bit wrinkled, but pale orange and delicious.

Probably because we were feeling raspberry-deprived, we planted ground cherries when we first moved to Piermont. They're so easy, they would probably thrive in a window box, and they keep producing fruit from June through September. Once you've picked the fruits, you can leave them lying around as snacks for visiting children (or adults). Just don't expect to have any left when your guests depart.

POHA PIE

(adapted from Euell Gibbons, STALKING THE WILD ASPARAGUS)

Preheat oven to 450° F.

Mix together:
*¾ cup **sugar***
*4 tablespoons **flour***
*1 tablespoon grated **lemon rind***
*½ teaspoon **ground cinnamon***
*6 tablespoons **water***
*1 tablespoon **lemon juice***
Boil until thickened.

Add:
*3 cups **ground cherries**, husked and washed*
Stir to mix.

Fill an 8- to 9-inch pie crust, dot with butter, put on top crust, and bake 10 minutes. Reduce heat to 350° and bake for 40 to 50 minutes more, until golden brown.

Without question, however, the fruit we grow that attracts the most attention is our fig, a feature of many Italian gardens in the Northeast, but one that requires attention. Where it gets seriously cold, figs have to be wrapped to survive the winter. Alan once did an evocative pastel called "Wrapping the Fig," which shows an array of curling fig leaves with a sweep of twine and a broken black rectangle swirling through them. It succeeds in capturing the energetic delight of wrapping one's arms around a pliant tree, binding it into a column, and swathing it for protection from the winter's blasts. The black rectangle referred to tar-paper, which is what Alan used to do the job:

twine first, to bind the branches together, then burlap pinned to-gether with nails, then tar-paper in a cone also pinned with nails, with the point open to the top to allow for air circulation. A bucket caps it off. If you have travelled through urban Italian neighborhoods in the winter, you may have seen these unnaturally ugly constructions.

So when we planted an offshoot of our Congers fig tree on the riverbank in Piermont, where it was visible from my office window, I announced that I didn't wish to spend the winter looking at a tar-paper teepee and a bucket. Alan relented and let me try something different, a rigid wire cage covered with burlap and filled top to bot-tom with fallen leaves. The first year was modestly successful—the tree was very small anyway and there wasn't much die back—but the tree got much bigger that year. We tried sewing the burlap inside a 6-foot-high tomato cage and lowering it over the bound tree (the curved upholstery needle I use to sew up the Thanksgiving turkey was accidentally left inside the cage all winter!). It proved nearly impos-sible to push leaves down to the bottom of the 6-foot cage through the spiderweb of string we had used to tie the branches together, and I worried all winter that we would lose the tree.

We didn't. Four decent-sized figs were already formed when the tree was unwrapped in April, and for a panicky week or so I thought that was it. Then tiny fig buds began to emerge from each leaf node, and as the branches lengthened, literally hundreds of baby green figs popped out, swelled and ripened into purple sweetness before the summer was over. For the first weeks after they began to ripen *en masse*, our abundant local bird population apparently didn't recognize figs as food, and the paper wasps didn't find them either. So we had them for ourselves—and for the many visitors who didn't even wait to be asked to pick. "You have figs . . ." they said as they started reaching for the fruit. Ultimately the wasps do find them, so we are forced to share, settling at times for wasp-scraped figs. Once they are discov-ered by catbirds, it's hard convincing *them* to share.

The first year the fig bore heavily was also the first year I had late raspberries, a coincidence that didn't initially prompt any special celebration. However, a friend looking over my cookbooks for some-thing special to do with the abundant fig crop found a Deborah Madison recipe for figs and raspberries in *The Savory Way*. My first reaction to the idea was that nothing could improve on solitary figginess or raspberriness, so why bother? Once again, I was wrong.

FIGS AND RASPBERRIES
(Deborah Madison)

Allow two or three figs per person. Wipe the dust off them, set them on their bottoms, and quarter them, from the top, cutting just down to the base. Press gently against the base to open the figs like the petals of a flower. Tumble raspberries into the centers, spilling over onto the plate. Sugar very lightly.

Very simple, but amazingly delicious. I think Deborah's figs were bigger than mine, though, because two or three of mine would look skimpy in a bowl. Seven to ten is more like it, and I put a raspberry in each fig and then tumble the rest over the top. This turns out to be a more-than-the-sum-of-the-parts combination—and all from the late fall garden! I definitely had enough figs before the season was over. I almost tired of them despite having served figs to anyone who would come to visit, so I dried some for the winter. Certainly their abun-dance and exquisite taste make a powerful case that seasonal eating isn't a sacrifice.

The year of the great fig and fall raspberry crops was bittersweet, however, because Alan missed it all. I wrapped the fig with the help of two women friends, the mother of two of my favorite children and an artist who wanted something fancier than burlap to cover the leaf-filled cage. I learned then what it felt like to clasp your arms around a fig, because Alan, the fig-wrapper in our family, had died in May, not long after the day when, sitting weak in a white chair on the river-bank, he had watched me free the fig for its summer production.

Now that I am living alone, in the last trimester of my life, and settled into what I hope will be my final home, I can see that it's now or never for fruit production. I planted a new Sungold to replace the young one we moved, which didn't like the flooding here and has since perished. I also now have a Johnafree (no-spray) apple, a self-fertile Asian pear, a cherry, and a peach. Decisions about planting a pear tree will wait until someone buys Mr. Kosenko's property. One of the garden catalogues is offering a kiwi that promises to bear fruit in a year. Hope springs eternal.

9

Friends Next Door

> And where does satisfaction come from? I think it comes from contact
> with the materials and lives of this world, from the mutual
> dependence of creatures upon one another, from fellow feeling.
>
> —Wendell Berry, *The Gift of Good Land*

UNTIL THE COMMUNITY GARDEN grew up next door, I had only three friends with whom I could share my gardening passion. My next-door neighbor Julia was one—until she died; a friend who had five acres and a gift for planting all of it was the other—until woodchucks broke her spirit. The third moved away years ago and we seldom talk, but when she came to see me after Alan died, she was bearing plants.

When we moved to the suburbs, most of my friends continued to be city people; most of my new neighbors gardened minimally—usually just mowing the lawn to "keep up the property"—and some of them didn't do that. Thirty-six years after I moved to the suburbs, the Piermont Community Garden changed all that.

A desire to share not only the joys of gardening but the importance of growing food had come over me before we moved to Piermont. I'm not quite sure what prompted the effort—being active in the not-very-active Congers Civic Association, perhaps—but Alan and I tried to start a community garden the year before we moved away by putting the following notice in the Congers Civic Association newsletter:

When my late neighbor Julia Hammer was growing up as Julia Zenovick in a home in the now-defunct town of Congers Lake, she remembered that everyone in her town and ours had a garden, since it was a long way by horse to the store. By the time Julia and I became friends, forty-odd years later, she told me she thought she was the only woman up on what people in her day called "Snob Hill" who got out and gardened. At least until I moved in. Then there were two of us.

Now, once again, I see more and more vegetable gardens around town. But lots of things have changed. Few people have anyone to turn to who is experienced in growing vegetables. . . . Even more of a problem is the fact that there are now lots of residents—townhouse dwellers or those with nothing but shaded land—who don't have a place for a vegetable garden even if they knew how to plant one.

It looks as if the time has come for a Congers Community Garden in which all of you who would like to garden can request a plot and be given whatever help you need to prepare and plant it.

We can expect help from Co-op Extension. But right now more than anything we need suggestions for a piece of land. Does anyone know of a site that is centrally located and is unlikely to be built on for at least the next couple of years?

Assuming land will be available, are you or your family interested in participating? The rewards will be not only community fellowship and rewarding aerobic exercise but fresh produce (and advice about how to cook it deliciously).

When we received not a single response, we tried again.

More about a Community Vegetable Garden

There's good news about the search for land for a community vegetable garden. Alex Bourghol has generously agreed to let the hamlet use the land he and his brother own on the north side of Lake Road across from their jewelry store. Before the Civic Association even thinks about next steps, we need to know whether there are people in the community interested in having a share in such a garden. Are you or your family interested in participating?

We followed this with a tear-off form on which people could indicate their interest, skills, and equipment. The next newsletter carried the results of our effort.

BETTER LUCK NEXT YEAR

If anyone out there is wondering when the Congers Community Vegetable Garden will begin to develop across the street from the jewelry store, the answer is, not this year. Our requests for indications of interest generated only one response. Perhaps the arrival of a new administration in Washington distracted you; perhaps you didn't want to appear in public in your gardening clothes; perhaps you hate vegetables, or would rather get your exercise in a gym, or. . . . Whatever the reason, no one wanted to help . . .

Fortunately, nature is generous. Another spring will come next year, and with it, another chance to start a community garden.

Another chance, but without Alan and me; for by then we had moved to Piermont.

We would surely have entered into village life there in any case—Alan volunteered immediately for the planning board—but what really "planted" us in the community was the fact that Piermont was over-ready for a community garden, although we didn't know it. In this Hudson River version of an Italian hill town, few long-time residents had flat land; owners of the new condominiums on the pier had no land at all. But we were deeply into gutting a house and creating our own garden, so it didn't immediately occur to us that we ought to do anything about *their* problem.

The impulse that actually initiated the garden was neither communal nor friendly. It was a splendid example of NIMBY—the Not-In-My-Backyard syndrome that the environmentally passionate are regularly accused of having. What was *in*—really *next to*—our backyard was a junk pile. I remarked earlier that 100 feet of our yard abutted an unpaved wasteland clogged with industrial-sized litter. Once part of a much larger parking lot for employees of the giant paper mill on the pier, the area had been deeded to the village when the factories were taken down and the pier subdivided. Since then what had been parked there included a number of telephone poles, two rusted cars, a boat trailer, a wrecked boat, a bulldozer, and a giant pile of plastic video sleeves, all of which disappeared by mid-summer into a forest of 8-foot-high great ragweed.

Enough space was left to park the cars of whomever lived in our house, and to drop the series of dumpsters which were rolled in, successively filled, and carted off to be weighed for tipping fees as we gutted the house. (That's how we knew that by the end of our first summer we had personally removed twenty-four thousand pounds of sheathing, plaster, lath, headers, footers, studs, and stuff.) We were deep into gutting by now, unaware as yet that the house would have to come down. Our plans had been approved by the planning board, and in the course of cleaning up our property I decided I should also police its immediate environs.

So I went out to the parking lot and began pulling what weeds I could, removing junk small enough to fit into one of the blue village trash cans, and mowing the area immediately outside the gate that led from our property to the parking area. One May day when we were thus engaged, our irascible neighbor to the north dropped by, pulled his cigar out of his face, and grumped out the appalling news that the mayor had asked him what it would cost to pave the area for village parking. Since Barry used the lot as his private junkyard for storing pilings, nonworking bulldozers, and other essentials, he had marked its entrance with a telephone pole on which was tacked a sign that read "Private Parking, No Trespassing." The mayor's question about paving the space for "public" parking was a direct challenge. "I told John I won't do it," he barked. "I'll block it with my bulldozer!"

Bad news! We had not anticipated having parkers as neighbors. "A next-door parking lot. That's all we need," I raged to Alan, frazzled as I was by the effort of house-gutting. "It's a beautiful sunny spot with a view of the river. It should be a community garden." Two days later, Alan bore the seeds of that idea with him to Piermont's annual Memorial Day Bluegrass Festival and planted them with his usual verve. Over the beer and hot dogs he was helping sell for Piermont's Civic Association, and accompanied by the sound of fiddle music, Alan brought the idea to a chemically sensitive young woman looking for allies in her fight for a pesticide-free village; to Barbara, the assistant mayor's wife, who headed the park commission; and finally to the mayor himself, who ultimately put the question "garden versus parking lot" on the agenda of the Village board meeting. A month and a year later, at the garden's first annual Summer Solstice celebration, Mayor Z. gestured to the flourishing garden behind him and told us that he had originally decided to let us move ahead if we could find twenty-five interested people. As he spoke, more than fifty gardeners were growing vegetables and flowers there, some of them sharing plots smaller than a modest bathroom.

From its inception, the Piermont Community Organic Garden— "To Nourish the Spirit" says the sign that marks the entrance—was intimately entwined with the fate of our dwelling, and with our lives. The day after we learned that our house had to be torn down, the board of trustees met and approved the use of the "parking lot" as a community garden if there was enough interest. Because the available 100-by-100-foot space had to leave us driveway access, Alan and I constituted ourselves a committee of two, allotting a 75-by-75-foot square to the community garden.

That fate was smiling on the enterprise became evident when Barbara found a local landscape architect willing to help us design the garden as well as the existing undeveloped park. Dan planned for eighteen raised beds, 10-by-8 feet, which would each be divided in half to make thirty-six plots measuring 9-by-10 feet. He also came up with attractive but expensive ideas for fruit trees, fencing, arbors, and work sheds, with the hope that what could not be paid for out of the parks budget could be donated by the members-to-be.

In mid-October, the plans were displayed to an excited crowd of potential gardeners, drawn to the village hall by an article in the quarterly village paper. Most of them had never seen the garden site. Sitting as it did behind two collapsing garages on the main street, it was not a well-trafficked area. So they oohed and aahed over the plans, asking excited questions and pushing to get started right away.

Painfully aware of the site's distressing condition, I protested that we were headed into winter. Fortunately, one of the would-be gardeners offered to get a speaker for an indoor winter meeting at which the ground rules of organic gardening could be introduced.

As five people volunteered to form an ad hoc steering committee, I wondered whether anyone's enthusiasm would survive their first look at the potential garden in its current state. Our original house having come fully down, the dumpsters that had occupied the site for months had been replaced by a ten-foot-high tumble of rough fill dug out to create the basement of our new house. Warming to the trashy opportunity, the cement company laying sidewalks in a neighboring private park had added their piles of rocky dirt to ours. The space was a disaster. The steering committee included at least one experienced gardener—me—and at least one gifted organizer-record keeper; two steering-committee meetings later, she and I were, by default, co-chairs of the garden.

By the time of the first Piermont Community Garden meeting in early January, the gardeners had, fortunately, still not focussed on the site. They were pleased to meet each other, get names and phone numbers, learn a bit about what they might plant, and hear a talk on the principles of organic gardening. Near the end of January, only days before Alan and I actually moved into our incomplete new home, the backfilling was finally completed. The house was no longer surrounded by a moat; it was now surrounded by mud. But the piles of rock and dirt that were supposed to disappear in the process still filled the community garden site, too rough to put around our elegant new house, our backfiller decided. He had brought in new dirt and the mess was still there. The gardeners' enthusiasm had meanwhile been stoked by a meeting where they were assigned numbered plots by lottery.

The landscape architect, a gifted organizer, planned a mid-March workday and ordered fifty yards of topsoil. In one day, he planned to have the eager gardeners lay out the paths, cut up the planking, nail together the giant boxes, and move them into place to be filled with soil.

The tiny village bureaucracy moved more deliberately, however, and when the village cleanup crew finally arrived with bulldozer and backhoe for a day of dragging, hauling, levelling, and raking, it was just three days before our planned giant work-party. The workers disposed of the boat, old telephone poles, boulders, videotape cases, and other less-identifiable trash. Then they levelled the rocky backfill and covered the newly virgin space with successive loads of wood chips that had begun to arrive once local arborists learned we were eager to have them.

Here is my journal entry for the bright and beautiful March day when thirty of us created an instant community garden.

MARCH 18—The garden work-party began at 9 A.M. and Alan and I had prepared the area that was our driveway with a picnic table. Coffeepots had been brought in the night before so we plugged them in early to get the coffee ready. Donuts were supplied and volunteers began to arrive to be organized by Dan into the work parties—rakers, measurers, sawyers, nailers— planned for at last Sunday's meeting. Wood had been delivered for making the beds and the area was now covered with wood chips that had been roughly levelled by the Piermont crew. One of the gardener's husbands arrived early with his saw to begin sawing the wood for the beds. A plan for making the beds had been worked out and everyone cooperated amazingly. The dirt-moving crew with nothing to do at the beginning began raking the site more level and taking off the longer branches that didn't get chipped.

Then gradually—or not so gradually—we began to distribute the 10-by-18-foot boxes around the space. Once the boxes were laid out, we began to haul the dirt with wheelbarrows. We got most of the boxes at least half filled, and at one point Colleen went around and put numbers on the boxes so people could see which one was theirs. It was very touching as people began to take possession of a little piece of land. Altogether a very triumphant day.

Two weeks later, the garden was fenced at the village's expense, a water line was run (through our basement to avoid another curb-cut from the street), and some of the gardeners who could wield a hammer and saw put together a shed along the north border of the garden.

As the soon-to-be gardeners continued to cart in soil to top off their own plots, we had another meeting in which I described a number of designs that would allow them to make most effective use of their small spaces and to avoid walking on the planting areas. Once their beds were filled, they universally ignored my suggestions—we had inverted Y's, concentric circles, beds divided into one-foot squares, and paths made of used brick, hay, wood chips, and stones. All of them were beautiful.

We also planned a common seed order for the first year and almost broke up over the division of the seeds; few gardeners yet understood that a pinch of tiny mesclun seeds would plant a row and a handful would fill half the beds in the garden. The assistant mayor's wife ended up with a mesclun lawn of which I strongly disapproved, suggesting repeatedly that she thin it by pulling some of the plants. She, however, happily cut lettuce for her entire family and all the guests she could invite, and was so pleased with what I viewed as her desperately overcrowded crop that she repeated it in successive years. Thus did I learn—again—that not everyone wants to receive what you choose to offer, and that pleasure does not only arise from doing it "the right way."

When the youngest couple in the garden, both teachers, both lovers of the outdoors, sat on a wood-chipped path one July evening and picnicked, leaning on the edge of the box that held their plot of land,

I knew we had given Piermont something more than vegetables and flowers. The garden meant not only proprietorship of a tiny plot of land down by the river, it also meant relationships. Even in this small village, it turned out, many of the newer residents felt isolated. Overnight we had given everyone the choice of fifty acquaintances, with the likelihood that some of them would become friends.

In my case, the garden was omnipresent, and the friendships lifesaving. One of my office windows looked out on the garden, and for the first year we lived there, I found it nearly impossible to stay inside when someone came to tend a plot. There was talking to do, advice to give, people to get to know. What could be better, as I said to my city friends, than helping people do something you love while making new friends in the community to which you have pledged the rest of your life?

When I suggested, mid-way through the first summer of gardening, that we should celebrate the solstice, the idea was eagerly accepted. So toward the end of the longest day of the year, fifty people gathered in the park on the river side of the garden, spread their blankets, and shared food and conversation. Those who could made music and the mayor and others said brief words of appreciation. And in one corner of the garden, Alan planted a pole he had carved years earlier in honor of Santa Cruz—a symbol that we were now at home here.

In Congers, Alan and I had been less ceremonial about the summer solstice, but we had always acknowledged the winter one, collecting fallen branches from the oaks to make a fire in our improvised fireplace, encouraging the slow-rising winter sun to appear at the close of the longest night of the year. At the end of our first year in Piermont, with a heavy snow on the ground, we invited a few of the gardening folks to join us for morning coffee and hot muffins by a tiny fireplace we had stacked up out of fire bricks at the end of our yard.

Blueberry Bran Wheat Germ Muffins

(adapted from Vegetarian Times*)*

Preheat oven to 400°F.

Beat well:
  3 eggs
Then add and beat:
  1 cup brown sugar
Add:
  1/2 cup oil
  2 cups buttermilk (or skim milk acidulated with 1 teaspoon
  vinegar or lemon juice)
Mix well. Add:
  1 teaspoon vanilla
  1 cup wheat germ
  1 cup bran
In smaller bowl, combine:
  2 cups flour
  2 teaspoons baking powder
  2 teaspoons baking soda
  1/2 teaspoon salt
Then stir in:
  1 1/2 cups blueberries

Pour flour/berry mixture into liquid ingredients, and stir until mixed. Spoon into greased muffin cups, and bake at 400° for 20 to 25 minutes. Makes 24 muffins. Make a whole batch; these freeze well.

For the next winter solstice we planned something larger. We had invited all the gardeners willing to venture out into the dark and cold to bring their own coffee and hot breads and join us. Then, a few days before the ceremony, we learned that Alan had a ruthlessly fatal cancer. So we built a giant fire, this time in our dirt and wood-chip driveway, and when one of the gardeners offered to do a Native American cleansing ceremony, I asked if she would cleanse our yard as well. We all held hands as the sun finally rose, and I tried hard not to believe that it would be Alan's last solstice. No one else knew.

And they learned only slowly, mostly from me since it was Alan's nature not to bring—or accept—bad news. When the truth could no longer be hidden, when Alan's pain and weakness would no longer allow him, or me, to go anywhere, it was the people I had met through the garden who began to bring meals and leave them on the doorstep, or write notes asking if they could shop for me. They loved Alan; he brought them sunshine. And Alan loved the gardeners.

Which is probably why, when he made what was to be almost his last trip outdoors, he went out the gate to the community garden to introduce his visiting family to any gardeners who were working their plots. He was yellow and gaunt and looked like death; I'm not sure what they thought. But he knew his priorities.

Eleven days later, the morning after Alan died, I went out and hung a large dried wreath over the arch that spans the gate leading from our driveway—and the community garden—to our yard. Across it I tacked a ribbon that read "Alan Gussow, 1931–1997." To all those people whose loving thoughts had supported me through the final days, it was a notice that the struggle was over. If we had still been in Congers, no one would have known.

That year, its third, was a bad one for the community garden. I think Alan would have wanted his energetic spirit to pass in that direction. Instead, some of the gardeners were so upset by his departure that they neglected their plots. On my own land, of course, I gardened for my life. It had become clear to both of us that the garden was going to be repeatedly flooded unless it was raised. So even as Alan was dying, I set about beginning the process of raising each of the twenty-two paved paths by setting the pavers atop a four-inch pad of sand hauled up in sandbags from the riverbank. When I finished raising the first path and realized it had taken twenty-five bags of sand, I did the multiplication—twenty-five times twenty-one more paths to go—and realized I had enough therapy to last me a long time.

Alan had insisted that we order twenty yards of topsoil to be dumped in the driveway and brought in to raise the beds once the paths were completed. And so it was that many of the people who came to see Alan for the last time helped him walk out to the riverbank to sit while they hauled sand or dirt for me. And after he died, and people wanted to help, they came and filled sandbags as we talked—sometimes a hundred bags were lined up on the boardwalk waiting to be moved and dumped. Alan surely would have approved.

Meanwhile, the community garden came slowly back to life. A new member, digging in the spring of the fifth year, gave us all a happy surprise. Here is my co-chair's e-mail message.

Sat. 10 Apr.1999, 01:37:18 EDT
To: Gardeners—

Work Party Sunday noon-3:00 P.M. for those who could not make it today. Digging and planting are on the agenda.

Today at the work party one of our members accidentally dug up a nest of three day-old baby rabbits. After consulting with a wildlife rehabilitator, I set a Havahart trap with the nest of babies inside. The mother was trapped this evening and will be relocated in a place under supervision of the rehaber where she can safely raise her young. This may or may not have solved our rabbit problem. There is always the father.

:-) *Colleen*

And as my own account of that weekend reflects, both the garden and I had by that year made a full recovery.

APRIL 11—End of a great weekend where I totally exhausted myself supervising the two work-days for the community garden. I came out of it feeling terrific. We got so much done, well done, and so many people who had been difficult were made cooperative by the fact that I just took for granted they'd help if pushed. The garden looks beautiful—Saturday was also a glorious day though today was cold and cloudy, and tonight it's raining. But it was very satisfying and I think the spirit of the garden has returned despite everyone's busyness. Hooray. Now, exhausted and satisfied, I'm going to take a shower and go to bed. I wanted to go at 7:00! Now it's 8:30 and I'm allowed.

Sometimes these days when my own peppers are producing so lavishly that giving them away to everyone who comes by doesn't help, I wander next door and spend a little time envying my fellow Piermonters with their tiny, tidy plots from which they coax amazing but manageable harvests—just enough of something for summer dinners three or four nights a week. It never ceases to amaze me what even a small piece of land lovingly tended can produce.

10

Gaining Ground

Out of the earth are we and the plants and animals that feed us created
and to the earth we must return the things whereof we and they are made
if it is to yield again foods of a quality suited to our needs.
—Robert McCarrison and H.M. Sinclair, *Nutrition and Health*

ALAN AND I HAD AGREED that we wanted to be cremated after death
so that no trees would need to be cut and no metals mined to make a
fancy coffin or even a plain pine box. So the evening Alan died at
home, his washed body was taken away in a bag by the undertaker,
sent to a crematorium and burned, and the ashes returned to me three
days later on what would have been Alan's sixty-sixth birthday. On
that day, Adam and Seth and I were having a small memorial service
in our garden for relatives and close friends. Adam had assumed that
I wanted to scatter the ashes in the river while the guests were present.
I didn't. I wanted to do it ceremonially but mostly privately. We had
a tense moment. Seth intervened. I won.

When the memorial service was over, Adam, who plays blues har-
monica professionally, demonstrated the glory of that uniquely por-
table instrument by piping us down the clover path to the boardwalk,
where we all stood and held hands for a few minutes. Then we went
inside to have beer and pizza. When both of us had had a beer, I went
over to him and said, "I hope you noticed that the tide was out and we
would have had to strew your Dad's ashes in the mud." To which he
smilingly replied, "Yeah, Mom, and there was a stiff onshore wind."

Several months later, Adam called to say he wanted to take some
ashes with him to Monhegan Island. It was the place that had beck-

oned Alan toward his life in art; we knew he wanted part of himself to rest there. I suggested that Adam come out from his city apartment early Sunday to join me and the family friends Alan and I had shared breakfast with on most Sunday mornings for twenty-five years.

When he arrived at the house, I pulled out from under the desk the heavy maroon plastic bag the undertaker's delivery boy had brought me months earlier. I had never looked inside it. Out of the bag I pulled a box and out of the box came an unlabelled can not quite large enough to hold a gallon of paint. We pried it open. Inside was a plastic bag full of a rough gray substance like small gravel. We scooped half a cupful into another plastic bag. Then we closed the plastic bag and the can, put the can back into the box, the box into the bag, and the bag back under the desk. Both of us were serious, but not sad. Then we drove to meet our friends for breakfast.

Later, on the way back to the house, I said, "Adam, I want to ask you something. You need to be honest with me. When we opened the can, I realized it looked sort of like bonemeal . . ." And Adam, not waiting for me to finish, said "You want to put it on the garden, right, Mom? Sure, that's okay with me." And I said, "Well, I do think your father would like that. I'd save some to put in the river, but I think he'd like to know his ashes were improving the garden."

Permission granted, I didn't act on my intention for months. It was the following January when I realized that the can of ashes was still boxed and bagged under the desk. It happened to be a lovely day, no wind, no rain, and I was alone. I think I hadn't wanted to open the can before. But once I did, it was easy. I went out like Demeter reaching into the can and scattering some of its contents on the strawberries and some on several of the other beds, saving two handfuls for the river.

Then I walked out to the boardwalk and emptied the can into the Hudson, telling Alan goodbye. It didn't feel as if he were there. But I was certain this was where he would have wanted to go, adding to the fertility of the garden, and moving with the Hudson out into the river channel, and to the sea. We both understood that soil is precious.

Much earlier, I remarked on the sense of urgency Alan and I had felt about testing out the growing properties of the soil at Piermont. We had good reason to worry, since the fertile garden we were leaving had been carefully built over time, out of a stiff red clay fit for a potter's wheel. The base soil of much of Rockland County is a fine clay rich in minerals, and capable of growing wonderful plants, but raindrops or footsteps or wheels can compress it into a firmness almost impenetrable to plant roots, air, and water. So over the three decades when we grew vegetables on our former south lawn in Congers, our task had been to loosen the soil by adding organic matter—everything nature produces with water and sunlight—after the initial mass of garbage, leaves, decaying grass, newspaper, and salt hay had been dug into our garden beds. Here is how B.V. Richardson puts it in *Introduction to the Soil Ecosystem*: "Soil organic matter derives from several different sources, being the remains of dead plants and animals and their excretory products in various stages of decomposition, the final stage being known as humus."

What's going on here is that nature—represented by billions of organisms—is passing what she's been offered through the cells of bacteria, fungi, protozoa, nematodes, mites, springtails, worms, and other organisms. As these organisms cycle chemical elements and energy, they help knit the clay particles into a porous mesh through which air and water can percolate, and roots can stretch and breathe as they search for the nutrients that will grow plants.

Given the incomprehensible complexity of this process, one hardly knows what to make of the news that one of the worm-like creatures that participates, a millimeter-sized nematode called *Caernorhabditis elegans*, has had its ninety-seven million-letter script read by British geneticists. Such "reading," one must presume, is a step on the way to modifying the little worm's genetic code. Since scientists admit that the humic end-product of this process is a mystery, one must hope they will be uncharacteristically cautious about any attempt to "improve" the elegant process in which *C. elegans* plays a part.

Composting—chopping up the collected garden trash, and mixing it with some animal manure in the right ratio of green and brown with the goal of producing humus—was one of Alan's favorite garden tasks. I'm not sure why. He wasn't driven by neatness as I might have been—converting unsightly piles of trash into a tidy binful of potential fertilizer is very satisfying. That was evidently not his goal, however, because when he finished, as his wife too often pointed out to him, he usually left the area surrounding the compost bins a mess of rejected stalks and other trash. He clearly loved the activity of it, running the lawnmower over piles of leaves, spent plants, and other garden remains to reduce them to fragments; vigorously forking the chopped remains into a compost bin; layering it with soil and manure (from a neighbor's pony in the pre-Piermont days); and wetting it down to heat up.

When the ingredients are an appropriately moistened collection of organic material—carbon-rich brown matter and nitrogen-rich green matter—they create a happy home for that mysterious universe of organisms I mentioned earlier. As the organisms begin to grow and multiply, they produce metabolic heat just as we larger organisms do. (One of the most exciting things I learned in biochemistry was that the body has to produce metabolic heat in the course of just staying alive, so its problem is getting rid of heat. That's why it's so easy to run a fever if the body's heat-dissipating mechanisms—such as sweating—shut down.) So one way you can tell whether you've made compost properly is to see whether it heats up. Alan unfailingly went out to check the compost the morning after he made it, digging his fingers down in to see if it was hot.

Perhaps the most successful gift I ever gave him was a compost thermometer—built a lot like a meat thermometer but with a very long prod. Alan loved it! He would build the compost, stick in the thermometer, and then report regularly on its progress—sometimes every two hours or so. Indeed, he even drew and painted what others assumed he intended to be metabolic heat, most famously on a postcard ultimately reproduced in an "artists' postcard" series. It showed some tumbled brownish mounds flecked yellow and dark brown with a blue-green puff going off the top of the page, and was titled "Well-rotted manure, steaming."

Several people reminded him that when manure was well rotted, it didn't steam any more, since by that time the organisms had done their work. He responded that his sketch was made in early morning when the sun was causing steam to rise from the dew on the manure. I can attest to the fact that he was right about the steam, since the pile of manure that was delivered to the community garden recently was very, very well rotted and when I went out in the morning to dig a cartload, it did steam—not, however, with metabolic heat.

Soil can also be built by cover-cropping; that is, growing things on it, and then digging them in. This is good for the soil not only because turning in living matter adds carbon and nitrogen, but because the fresh plant material provides food to that universe of creatures I mentioned earlier. I cover-crop with soybeans and clover; with buckwheat, which is a beautiful and fast-growing plant; and, unsuccessfully, with winter rye or oats. I recently sowed oats again with the usual frustrating result.

SEPTEMBER 27—I wanted to write this morning about sowing what I kind of hoped were wild oats (according to the label, they were actually Cayuse oats). Remembering earlier attempts, I carefully retrieved each spilled seed visible on the brick path and put it back onto the bed, which I then over-sowed with buckwheat and covered everything lightly with salt hay in the hope of concealing the oats from the little birds. When they found the last bed I sowed with winter rye, they not only ate the seeds, but scratched away at the surface until they had hopelessly scattered the whole effort. As I tried to cover every last seed this time, I remembered Doug's remark when he watched me trying to plug a muskrat hole on the riverbank: "Remember, Joan, they're professionals."

They are, and they proved it once again. Next morning, the hay had been scratched up and every single oat seed located, leaving empty husks scattered all over the bed. So although I'd like to use grains as cover crops, I have to make do with what the birds will let me grow.

Plants that serve as cover crops have various characteristics, of which one important one, as the name suggests, is to keep the soil covered. Especially over the winter, this prevents the soil from being packed down or eroded by rain or heavy snow, and gives that mighty army of living organisms something to work with during the cold months.

Aside from air and water, the nonliving part of the soil is made up, of course, of the variously sized remains of an assortment of rocks, ranging in size from large sand grains to extremely fine particles of clay. The ideal soil is what is called a sandy loam—made up of just the right proportions of small and large rock particles and organic matter. When our major gardening was still taking place in Congers, before we actually moved to Piermont, I worried a lot about what the soil would be like when we got here.

SEPTEMBER 12 — Today I harvested the last potatoes, Purple
Peruvian, Haida, leftovers from last year planted in the southern-
most bed. As I was arm-deep in the soil harvesting the Purple
Peruvians (which in the fading light look like dog turds!), I
realized that what I will miss most about this house is the soil! I
realized how well I know the rich deep soil we have created, and
how different the soil at Piermont is. But soil is a choice. We will
have rich deep soil there too!

As luck would have it, the soil at Piermont, once we had pried out the rubble with which the land had originally been stabilized, was sandy loam.

Taking the living earth seriously means taking seriously our re-sponsibility to protect her skin. Estimates for Nature to grow one inch of topsoil range from thirty to one thousand years, although any ardent earth-tender knows she can do much better than even the low figure by providing more food to the army of organisms that generate humus from waste. Which is why we help Nature along. Most non-farmers, I suspect, don't think much about soil, since they are used to thinking of it in flower-pot quantities. "Potting soil" can be bought at the garden supply store, but you can't grow acres of crops on soil from bags; it has to be built and conserved onsite.

It was knowledge of that fact, I'm convinced, that made me resist buying a truckload or two of topsoil to raise our new yard when we realized that it was flood-prone. No one can say we weren't warned. Three weeks after we took possession of the Piermont house, Barry's son-in-law stopped by to tell us that the town was planning to bring up the level of the parking lot south of us, and that when they did that, our yard would be a bathtub.

Alan took the warning seriously, and with good reason, as is now evident. The parking lot remains unfilled, and the Community Garden now buffers the yard, but we *are* a bathtub; floods, small and large, have been frequent. Nevertheless, I continue to be glad that I successfully resisted Alan's urgings to quickly plump up the yard with purchased topsoil, although the reasons for my intransigence were not clear to me at the time.

Looking back on the contest from a distance, however, I can identify two reasons—no, three—that I fought so hard. The third one was money. It would have cost several thousand dollars to truck in enough topsoil to cover our yard to any depth, and at that point, the balance in our bank account was sinking like water in an unplugged drain. But we could have mortgaged ourselves for dirt if we absolutely had to.

Then there was the fact that out toward the river, we already had some traces of what might be reassembled into a beautiful garden, including plants that could be moved around and tested in various spots. I didn't know how to impose a pattern on four thousand square feet of raw dirt. Although Alan was used to creating patterns where none existed except in his imagination, he never brought those skills to bear on the yard. And I didn't have his creative gift. Faced with a blank slate, I found it hard to think. I was good at taking what existed and altering it to my purposes—making do. I was appalled at the thought of digging up everything that was out there and starting literally from scratch on a slab of dirt.

Reflecting now on my stiff resistance to trucking in topsoil, however, I'm certain there was a much more important reason, one that I could not have articulated at the time: Bringing topsoil from somewhere else instead of building it on site doesn't fit my picture of how the world ought to work. Hoisting bags of sand off the river's edge to raise the paths has seemed natural to this place. Diverted by an upriver bridge, the tides sweep sand onto our backyard beach, where it builds up faster than we can remove it. But buying topsoil, as I did recently in desperation, is transplanting fertility from some other part of the earth to my own. That symbolizes to me a destructive pattern of earth-use by which we rich folks have built our civilization, and I want to participate in it as little as possible.

Most of us don't live, and don't want to live, where coal or chrome or copper or gravel are wrenched from the earth to provide us with heat or toasters or wiring or foundations, and so the costs to the earth and to its living skin where those things are mined remain invisible to us. So does the true cost of our food, produced around the world often by people who are too poor to eat well, on cropland they might otherwise use to feed themselves. We can resist participating in this pillage by living frugally, buying and replacing as few material objects as possible, and by trying to eat from farms close to home. In the garden, I figure, we can do it by not stealing topsoil from somewhere else, but by building it ourselves.

Which explains why I spent a recent morning hauling in cartfuls of wood chips and manure from the piles that get delivered to the community garden and mixing them with bagfuls of rocky dirt—this is clearly dirt, not yet soil—to make a mix that will raise my planting beds still further. This dirt is foundational stuff, dug from under the home of friends here in the village, when they discovered that the beams supporting their house were resting on the ground for the convenience of termites. Greg extracted the dirt, sandbag-full by sandbag-full, through a trap door in the floor of the dining room, and then had to dispose of it because he and his wife had no place for it in their small yard. I initially offered to take the rubble-filled sandbags to use as barricades against the floods. When I opened one up, I realized that what I had was not really rubble, but dirt. Good old dirt, mostly clay, probably, and some rocks. The clay seemed akin to what originally filled our Congers garden. Add some organic matter and it could become soil!

Nature grows trees, wind lops off their branches, and our village reduces them to manageability by making wood chips; it seemed not only ecologically responsible but positively magnanimous for me to use them up making soil from dirt. Much of our yard, from the higher area near the house down through the patch given over to blueberries and raspberries, was built up with wood chips—first from our own willow and subsequently from other trees toppled by storms in the village and reduced to chips. In a year or so, they turn into woodsy soil, courtesy of decomposers similar to the ones that make compost from garden trash.

Their efficiency in converting wood chips shows how intimately the lives of these tiny organisms are tied up with our survival; by cleaning up whatever dies they not only keep the place tidy, they recycle the nutrients we all live on. As biologist E.O. Wilson has pointed out in *Biodiversity*, humanity would probably not survive more than a few months if just the arthropods, the phylum that includes these organisms, were to disappear:

> . . . the land surface would literally rot. As dead vegetation piled up and dried out, closing the channels of the nutrient cycles, other complex forms of vegetation would die off and with them all but a few remnants of the land vertebrates.

When I layer the sloppy pungent collection of kitchen waste accumulated in my garbage pail into the compost, it disappears sometimes within two weeks. In winter, before the soil has frozen deeply, I sometimes bury it directly in the garden beds where the organisms who live in my soil will dispose of it. Several community gardeners are doubtful when I urge them simply to bury the remains of plants when they're cleaning up in the fall. One who did, a landscape architect who is a genius at designing with plants but knows much less about growing them, announced delightedly that he had done as I suggested with some dead plants, and when, a month later, he turned over the ground where he had buried them, nothing was there but soil.

One day as I was walking past the community garden, I realized that the two women working there were upset about something. "There's a dead rat here," they said, pointing down. Sure enough, a water-soaked rat corpse was lying in the path. I had someone with me who was even more earthy than I. "Pick it up with a shovel and put it in a plastic bag," she said. "Uuuu!" their faces said. "It's good fertilizer. Put it in the compost," she threw at them, and then drove off. They stood there looking quite distressed. So I went and got a shovel from the shed, scooped up the dead rat, and made one of the gardeners hold a plastic bag open so I could dump it in. She looked away while I did the deed. Then I took the bag, tied it shut, and put it in the garbage can outside the garden. It will make its way back into the nutrient cycle from there with more difficulty than it would if I had put it in the compost. I *should* have put it in the compost, but that would probably have ended my friends' enthusiasm for gardening.

Since gardening has given me such an intimate relationship to dirt and its ingredients, I'm continually surprised by the anxiety that contact with the possibly contaminated seems to cause people. Most people who visit my garden do not have my positive relationship to dirt. They're always a bit startled when I graze in the garden, picking and eating one leaf or another. And when I pull a carrot, wipe off the clinging soil on the clover path, and offer it to them to eat, they glance around for a sink.

I suppose it's inevitable that people raised with little contact with soil, or with the process whereby even garbage can be transformed, think of all dirt as simply the opposite of clean. That might not matter if the way people thought about soil didn't affect their attitude about what's clean—and what's important. But our fundamentally negative view of "dirt" means that we don't really understand the need to protect it. Dirt on the windowsill, dirt on the front steps, dirt on the patio, is to be wiped or swept or hosed. What you wash off your produce, invisible or not, is dirt. Mommy shouts at her little boy, "Don't put that in your mouth, it's dirty." And if a positive thought is given to dirt, it's simply what underlies our tennis courts, roads, foundations, golf courses, or, closest to home—lawns. The fact that soil is the basis for life on the planet is largely forgotten, with consequences that were vividly illustrated only recently in our own village.

Piermont is much like a coastal Italian hill town—except our ocean is the mighty Hudson. Most of the houses are not on the flatland next to the river where I live, but stacked along small winding roads up the flanks of the steep woodsy hillside behind me. When storms hit, the worst damage almost always occurs right along the river. A northeaster or a hurricane churning up from the south lowers the barometric pressure and pulls up the tide by a couple of feet, and then blows in along with torrential rains. So when a huge hurricane came plunging up the coast and all I got was twelve inches of water in my yard—no damage to the boardwalk, no floating boards or logs or plastic—I didn't think to wonder what had happened elsewhere in the village.

I should have been alerted, I guess, by the fact that the water filling my yard—clear in the early afternoon—turned muddy before dark. But the electricity went off about then, and my bedroom ceiling started to leak, so my thoughts were elsewhere. I live almost exclusively with my back to the street, in the part of the house that faces the yard and the river, so I didn't notice what was going on behind me until someone appeared at my door the next morning to ask how I had made out. It turned out that this time the hillside had taken the biggest hit.

When rain falls on a forest, or even a single tree, the trees' leaves take the impact, allowing the water to come down gently enough to soak into the soil, which is held in place by the trees' roots. In recent years, many giant "river-view" houses have been built on lots gouged into the steep Palisades, uphill from the major road that runs above the village. Their wealthy owners all cut trees, of course, so they can enjoy the view of the river they have paid so much for. But when trees are cut and a house planted on a steeply sloping lot, a driveway paved, and a deck laid out back, heavy rain that falls on all these impermeable surfaces runs off and pours down onto a few square yards of soil— most of it covered with a (largely impermeable) lawn. What began as a heavy rain then becomes a river that rips away everything in its path.

So when water coursed down the hillside past these treeless mansions and onto the road, it took soil as it went. Following the path of least resistance, it ran through the front doors and out the backs of four houses newly built just below the road, depositing mud wherever it met an obstruction. Then it raced downhill, carrying everything moveable with it: roads, backyards, retaining walls, garage roofs, and, by luck alone, no houses—this time. When the flood reached flat land, the road and the houses adjacent to the river, it spread out and settled, blocking the main street with mud and boulders, filling the front yards and basements of the riverfront homes directly in its path with brown sludge, and flowing slowly down the street in my direction.

As the mud flowed past my house, it filled the sidewalk and my narrow front border, doing no damage. The worst of it flowed by, poured into the parking area south of my house, and then down onto my dirt and wood-chip driveway, which it covered with two inches of mud. Word got around town that I was the only homeowner in Piermont happy to have received this soil bounty; the driveway needed raising anyway. My plan now is to sow clover there, since it's obvious that we need to build topsoil wherever and whenever we can.

11

Varmints

It's astonishing actually, how much anger an animal's assault
on your garden can incite. It was not as if I were liable to go hungry
as a result of his depredations, after all. No, this was no longer merely
a question of vegetables or even self-interest. This was about winning.

—Michael Pollan, *Second Nature: A Gardener's Education*

READING AN EARLY DRAFT of this book, one of my sons informed me
that the hard questions needed to be answered up front. I've tried to
do some of that as I went along, but I decided I'd wait a while to take
up the hardest question: Why, although I seldom *eat* animals, do I feel
justified in killing them? The simplest answer—that the 1,000-
square-foot space on which I produce the basics of my diet is too small
to share with competitors—won't satisfy anyone, not even me. So it's
probably time for the truly complicated story, *stories* really, of how a
small producer (or at least *this* small producer) has had to learn to
think about death and wildlife.

Wildlife comes in all shapes and sizes, but in a small garden, the
arrival of anything that competes for your vegetables (or your space)
is quickly obvious. Alan was as scrupulous as I was about preferring
pests to pesticides on the crops, but he never liked to be surprised. So,
in the rest of the yard, he usually acted immediately to spray, set up
traps, or otherwise eliminate competing wildlife. Since his death,
however, I have rediscovered that my own instinct is to work toward
peaceful coexistence. The summer after he died, for instance, I became vaguely aware of being on the flight path of outgoing wasps as
I went in and out of my toolshed. (Allow me to comment here on the
joy of finally having—in my seventh decade—an actual toolshed. Not
a lean-to with a pegboard on the wall and snow indoors in the winter,

but an honest-to-God toolshed with two doors that latch and places to hang almost everything.) I had left the toolshed doors open overnight a couple of times and, noticing the wasps, reminded myself that I shouldn't do that any more since "varmints" might invade the indoor space and set up housekeeping.

Then one day, dashing into the toolshed once again, I looked up and saw that it was too late. Fastened to the angle between one of the rafters and the low roof was a soccer ball–sized paper wasp nest with several wasps working on it. Almost immediately, I noticed that on the opposite side of the same rafter was a mud tube, less than an inch in diameter with a single large round hole in it. How had I missed seeing them earlier?

My first thought was to wonder where Alan had left the wasp and hornet spray he routinely used to dispatch such uninviteds. My second thought was to wonder whether either nest really needed to be zapped. I had been going in and out of the shed for weeks without knowing they were there. The wasps and I (and whoever had produced that modest mud tube) appeared to have worked out our respective schedules. I had been considerably more menaced in Congers by a robin, who, having brazenly woven a nest in a clematis vine that bracketed our entrance, attacked anyone who walked past it.

As I contemplated simply accepting the wasps, I realized that, as was the case in so much else, my own impulse to let things happen had often been at odds with Alan's need to make sure nothing got out of control. If he were alive, I might have urged him to let the stinging critters stay. But he would have argued that they were in a bad location, right over the hanging scale in which we weighed our produce, and thus dangerously likely to sting him. He had been stung in the past, and I would have decided that it was not worth the effort to prevail. If I had, he probably *would* have gotten stung, and *then* we would have had to kill the wasps. I decided to trust my instinct to leave the nest and be extra careful weighing the produce. I never got stung. The beautiful paper ball is still hanging there, but no one has lived in it since that first year.

I thought back to June, just after Alan died, when the yard began receiving visits by what I took to be a raccoon, given the critter's cleverness in removing the lid of the garbage can. His (or her) visit began with the aggressive disarray of all the wood-chip mulch around my azaleas. It had been rummaged through, piled in windrows, burrowed into. I pushed it all back into place, cursing a bit, and the next night it happened again in another spot piled with wood chips, then all through the long wood troughs in which I grow asparagus.

My first impulse was to blame a skunk, since skunks had been omnipresent in our summer lives for years, rooting around the yard for grubs and worms. But skunks are not designed to lift the lids of garbage cans. This visitor removed the lid each night and tossed the garbage about. We have a trap, though I wasn't sure how to set it; trap-setting had been one of Alan's tasks. But we also had some fox urine (yes, you can buy it—I have tried to remain ignorant of how it is collected), which is intended to give pause to smaller folk.

So I put some fox urine on a cloth under the lid of the garbage can, put another lid over that and weighted it all down with a heavy metal bar. Then I sprayed fox urine on strips of sheeting and laid them down in all the places where my nocturnal visitor had been working. It took several nights. The first night the heavy metal weight was knocked off and the garbage pail lid was flipped, but after that the garbage pails were avoided. And then one day there were burrowings in the wood chips outside the garden gate and after that there was no more activity in the yard. I like to think *my* cleverness prevailed. Maybe the raccoon just got fed up with my boring vegetable garbage. It's probably worth noting here that fox urine does not seem to deter skunks. I think they have, wisely, a bad sense of smell.

I've opened this chapter with friendly insect and animal stories to let you know that where garden critters are concerned, I do aspire to coexistence. I have my limits, however. One of these is woodchucks. To anyone who has had a woodchuck in a garden, nothing more need be said. If you haven't seen one, I need to tell you that a full-grown woodchuck is about the size of an English bulldog. It is very persistent, can dig amazingly deep and fast, and has a huge appetite. A woodchuck can wipe out an entire bed of broccoli in one night—sometimes by eating it down to the ground, sometimes just by covering whatever hasn't been eaten with dirt as she makes her den.

Raiding *en masse* from the adjoining woods, woodchucks once convinced a passionate gardener friend who is both hardworking and durable to give up gardening. She had devoted time and considerable energy to creating a lovingly lush English perennial garden, growing all the plants from seed. Then the woodchucks discovered it. She tried smoke bombs, dogs, shotguns, and prayer. Finally, she gave up gardening altogether, since no matter how many woodchucks she trapped and took miles away, no matter how many repellents she tried, her garden was simply destroyed. They ate everything.

In Congers, we had gone to enormous lengths to keep woodchucks from denning under our lattice-enclosed porch, including covering every inch of soil with chicken wire and snow fencing. Still they came. Ultimately, Alan and I bought a Havahart trap, but we only once caught a woodchuck in it. Two others we killed by being faster and meaner than they were—I won't tell you how because it offends even me. But when all else failed, we hired a professional. We didn't like him much. He seemed to enjoy killing. And the point was not the killing. The point was to save our food.

It's interesting that even non-gardeners who think woodchucks are cute (no serious gardener thinks a woodchuck is cute) have no qualms about killing rats. Since rats seldom do serious damage in the garden, I'm much less urgent about their dispatch. Eventually, however, we had a bad rat year in Piermont, and a neighbor told me about Roger of "Ecological Pest Control." I first called Roger after a meeting at which several of our next-door community gardeners reported seeing rats climbing their sunflower stalks and defiantly staring down at them. Rats come with the river, of course, but that seemed a bit much.

The whole summer had been trying, even for an enlightened riverfront dweller. The rat influx was undoubtedly caused by construction on the rocky man-made promontory, the "pier" that gives our village its name. This four thousand-foot promontory built on piles reinforced with earth and stone had been built in the 1830s as the southern terminus of the New York–chartered Erie Railway. Through the years, it had supported roundhouses and factories, but today's building standards apparently demand a firmer footing. To consolidate the rocks and soil for the foundations of the condominiums they were hired to build, the construction workers were spending their days repeatedly raising and dropping multi-ton weights. The rats probably decided they should look elsewhere for homes (no doubt the occupants of the next-door condominiums were thinking the same thing).

So the community gardeners were not happy—nor, really, was I. Out in the garden, I felt as if I were being watched. When Roger came, he informed me that I was. Moreover, the rats had taken to rather assertively voting their preference among our tomatoes. The largest and sweetest variety in the garden is called Old Flame. The fruits look like small pumpkins and must be harvested by cutting their heavy stems with pruners, since they are too tender to be yanked off when ripe. They are simply stunning when sliced, with alternating gold and red cells. The rats chose Old Flame as their favorite, so for a while each tomato had a bite out of its bottom. This encouraged the rest of the tomato to rot and stink, as rotten tomatoes do.

So Roger came. Roger was so discreet about dispatching rats that no one ever saw a trap, nor did I ever see Roger until I asked him to stop by. He was nattily dressed in an incredibly clean uniform, and nice. Now that the construction is almost completed, the rats seem to have returned to their original homes and I no longer feel watched in the garden. I was also finally able to pick several untouched Old Flame tomatoes. This tomato is definitely one to display decoratively, simply sliced, and served with slices of mozzarella and fresh basil leaves. Anything else would be—hmm, overkill.

You could say that rats and woodchucks are the easy calls, either deeply detested on the one hand, or devastatingly destructive on the other. After that, it gets harder. Skunks, for instance, are cute, and only mildly damaging. We caught only one woodchuck in our Havahart trap, but we caught a lot of skunks. Skunks tend to carry their smell around with them, and they're a garden undesirable because they can do a lot of damage rooting around in the dirt. But we began catching them in Congers with no intention of doing so. We set our trap baited with peanut butter and salami to catch whomever was digging in the garden, thinking it was a woodchuck. Next morning, I looked out the window and saw that the trap had been sprung. Success! I raced outside—and stopped short a safe distance from the trap. Inside was an unmistakable black and white animal. *Now* what? Trapping the skunk was obviously only the beginning of our problem. How did we proceed from there?

Alan went out suited up in his oldest pants and shirt under a pale green shop smock my father had deeded him. Hooded, gloved, and holding a large sheet of plastic gingerly in front of him, he approached the heavy metal mesh cage, dropped the sheet of plastic over it, and waited. Nothing happened. Then he lifted the plastic-draped cage by its handle, and I advanced to wrap the plastic under it. Since the ends of the trap are solid metal, the skunk-filled trap was now entirely enclosed. Still no spray. So Alan took another sheet of plastic, enclosed the trap even more thoroughly and tied it up with rope. No spray.

In those days, there were no laws prohibiting removal of wild animals from your property, so he tied the wrapped cage onto the bicycle rack on the back of the car, and together we drove it out into the nearby woods. There, we very cautiously reversed the procedure: untying the rope, then pulling off the layers of plastic with a long-handled rake as we moved quickly away. The skunk just sat there, entirely at ease. Using a long rake, we released the wire that held the cage door shut, and opened the door. The skunk ambled out, never looking back, and headed into the woods.

After that, it got easier. Which was good, because that summer was a humdinger for skunks. We caught thirty, almost one a day for a while. Alan even called the local paper and a reporter came by with a photographer to do a story on Alan transporting skunks. The photographer used a telephoto lens, though, not wishing to take any chances. Personally, I never got over the nonchalance with which a skunk who had been trapped, wrapped in plastic, transported two miles on a bike rack, and released in strange territory would walk out of the open trap and stroll away. Nothing like wearing a lethal weapon, I suppose.

Those were good years for gardeners and for skunks. Everything became more difficult when we had a rabies epidemic. Raccoons were the creatures of concern, but the county passed an ordinance prohibiting removal of any trapped animal from your property. After that it was either let it go in your yard (after instructing it in garden etiquette, I suppose) or kill it. For a while, in Congers, we just kept breaking the law, intending to plead ignorance, letting the skunks go in places where we hoped the police wouldn't be patrolling. Ultimately, we learned from our friend with the woodchuck problem that she was drowning her woodchucks in the lake that bordered her property. Once Alan took our trap over there—illegally.

At this point, I need to insert a warning for those upset by the death of any wild creature for human convenience and/or survival. I am one of you. But once we had been barred by law from simply taking animal invaders elsewhere, Alan and I did, unwillingly, kill animals we trapped, just as farmers have always had to do. The alternative, giving up vegetable gardening, didn't seem like a real option to us. But my students taught me several years ago how deeply offensive any animal death can be to many urban people.

Before we get to my most personal slaughter story, therefore, I want to take a breather and talk about human and animal life. Some years ago, I was asked to join the board of an organization promoting vegetarian diets, and refused on the grounds that I hadn't yet decided whether vegetarianism was environmentally appropriate for the health of the planet. So when I was asked not long afterward to prepare a paper for a vegetarian conference about the environmental consequences of vegetarianism, I jumped at the chance.

At the time, a very popular book was promoting the idea that if we stopped eating beef, the whole planet would heal. I found the author's arguments naive and unconvincing, and wanted to explore the animal/human relationship in my own way. I posed myself the question: Would the world be better off environmentally if we all became vegetarians? I knew that when I finished my paper I would either be a vegetarian—since I have to live by my beliefs—or I would know how to explain why I wasn't.

My explorations led me to conclude that vegetarianism on a global scale is, and, always has been, impossible. Inuits, to take the most obvious example, could not survive as vegetarians. But there was much more. The idea that the earth would be a more fruitful place if all of us stopped eating animals and their products is simply wrong. This is so, among other reasons, because ruminants (animals who have bacteria in their guts that allow them to make use of plant matter humans can't digest) can graze land not suitable for growing crops. Banishing livestock would reduce the planet's overall supply of food and cause the humans who depend on animals to starve.

Moreover, if we unilaterally declared peace in regard to other living things, they would not reciprocate. Multiplying freely on land formerly grazed by livestock, wild animals would compete even more seriously than they presently do for the vegetable matter we would need to stay alive. So, while American meat is an undoubted scandal—raised, slaughtered, and processed in ways that are cruel, dangerous, and dirty—animals, domesticated and otherwise, are essential to the functioning of the planet. If we turned our livestock loose and simply allowed them to roam freely, they would eat our vegetables and we would starve.

I learned in a dramatic way, however, that many intelligent, environmentally concerned people are shocked by this biological reality where food production is concerned. It happened in "Nutritional Ecology," a course I have taught for years, in a session called "The True Cost of Food." I was trying to help students understand that our food costs much more than the few dollars we spend for it in the grocery store. Welfare, for example, is one of the long-term fallouts of the agricultural industrialization that drove many poor southern blacks off the land where they grew food, into urban dependence. Groundwater depletion (encouraged by subsidies), water polluted with nitrogen fertilizers and pesticides, soil erosion, and salinization are other uncounted costs of food production. And so is death, of insects, animals, birds—and even humans.

In presenting these ideas to the class, I used my own garden as an example, describing the dilemma Alan and I faced regarding animals we caught on the land that produced our food. Now that we lived on the river, I told the students, it was somewhat easier because we could drown animals if we had to. Near chaos broke out in the class. One of the students cried out in an anguished tone, as if she had just discovered that her teacher was a serial murderer, "I can't believe you'd drown an animal. How could you? When my cat caught a mouse, I took the mouse to the vet."

We had a problem. I insisted that we needed to respect all points of view, and let the deeply upset mouse-woman and the other students dialogue with each other briefly. Then I announced that we would spend some time in the next class session talking about animals and food. After that, I went home and thought hard.

The following week, I started off the class by telling the students how disturbed I was by the level of feeling I had generated. Then I reminded them that the class was called "The True Cost of Food," and that the issue of animal death had come up because of a hard truth: Whatever you choose to eat, and wherever you get it, the true cost of your food will, almost inevitably, include death.

Every time any of us eats, I told them, we are benefiting from the killing of something—insects, birds, animals, even humans—not just the plants we put into our mouths. Death is one of the true costs of our food. Death does not come merely to animals trapped, shot, or poisoned by farmers protecting their crops. It comes as well to creatures whose life spaces and local ecosystems are usurped by the vast monocultures of modern agriculture. Death also comes to workers and their children in Central America, forced to enter fields too recently sprayed with pesticides, to women and children going hungry as the food they grow is sold north for badly needed cash, to peasant families left without income as a multinational company refuses as "below standard" a broccoli crop intended for our freezers.

Vegetarianism may be a wise and moral personal choice. But not because it does not involve death. One could live one's whole life as a vegan—eating no meat, using no animal products—yet animals and sometimes even people will have died on one's behalf. You can't control nature without inflicting pain. We have been shielded from that pain by distance. Unless we know where every mouthful of our food comes from, and none of us does, we have to be honest enough with ourselves to acknowledge that its production has at least indirectly involved killing.

Only a few farmers still grow crops in the county where I live. One of them is named Smith (really) and he grows corn and pumpkins, among other things. Pumpkins are a good money crop that allows him to stay in business. In our rapidly growing county, we have lots of places where old woods edge new clearings (crow heaven) and lots of road-kill (crow food), and as a result we have lots of crows. Farmer Smith has suffered major losses of corn to crows. And he has had to hire schoolkids to stand in his fields to drive the crows away, since otherwise they come down and put a hole in each pumpkin—which makes them unsalable.

Smith is a small-scale farmer, and he is losing his livelihood. This is an example of the fact that the heaviest consequences of the expansion of the suburbs fall on the people who are trying to protect open land, and who probably have the greatest respect for other living creatures. Should Smith stop trying to grow food in the face of crow damage? That will simply leave us with one less local source of food, banishing to somewhere else the necessity to deal with varmints if we're to have food.

Most native peoples killed animals and used every part of them, respecting and honoring them as they did so, recognizing that the animal's life was given up for theirs. To be responsible toward animal life is to want to know how the animal that provides your milk or meat—or leather—is raised. Modern livestock raising is, for the most part, a horror. As "units of production," sentient creatures are jammed together in cattle feedlots, hog factories, and chicken tenements, shot up with hormones and antibiotics so they can survive the stress, then disassembled in slaughterhouses where the workers are as brutalized as the flesh they cut. The devil is in the details, and knowing your farmer is important whether what she grows for you is beef or beans. Thoughtfulness about your *diet* has to include asking yourself what happens to all the lives that produce your food, whoever and wherever they are.

It's worth noticing that, except for the mouse-woman in my class, most people don't seem to get upset about the deaths of rats or mice even if they deplore the killing of animals much less familiar to them. That's because rodents are agreed-upon pests—and a pest is something that competes with us for food and shelter in our own households. Apparently a garden is different, at least to city folks. One of my students told me that following the event in class, she had talked to a number of her friends who were, like her, vegetarians. They all agreed that killing an animal to save your garden was wrong, but that it was different if someone else did it. So it seems to matter a lot how personally involved you are in the killing.

JULY 1998—We always battled the birds for blueberries and raspberries, and this year is no exception. They penetrate the nets with regularity and flap around inside waiting for me to release them. Which I always do. But this year I've been feeling especially assaulted by "wildlife" in general. The other day, the patch of low-growing evergreens under the maple tree was covered with small branches fallen from the maple, not dead branches, but perfectly healthy young growth with ten or twelve full-sized leaves each. What on earth was going on? A friend came by, looked up, and said, "There's a squirrel up there." Sure enough, a squirrel was racing along one branch and then making a daring leap across to the adjacent one, carrying in her mouth a maple branch. Eventually we located a nest of browned-off leaves in a high-up crotch of the tree. Evidently the squirrels were gnawing off young branches for their nest and failing to catch them as they fell! They probably managed to get one branch to the nest for every four they chewed off. It seems unnaturally inefficient, but I suppose nature has something in mind. Fortunately, the tree is large and can handle the pruning.

I could have viewed the squirrels with no more than amusement if they had stopped there, but they didn't. They stole all my peaches (it was the first year the peach tree had borne; they looked beautiful) and all my Asian pears but a single damaged one. After the squirrels came the skunks, and after the skunks came an honest-to-God woodchuck (ate all my soybeans—no green soybeans in this year's winter diet). Then came an animal control man who caught three skunks and the woodchuck. Then came a possum who destroyed much of a newly emerging parsnip bed, too late to replant for winter parsnips. (The story of his/her dispatch follows shortly.) A period of peace followed.

Then the next-door community gardeners noticed a bunny (two bunnies—five?) and I noticed that the tops of my fall crop of sugar snap peas were chomped, as were the tops of all my last crop of green beans. Someone was also beginning to work on the carrots and parsley—and, outrageously—on the tops of the fifteen parsnip plants remaining after the possum disruption. Then came large pits dug in my orchard area and on the riverbank, and while I was patching them, I noticed that the broccoli tops were being eaten. Woodchucks don't dig for grubs and worms; skunks and possums don't eat broccoli (nor do rabbits since the plants sit up too high for them). So I am setting traps—with anger—and calling the animal control man again. I eat what I grow. I had looked forward to the fall crop of peas since the spring one was decimated by slugs, and the broccoli loss, like the soybean wipe-out, will reduce the winter's frozen green-vegetable supply. Until I catch whoever is responsible, I've put cages and netting around all these plants so the garden looks under seige. And it is.

Which brings me back to the possum. When I noticed that something had rooted around in my wood-chip mulch, and, more unacceptably, nosed into my newly planted parsnip and carrot beds and uprooted the seedlings, I knew something had to be done. Assuming I was dealing with a skunk, I set the trap with dog food and went to bed. Next morning, the trap had been sprung . . . by a possum. It was a small one, but decidedly a possum, with a long rat tail and a little snarly face edged with pointy razor-sharp teeth. What to do?

Coming face to face with trapped animals isn't too unsettling when, unlike skunks, they don't carry mace. But deciding what to do *after* a face-to-face encounter is harder, since you could illegally hide a possum in the car and drive it away to release someplace without risking olfactory pollution. However, the illegality of removing the animal to a nearby woods was not a trivial matter on this occasion, since the County Health Commissioner was rooming in my house at the time, and such activity would, at least, have embarrassed him. Alan and I had not really resolved our what-to-do-with-trapped-animals-problem when we left Congers. But when we got to Piermont, we realized that living by the river gave us the same option our lakeside friend had used: drowning.

So once we got to Piermont, Alan took responsibility for drowning marauders—or trying to. One trapped skunk was kidnapped by some compassionate visiting friends and released illegally in the woods in the dark of night. Another was seen swimming across the river toward Westchester shortly after the trap was lowered underwater. Now that I was alone, drowning was easier to decide on than to actually do. But there seemed no other option. Calling animal control simply meant paying someone else a significant sum of money to do—probably by firearm—what I shrank from doing by water. My only choice seemed to be the manner of death and the directness of the responsibility.

But if a drowning had to be done, I didn't want to be seen executing it, so to speak; I decided to do the deed before dawn or near dusk. But there was a problem. When the tide is out—twice every twenty-four hours—I have a beach where no one could drown. When the tide is in, the water is three to four feet deep right off the boardwalk. I needed the tide to be in. I went to look at the tide charts and discovered that the tides were high in mid-afternoon and the middle of the night, and low when I would have chosen to act. I would either have to rise in the wee hours before the tide fell too low, or do the deed in early evening when the tide had risen high enough, just before darkness fell. I decided on the latter.

I made sure the cage was out of the sun for the day and tried to concentrate on other things. As dusk fell and the tide began to come in, I went out and tied a rope to the hard-wire handle on the top of the cage. Then I draped everything with a piece of black plastic in case of onlookers, and carried the cage and its possum out to the boardwalk. Ever since the Tappan Zee Bridge had been cast across the widest part of the Hudson in the 1950s, sand had been piling up on the riverbanks below the bridge, raising them higher and higher. My boardwalk—built within the last fifteen years—stands well above the level of the old river bank. But a foot or so below it, jutting out over the water 3 feet or so above the sand at low tide, are the remains of a small dock built in a much earlier era—two 2 x 6 planks, 12 feet long.

When I got out to the boardwalk with the cage, the tide was up just far enough to cover the cage, but not the planks. So I lowered the cage into the water, held onto the rope, and sat down crosslegged at the edge of the boardwalk to wait. How long? Fifteen minutes? I hoped no one would come into the park to my right, look over the fence and ask what I was doing. I hoped no one would walk down to the river from the house to my left, not Barry who considers himself unelected mayor of the village, not his friendly landscaper tenant with his two little full-of-curiosity daughters. So I waited, tensely.

About fifteen minutes into the wait, heavy waves from something churning up the river a mile or so out began sloshing into shore, tossing the cage back and forth and threatening to wash it away. I decided to haul it in. It was heavy, filled with a wet possum and—half-way up—with half a trap of water. I heaved. The rope broke, and trap and possum dropped back into the water.

There was no way I could reach the handle on top of the trap from the boardwalk, so I lowered myself down onto the narrow projecting planks, leaned down, and tried to get hold of the handle. The trap was being sucked out into the river, it was getting dark, and I had to grab fast, as waves washed the trap back and forth, pulling it out a bit each time. The rising tide began to wet my shoes and the bottoms of my pants. It crossed my mind that I might fall in, and that the young possum in its trap and the sixty-nine-year-old woman might both be found the next morning, drowned in the Hudson, an Edgar Allan Poe story in the making. Hanging onto the edge of the boardwalk, I finally got hold of the trap and breathlessly heaved it out of the water, onto the plank with me, and then up to the boardwalk, where I followed it. Done.

It had been Alan's practice to dump a drowned animal into a black plastic bag, seal it up, and put it in the trash can outside the next-door community garden. But by now it was full dark. I knew the possum's sharp teeth couldn't harm me anymore, but I was daunted enough by my stupidity in using old rope to hold the trap to decide I would wait till morning to finish the job. So I moved the trap and its now-dead occupant back to the place where I had caught it, near my south fence where it was nearly invisible to anyone looking over, and went inside. Next morning, early, I walked out with my black plastic bag to finish what I had started. The possum was alive.

I will spare you the details of its last day on earth. It probably had pneumonia from its immersion—I am tempted to say one can play possum only so long—but I fear any attempt at lightheartedness might offend those who are already feeling pretty bad about this story. I felt awful at the time, but in the end, one can probably only live in the present world by keeping one's sense of humor. The possum hung on until late afternoon, when it expired. Feeling decidedly like a killer, I sealed it in a black plastic bag and put it in the community garden trash can. It should have gone into the compost pile, but I just couldn't bring myself to do that.

I once saw in a gardening magazine a columnist's response to a letter writer who had berated him for putting a dead woodchuck on his compost pile. "How can anyone claim to respect nature and do a thing like that?" the animal lover fumed. "Madam," he replied, "it is precisely *because* I respect nature, which functions by recycling plants and animals, that the woodchuck belongs on the compost pile."

So now you know. We're all killers. We either do it personally or through surrogates, but we simply can't avoid the fact that, if we eat, killing is being done on our behalf. I am personally happier—no, not happier, more morally comfortable perhaps—taking some responsibility for what has to be done if I am to survive. It is hard to be a farmer, even a mini-farmer who takes production seriously. One can readily feel under seige. So I keep my sense of humor, but I don't take the killing lightly.

As the narrative above reflects, the possum came mid-season. Much later, when I set the trap for what I hoped would be the last skunk, I heard from an acquaintance that there was an animal rescue person in the county who would come and take away (kindly though illegally) whatever I caught and release it in her yard. So I called her. I indicated that because of the laws about animal removal, I had had to dispatch one of the creatures I had trapped on my land, but that I preferred not to if she would take them away, legally or otherwise. Her first response was a bitterly hostile attack about my being a murderer, so I was glad I had thought through the issues for my class. In the end, I convinced her that I was calling her precisely because I didn't like killing animals. She came; she coaxed the baby skunk I had trapped into a spacious cage that she carried gently to her car and took away to release in her own yard. After I gave her some freshly picked tomatoes and green beans, she even smiled.

I respect her position. But when in the course of our initial argument, I pointed out to her that farmers killed animals in her name, she shot back that I wasn't a farmer. And I shot back, "But I raise my own food. Should I not do that?" Is slaughter forgivable only for the large commercial grower who produces her food? What will I do the next time I catch something in the trap? I'll probably call her again. If it's a woodchuck, however, I might call the animal control man. I don't know. I only hope that I am, as I believe, facing my killing head on.

12

Eating My Yard

Let her dyet proceede more from the provision of her owne yarde,
than the furniture of the markets; and let it be rather esteemed
for the familiar acquaintance shee hath with it, than for the strangenesse
and raritie it bringeth from other Countries.
—Gervase Markham, *The English Hus-wife*, 1615

I STRUGGLE TO KEEP other species from grazing my yard so I can do the harvesting. But even when Nature and her creatures cooperate fully, I don't come close to feeding myself; Alan and I never did. I do try to live as much as possible on what I grow, and this book is all about when, where, how, and, perhaps most of all, *why* I try to do that. But the extent to which I'm not self-sufficient reminds me constantly that I depend, as we all do, on neighbors—increasingly remote neighbors—to carry on for us the demanding work of food production. Because farmers keep planting and harvesting, tending trees and vines, and caring for animals and birds, none of us is required to survive on our own production capacity.

Consequently, the invisibility of these people as the *source* of our food never ceases to alarm me; witness a commentary by Dave Hage recently published in *The Nation* asking why taxpayers should be rescuing farmers who are once again in financial trouble. The first answer, the author says, is because Congress always responds to the farm lobby. "A second answer is that a government should cushion its people against the cruelties of the market." I'm waiting here for him to mention the fact that farmers grow our food and we'd starve without them, but he says, "Finally, farmers give the nation a certain economic and social diversity. They provide a counterweight to the grain and meat-packing giants that control our food production, and they undergird a rural culture that millions of families still find preferable to suburbanized America." I'm certain that this writer knows that we need farms to produce food, because he's located in the middle of farming country, but he seems to feel no necessity to point out that these providers of economic and social diversity, these undergirders of rural culture, feed us.

I don't at the moment grow grains or any animal products (flesh, eggs, milk), and I eat—among other things—bread and muffins, homemade granola, eggs, milk, lots of cheese, and a little meat. I also eat more fruit than I have yet been able to grow, though I'm trying. And I don't grow all my own fertility. According to calculations by intensive-grower John Jeavons, who has thought more about saving our planetary soils than anyone, I would need to plant at least half of my garden beds with compost crops to produce on site all the nutrients I need to keep the other half growing vegetables. So I bring in manure and wood chips as I've reported, add chopped-up newspapers to my compost pile, and supplement with purchased blood meal, bone meal, ashes, and mineral powders.

Some small-farm families grow almost everything they eat, but most farmers don't. The great majority of U.S. farmers have been convinced that growing their own food is a waste of land—which could better be planted with crops they can sell—as well as a waste of time, because everything can be bought fast and cheap and even ready to eat. The bargain chicken the farmer eats, however, may have grown up on feed she sold off her farm. That sort of logic has led to lots of farmers going broke and others depending on food stamps, since low prices for the "raw materials" that are turned into processed foods translate into even lower prices on the farm. Cheap chickens mean even cheaper corn.

There is an article much quoted among people concerned with creating a food system that the planet can support indefinitely. In it, a University of Maine economist named Stewart Smith points out that the farmer's share of the food dollar has declined so steadily since 1910 that if the trend simply continued, there would be no more "farming" in agriculture by the year 2020. His graphs show that by then our food dollars would go entirely to pay for the inputs (fertilizer, seed, pesticides, herbicides, machinery, interest on debts, etc.) and for the cost of getting the food from the farm through the processing plant and the supermarket to our table (transportation, processing, advertising, retailing). These pre-farm and post-farm sectors are where more and more of the money flows. Smith called his paper "Is there Farming in Agriculture's Future?" This trend makes it hard to understand the government's reluctance to help keep farmers solvent. Someone, of course, will need to produce food, but maybe our leaders have decided that losing our farms is just one more instance of "progress" that can't be stopped. Perhaps they have concluded that we'll get our food from poor countries south or east of us where farm workers are paid so little that food cheap enough for us rich folks can still be produced profitably.

Because my "farm" is only 1,000 square feet of growing space twenty minutes north of New York City, I couldn't really feed myself if I wanted to. But I do grow all my own vegetables, and I therefore eat differently than most people—better, I think. In deciding what to eat, I bind myself to the seasons, augmented by what a small upright freezer will hold. And—what impresses me most—I'm almost always able to plan meals for myself and for frequent guests based on what's fresh in the garden or what's stored in the cold cellar or the guest bedroom closet. I eat fresh tomatoes between July and December or January when the last one harvested green has turned red (dried tomatoes or frozen sauces take me through winter and spring). Sometimes on a cold morning I have a roasted sweet potato for breakfast. I eat no lettuce when no lettuce is in the garden or cold frame, and in its place (in tacos, for example), I use chopped kale. And for salad? I'll get to that.

What do I grow? Always potatoes (six or seven kinds) plus sweet potatoes, tomatoes (several kinds), a variety of hot and sweet peppers, eggplant (short and long), zucchini, green beans, dry beans (pinto, scarlet runner, and black), storage onions (red and yellow), leeks, garlic, carrots, parsnips, kale, spinach, lettuce, mesclun, edible-pod peas, green soybeans, broccoli, parsley, basil, and other herbs. Sometimes cabbage, beets, turnips, collards, leaf celery, ruby chard, and butternut squash. Depending on which of these things is available, I plan my meals, augmented mostly by cheese, eggs, milk, bread, and grains. The mix is obviously nutritious since I am, at seventy-plus, absurdly healthy. And, hearing no complaints from guests, I assume that they find my seasonal local meals as delicious as I do.

As to how this works out in practice, there I was on July 3, having just come home from the supermarket with tortilla chips (I'm not perfect!), eggs, apricot and grapefruit juice, English muffins, and . . . Coca-Cola (I'm *really* not perfect—and I had someone coming who would ask for it). I also had to get bottles of seltzer, because the man who brings me a wooden case of ancient heavy-glass spritzer bottles when I need them seems unaccountably to have disappeared. That was my Fourth of July shopping. I was at the market early, when other people were loading up with bags and bags full of meat and buns and snacks and the like. And I was a little anxious, because I was trying, as usual, to make things from my garden the center of a meal for seven or more.

Watching those other shoppers line up with two or three cartloads of groceries, I realized how odd I was. And, feeling a momentary twinge of self-pity, I understood that it was hard to do what I was trying to do, to count mostly on what I had grown, and thereby symbolically to use only what belonged, at any particular time of year, in the place where I lived. Then I walked over to get my tortilla chips, and realized what *hard* really was. Because I don't watch television or read women's magazines, I don't see food advertisements. This means that I don't know how to decide which of the dozens of different kinds of tortilla chips—bite-sized, restaurant-style, white corn, yellow corn, chili-lime, avocado–sour cream, and so on, filling half the length of a supermarket aisle—I need to buy. Why would I want circles instead of triangles? What does it matter if the chips were made with all-white corn? Why would I buy chili-lime–flavored chips if I'm going to serve salsa with them?

Then I realized that the store had twenty aisles of such time- and energy-sinks, centers of artificial diversity that raised silly questions and induced you to occupy your mind making non-essential distinctions—non-essential, but necessary if you were going to escape the store without simply fleeing. I don't have to do much of that kind of choosing—and I won't starve if I simply flee. Many of my choices are made for me by the seasons, and by my once-a-year planning for what I will grow. And stressful as it might be to wonder if I can put together a meal for seven at the beginning of July, before the tomatoes and peppers and eggplant have fully begun to fruit, it is, on a profound level, easier than the alternative.

We're going to start our Fourth of July meal with those tortilla chips (not local, I'm afraid), and a "fresh" salsa made from some tomatoes I froze whole last year, and some roasted hot peppers and salsa cubes both left in the freezer—stuff I need to get rid of before the new crops of tomatoes and peppers come in. We'll also have a really seasonal offering that will be the most popular appetizer, the last of my sugar snap peas, briefly steamed whole and dressed with my home-dried tomatoes softened in balsamic vinegar. For the main event, we'll have Grilled Andouille Sausage and Sweet Potato Salad (lots of last year's sweet potatoes still occupy the guest room closet), some kind of bean salad (I have lots of pintos, some black beans, and a handful of white beans that I'm taking the trouble to cook separately so the dish will be more interesting to look at). We're also going to have a frittata made with various garden greens (beet, collard, kale, lettuce that's bolting from the heat), scallions, and herbs, with some lime juice from my home-grown limes (the tree comes inside for the winter). If I can find enough unbolted lettuce that my fellow community gardeners don't intend to pick, I will also have a salad, but it's not the best time of year for that. Lettuce and spinach don't like 90-degree days any better than I do.

As it turned out, I burned the white beans getting distracted by all the different things I was trying to do. But when I looked in the freezer, I discovered that I had some snap beans left over (with the fresh ones already coming from the garden), so we had a salad of black and brown and green beans. And I never made the lettuce salad because the peas were such a hit that everyone was almost full before the main dishes were served.

I recognize that it's a fairly quixotic enterprise on which I have set out. Trying to grow as much as possible of what we eat began as a way to prove to myself and others that eating locally year-round did not imply a season of cabbage and old potatoes, even if you lived in New England. I demonstrate that every time I serve a splendid meal in the dead of winter. But the impulse to make such a demonstration grew out of my conviction that we all had to relearn our dependence on the land, getting to know and count on people who worked the land around us, farmers who were not-too-distant neighbors.

So my ultimate goal is to keep local farmers in business by increasing their customer base. Obviously, I would do this more directly by buying their food than by growing my own. So I'm much less troubled by the fact that I can't grow everything I eat than by the fact that I mostly can't support local farmers by what I buy; it's usually easier to grow it myself than to find food that is locally grown.

One day last summer, I went to the nearest giant supermarket to pick up a couple of things and realized that I wanted apples.

AUGUST 6 — I found myself feeling profoundly misplaced as I walked through, chilled from the open freezer cases, in a kind of trance since the store was largely empty, wondering who bought all these things. The number of choices is simply overwhelming. . . . I started peering into other people's carts and wondering how they decided which of the sizes and flavors and shapes of things they chose. I got Brita filters and oat bran muffins (there must be 14 flavors—I get mine because I can't get whole wheat), but gave up at the frozen food section, which was even more overwhelming— and cold (all those chilled aisles using up electricity whose production helped warm the planet!).

And then I got some apples even though they were utterly

placeless. I went to someone in the produce section and asked whether there were any apples from New York state. He looked at me absolutely blankly and said "WHAAT?" I said, "Are any of your apples local, from this state? I like to support local farmers." "I have no idea," he said with obvious disinterest. "It might be on the box they come in." And I realized suddenly that I didn't have the energy to ask to see the manager and make the fight. I'm a single "old lady"; the manager could have looked in my cart and seen that I don't buy enough to be a "valued" customer. In that brightly lit twenty aisles of stuff that I mostly don't buy, I felt too alien and isolated to make a useful fuss.

So I bought Macintosh apples, and for all I could tell, the ones I bought might well have been shipped across the country from Washington State, although Macintosh is a New York State standard. But I wanted to make Apple Pan Dowdy with my home-grown blackberries the next day, and, after an hour of driving around New Jersey vainly looking for a simple bamboo blind (ah, yes, the suburbs!), it seemed wasteful and irrational to drive five miles north to Davies' Orchards to get local apples. The energy cost—fossil and human—would have been absurd.

How difficult and time-consuming it is to try to live simply in this culture of frenzied consumption. ShopRite was a kind of epiphany. I felt as if I simply didn't know how to shop there, how to make choices, how to find things. It made me feel helpless and alien. And how in hell do people make rational choices from among all those bewildering and complex items?

And when I came home, the four hay bales I had ordered for the community garden were sitting at the end of my driveway, so I put away the groceries and then went outside to clean up the shed before the bales were moved in. I did that, reordered it, swept it out, and felt great about how it looked. I weeded some in the driveway, then I went to tie up the tomatoes that were not in cages. . . . I found myself so peaceful and happy and open-hearted at that task. I realized that ShopRite had really made me crazy. It was all so artificial and had nothing to do with food. I am over-whelmed with the realization that for most people, ShopRite is their experience with what passes for food: dead, uniform, odor-less, and sanitized. How do we make people raised in such envi-ronments remember what food is? And how do we help them re-member that it takes farmers to produce it?

The simplest and best idea I ever heard for beginning to support local producers is to spend at least $10 a week on local food, and for a few months in the summer I can do that by going to the farmers' market that a friend started in a neighboring community. There I can buy locally baked bread, farm-raised trout, locally produced tofu, lo-cal cheese, local corn (which is too space-consuming to raise in my little garden), and fruit. I can also buy local cheese and butter at the small market in my community. And I've found a nearby place to buy local tortillas, which come fresh, three dozen for $1, produced for the large Latino population in the area. (I could have *made* local tortilla chips for Independence Day!)

But fruit remains a dilemma, especially in the winter. I paid $2.90 for a box of clementines at my nearby oriental market in January—well aware that they had been shipped in from Spain. As I stood peel-ing one this morning, I found myself thinking about the unsweetened grapefruit juice I regularly hunt for in the juice section of the super-market, and my mind flipped to the issue of making responsible choices. The juice section is, of course, just one aisle of the product playland most markets have become, thirty running feet or more, loaded from floor level to its topmost shelf with canned and boxed mixes of fruit concentrates, sugar and water whose often fanciful names give only the slightest indication of their actual contents.

Even my grapefruit juice is not simply grapefruit-squeezings, but "filtered water and grapefruit juice concentrate." Here at least, the name on the package tells me fairly well what I am getting—"Un-sweetened Grapefruit Juice"—and in smaller letters underneath, "from concentrate." But the juice is distributed from Chicago and carries no indication of where the grapefruit was squeezed, so I have to take all this on faith, and on signals from my own taste buds, which remain attuned to actual foods. Are most breakfast drinkers, their taste-buds blunted by "juice cocktails," prepared to detect fraud?

What was on the label of the "orange juice" made with "watery orange byproducts," sugar, and unapproved preservatives, which was discovered quite by accident several years ago to have been distributed in twenty-five states? It was manufactured in Michigan from concentrate supplied by a Chicago corporation from juice presumably extracted in Florida, California, or some other orange-growing region whence it made its way to Chicago. One can only hope that this well-travelled mixture was not marketed as "fresh." Are enough consumers left who have drunk "real" orange juice to notice?

The adulterated juice news story reported that the Food and Drug Administration was "committed to pursuing adulteration cases," but knowing what I know about understaffing at the FDA, the moral I drew from this depressing story was that if you ate from the standard U.S. food supply, you couldn't hope to employ enough policemen to make your food trustworthy. In a global marketplace, your eating and drinking really can't be protected from economic fraud or worse, however hard the regulatory agencies try.

When I peeled my clementine this morning, however, I wasn't worried about its safety or integrity. I simply wished I knew something about how many miles that fruit had traveled to get to me; I wished that something in the store could let me know its unit cost in environmental terms. I can't be self-sufficient, nor do I think I need to be. But I want to be ecologically responsible, and I would like to know which of my choices—from that juice rack, for example, or from those bins of fresh fruit—would have imposed the least burden on the environment. What did it really cost to get that pear juice to my grocer's shelf? the peach nectar? the cranberry juice (from concentrate)? Water *is* heavy to ship. Making concentrate from fruit where it grows and adding water locally would make travel sense. But adding water in Chicago and sending it east seemed not to—and where was the concentrate made?

On the face of it, apple juice would seem the winter beverage of choice in the apple-growing state I live in. But I am wary of that since the time I bought a small carton of "100% pure apple juice" from a Manhattan mini-mart and discovered on the label that it was made of concentrate from West Germany, Austria, Italy, Hungary, and Argentina. Now, I only recently learned, China has set out to be the world's leading producer of cheap apple juice. If we want to be responsible to ourselves and the planet, then the best most of us can do most of the time is to shorten the chain from the farm to our table, get as close to the producer as possible whenever we can, and for the rest, until the food system unwinds, take a chance on regulatory agencies we really don't trust.

I'm okay for vegetables year-round, pretty well off for fruits in the summer, resigned to using "imported" grains and their products (although I try not to buy pasta sent from Italy). I buy unbranded bread baked either in this county or at least in the region, but I don't know where the ingredients come from. I make my own granola from organic rolled oats, New York State–produced honey, organic cold-pressed unrefined corn or peanut oil, and a variety of nuts and seeds whose provenance I don't know (though my organic sunflower seeds come from farmer friends in North Dakota). And I buy sardines from Port Clyde, Maine, if I can find them, because that's the port from which the mailboat to the Maine island I know best leaves, and it's as local as I can get. Since New York is a dairy state; I ought to use mostly local dairy products. But except for New York State cheddar, goat cheese, and butter, but until recently I had been opting for convenience over conscience.

When our children were young and we were very poor, I started making milk from skim-milk powder, and kept doing it long after it was a budgetary issue. I was troubled by the fact that the cows whose milk was dried surely weren't local and the system has never paid a decent price for their product. But I drink almost a quart of milk a day and often run out just when I want to make myself a cup of warm milk before bed. The store within walking distance is closed then, and I've told myself that driving farther afield just for milk is environmentally irresponsible. Fortunately, someone heard me say this and asked the obvious question: "Why don't you buy local organic milk for most of the time, and keep powdered milk around for emergencies?" Amazingly simple. Now I can help my state's dairy farmers—who are going broke even as I write—and still have my bedtime toddy.

And then there's the critical issue of salads. Mention local eating in the Northeast, and one of the first things most listeners want to know is what they would do for salad, by which most people mean, of course, something like the standard American salad of iceberg lettuce and tomato. If people are surveyed about how important it is for them to have certain fruits and vegetables fresh year-round, they rank lettuce and tomatoes among the most important.

It's certainly not nutrition that's driving this need. When I learned many years ago that per capita consumption of iceberg lettuce was twenty-five pounds a year, I looked up its total nutritional value. A year's supply of iceberg lettuce contains pitifully few nutrients; three to four days worth of iron, for example, and enough vitamin C for a week and a half. Yet many people seem convinced that they cannot satisfy their daily nutrient requirements without an iceberg lettuce fix.

I was so intrigued by the question of how a watery crunch of lettuce and a sectioned orange golf ball had come to represent salad that I did some research and found out that the word *salad* derives from the Latin for *salt*, and according to Maguelonne Toussaint-Samat's *A History of Food*, was first applied to a dish "popular on festive tables in fifteenth century Milan." It was a very liquid, very salty ragoût, "flavored with preserves, mustard and lemon, and decorated with marzipan." That sounds really awful, and it sure ain't lettuce.

Looking further, I came to the conclusion that the word *salad* had arrived later than the idea of eating dressed raw greens, which goes back to antiquity. Indeed, Waverley Root and Richard de Rochemont begin their history *Eating in America* with an observation that when Columbus discovered America, the Indians "were given to greens . . .

which they ate raw, as salads, or popped into whatever happened to be cooking." Obviously the "Indians" were not eating iceberg lettuce, but local greens, in season.

What salad evolved into when the home economists got hold of it toward the end of the nineteenth century comes close to a return to ragoût with marzipan. By 1920, Fannie Farmer's *Boston Cooking School Cookbook*, then in its tenth edition, contained ninety-seven salad recipes and fifteen dressings. Here is one of the recipes just as presented:

Bershire Salad in Boxes

Marinate one cup cold boiled fowl cut into dice and one cup cooked French chestnuts broken in pieces with French Dressing. Add one grated red pepper from which seeds have been removed, one cup celery cut into small pieces, and Mayonnaise to moisten. Trim crackers (four inches long by one inch wide, slightly salted) at ends, using a sharp knife; arrange on plate in form of box, keep in place with red ribbon one-half inch wide, and fasten at one corner by tying ribbon in a bow. Garnish opposite corner with a sprig of holly berries. Line box with lettuce leaves, put in a spoonful of salad and mask with Mayonnaise. Any colored ribbon may be used and flowers substituted for berries.

I found my stomach clenching with pity at the thought of a struggling homemaker trying to tie those crackers into a box with a red (or some other color) ribbon with a bow at the corner.

The salad entries in the 1934 edition of Mrs. Simon Kander's *The Settlement Cook Book* are equally appalling and require a level of obsession and skill that would daunt Martha Stewart. If "salad" in the "New World" had come to this by the early twentieth century, iceberg lettuce and tomato was surely a victory for women's liberation and nutrition.

But we have choices, even in the cold Northeast, that are neither well-travelled iceberg lettuce or Bershire Salad in Boxes. My salad research led me to Meta Given, whose *Modern Encyclopedia of Cooking* had sold 500,000 copies by the time of its sixteenth printing in February 1954. She tells us that

> people have been enjoying the foods that go into salads for four or five thousand years. . . . Raw vegetables were included in the menu for a number of reasons: their crispness was a pleasant contrast to the soft foods in the meal; their fresh flavor seemed to highlight the whole meal; they were usually slightly tart and peppery and perked up the appetite for the foods that were eaten with them, and they were beautiful in color and form and pleased the sight as well as the appetite.

So winter salads need to be beautiful in color and form, slightly tart and peppery, and crisp—boiled or roasted beets marinated with raw onions, root vegetable slaws of infinite variety, cold dressed grains and lentils brightened with sundried tomatoes softened in vinegar, seasoned puréed dry beans with nuts for crunch—all of them more delicious and usually more nutritious than iceberg lettuce. These are some of the alternatives to winter greens in the Northeast winter.

But there is another responsible solution to the salad problem. On the Maine coast, Eliot Coleman grows "candy carrots," tiny little spears of sweetness, and a variety of cold-tolerant greens in an unheated greenhouse, with the vegetables inside covered with a light-admitting spun fabric for extra cold protection. At my house, twenty minutes north of Manhattan, I don't even have to work that hard. I have a cold frame covered with an old 3-by-6-foot storm window that I don't manage very carefully. Mostly I just leave one edge propped open to keep the plants from overheating on sunny days when the inside temperature can go up into the nineties.

JANUARY 14—I went out and picked a salad today. The Lollo Rosa lettuce and frisée in there is just perfect, and beautiful. Untouched by the 10° nights! A woman called about coming down to see my cold frame—saying I was the only person she had found in the Hudson Valley who had anything growing!

And out in the garden, not in the cold frame, but under a light cover of that same spun fabric (called Remay), I have a bed full of mâche, a small compact rosette of leaves that seems entirely undaunted by the cold. If I can produce these greens, farmers can grow them for all of us, but only if we're willing to pay them a reasonable amount to do so.

13

Lessons from the Tomato

The homegrown tomato requires no fuel in its transport, no packaging to be
sent to the landfill, no political decisions about who will be allowed to work
the fields or what level of pollutants is acceptable in our groundwater.

—John Jeavons, *How to Grow More Vegetables*

THE ITEM ACCOMPANYING iceberg lettuce in the standard winter
salad is the sliced or sectioned orange golf ball deceptively called a
tomato. Everyone over fifty knows that the tomato used to be a soft,
juicy, sweet-sour fruit—which has been legally designated a vegetable
because, unlike other fruits, it is not normally eaten for dessert.
Grown in home gardens more frequently than any other food, it used
to be eaten fresh only in season, through the hot summer and until the
first fall frost. In the heat of summer, real tomatoes could be sliced or
cubed and made into salads or a variety of uncooked sauces that surprised your taste buds. During the other seasons, they could be consumed canned and frozen, sauced and relished, dried and pickled, and
otherwise preserved.

Science has converted this succulent summer treat into a hard,
orange, bland, starchy ball that can be sliced or sectioned and served
"fresh" any time of year. It *is* served, insistently as I said, combined
with iceberg lettuce in a distinctly American salad that derives its only
taste from its heavy lather of dressing. Tomatoes have been bred to
tennis-ball texture because the authentic ripe tomato is a tender and
vulnerable object that resents being shipped.

The ordinary tomato is hard when it's green and softens because it
produces an enzyme that breaks down pectin as the fruit turns red or
orange, and sometimes yellow or purple. Jelly-makers may remember

that pectin is the substance that determines whether jelly sets up; pectin in a tomato makes its cell walls stiff. While the tomato pectin is disassembling in a ripening tomato, other transformations are occurring that push its flavor from bland to exquisite. Breeders have worked hardest, however, not to improve tomato taste, but to create tomatoes that are both handsome and durable.

One night a couple of years ago, a friend brought me two "vine-ripened" tomatoes to go with a dinner I was cooking for him. It was mid-February, and the gift tomatoes looked gorgeous. But when I picked one up, it was unyielding, its pectin fully intact. We agreed that we didn't want to eat the hard tomatoes and had some of my sweetly delicious just-dug carrots instead. When my friend left, he took one tomato with him and left one for me; we agreed that we would check with each other to see when they were ready to eat. That was on a Friday. On Friday two weeks later, my guest tomato was unchanged. It still didn't yield to the press of my thumb. Greg had forgotten about his and suspected it was lost somewhere in his car. Three days later, I wanted to make a tomato and cheese sandwich and figured it was now or never. So I sliced the tomato. The texture wasn't bad, but it had no taste.

Just before frost every year, sometime in October, I clear out my tomato vines, picking all the red tomatoes, all the ones turning pink, and the largest of the really green ones. The smaller greens are left to freeze. The year of the guest tomatoes, two Montanans were here helping me with the last harvest, and they picked everything—three 5-gallon bucketfuls of tomatoes including all the golf-ball-sized green ones that aren't supposed to ripen, ever. I can let unripe fruit freeze, but find it very hard to waste it once it is picked. So I laid out the green tomatoes on screens in my cold cellar where they get a little light and put some of the nearly ripe ones in a kitchen drawer to use as they turned full red.

Many years ago, I read that if a tomato is going to be flavorful when it's ripe, it can't be picked before it has begun to "break," that is, show a little pink. The fact that they are sometimes picked too green is supposed to explain why those orange globes in the supermarket have so little flavor. I save my larger green ones anyway, and if they make it all the way to red without rotting or drying up, they get cut up into sauces to add tang. Or, I make Spicy Fried Egg and Tomato, a recipe that can redeem even a less-than-perfect fruit.

SPICY FRIED EGG AND TOMATO
(*Colin Tudge*, FUTURE FOOD)

Chop fine:
> 1 **mild green chili pepper** (*Anaheim, poblano*)

Fry lightly in:
> 4 tablespoons **unrefined corn oil**

Stir in:
> 1 teaspoon **cumin** (*or more!*)

Fry another minute.

Now cut in half:
> 8 **tomatoes**

Add them to the pan with:
> **salt and pepper** *to taste*

Fry lightly on both sides without letting them burn.

When the tomatoes are soft, lift them out onto a heated plate, and keep warm while you fry in the remaining cumin-filled oil:
> 4 **eggs**

Serve immediately with two tomatoes for each egg.

My tomatoes that bumper year were remarkably unblemished when I brought them in. I lost only a few to rot, and even the small entirely green ones ripened. Late in January, only a few weeks before my guest arrived with the big red fellows, I had made a sandwich with the very last of my own tomatoes picked months earlier. So when I got around to eating my gift tomato, I had something to compare it with. My tomatoes won hands down. They had that mix of acidity and sweetness that makes a real tomato. Of course, there was more acidity and less of the sweetness that the sun generates. These closet-ripened tomatoes couldn't compare to the ones picked fresh off the vines in summer, but they were vastly superior to that sturdy red sphere that only looked like a perfect tomato.

I learned from this that if economics allowed construction of storage spaces appropriate for ripening tomatoes into winter, we could have a much longer run of quite-acceptable local fruit even where it's cold. Such rational solutions will be affordable, unfortunately, only when we count the costs to the environment of moving tomatoes across the country and decide that high quality local food should cost more.

The refrigerator is almost as hard on tomato taste as the scientists have been. When one of our tomatoes is damaged but salvageable or when I can use only half, I reluctantly put the remains in the refrigerator. But I never eat them raw. Real tomato taste and texture are gone, so the tomato remnant goes into a sauce where the fresh tomato flavor is lost anyway. Panzanella is something easy and wonderful to do on a hot day with a tomato that has never been chilled.

PANZANELLA

In a large bowl combine:
*1 pound ripe juicy **tomatoes**, cored and cut into ½-inch chunks*
*¼ cup finely chopped **red onion***
*¼ cup finely chopped fresh **basil***
*1 or more cloves **garlic**, crushed*
*5 teaspoon extra virgin **olive oil***
***salt and pepper**, to taste*

Add:

*1 ½ cups stale **Italian or other serious breads**, cut into ½-inch chunks, soaked for 15 minutes in water, and squeezed dry*

Toss to blend, season to taste, and serve at room temperature. Delicious!

Several years ago, someone wrote to the *Washington Post* saying that the soft and juicy backyard tomato was an act of subversion, because it's a reminder of what a tomato ought to taste like. Actually, the effort to recapture for commerce the taste and seductiveness of the old-fashioned tomato has engaged some good scientific minds over the last half-century, which probably helps explain why the tomato was one of the earliest and most publicized of the foods subjected to biotechnological "improvement." The FlavrSavr tomato, called the McGregor when it briefly hit the market, came from Calgene Inc., of Davis, California. It's entirely appropriate that this community was a leader in the new effort to make tomatoes "ripen" without softening, since the University of California at Davis is the home of the hard, square, tasteless tomato, bred for efficient packing.

When a tomato has grown large enough to ripen, an enzyme called polygalacturonase or PG is produced. This enzyme breaks down the pectin in the cell wall and allows the tomato to turn red, squishy, and luscious. Using the magic of genetic engineering, the Calgene company took the gene for PG out of the tomato chromosome, turned it around so it didn't work normally, and replaced it. While the fruit went on developing the acids and sugars that contribute to ripe tomato taste, the tomato's pectin would remain mostly intact, although enough functioning enzyme was supposed to be left that the tomato would *eventually* soften.

I served on the Food Advisory Committee of the FDA when that agency held hearings to consider whether this tomato—the first genetically engineered vegetable to enter the U.S. market—should receive FDA approval. As genetically engineered products go, this seemed a relatively safe one since no alien gene had been introduced. Well, one alien gene that we know of *was* introduced, but I'd like to ignore it for now since it's irrelevant to this part of the story.

Let's just accept that this particular invention seemed relatively safe for human consumption, and that it was hard to raise human safety questions that the company and the FDA hadn't already settled. Moreover, the questions that concerned some of us didn't seem to come under the FDA's mandate to protect the *safety* of the food supply. Owning genes, for example. Calgene owns the gene that keeps its tomato from getting soft. Was it really a good idea to allow a company to own a gene that God had made and human farmers had favored over time? What would happen to farmers growing tomatoes with genes that didn't belong to Calgene? They'd have to ship their crop when the tomatoes, not the market, were ready. Wouldn't they be wiped out trying to compete with a tomato that could look ripe for weeks without spoiling? We had other concerns as well, but none of them seemed likely to derail the FDA's approval process.

At a break during the FDA hearing on the FlavrSavr, I asked a Calgene PR person whether I would be breaking the law if I got hold of one of their tomatoes, saved the seeds, and grew them. She went off to find out, came back, and said, "Yes, but we probably wouldn't prosecute." Now, saving one's own seed is an ancient tradition among farmers and gardeners. Being able to save your own seed gives you independence from seed companies and allows you to plant a crop even if you don't have any money at planting time. In the nineteenth century, the Department of Agriculture encouraged farmers to save seeds and to send in samples of their best ones, which the Department then distributed to other farmers to use in developing their own varieties.

That free exchange, which stimulated farmer innovation in breeding different seeds for different regions, lasted only until the seed companies decided it wasn't fair to industry for the government to give away free seeds. Ultimately, Congress was induced to pass a series of laws that allowed seed companies to patent their varieties, on the grounds that without patent protection, they would have no reason to innovate. Although seed patenting does not seem to have encouraged real innovation as we were promised, it has encouraged the sort of "mine's better" promotion designed to convince American gardeners that white marigolds, purple cauliflower, and the largest and newest anything are best.

Where innovation really counted, in production agriculture, the number of varieties being grown has plummeted since seeds have been patented. By 1980, for example, 97 percent of the vegetable varieties that U.S. commercial seed houses were selling in 1903 were not in the collection of the National Seed Storage Laboratory, the largest U.S. seed bank. What this has meant for individual crops is alarming. In their book *Shattering: Food, Politics, and the Loss of Biodiversity*, Cary Fowler and Pat Mooney report that of 497 varieties of lettuce commercially available in 1903, only 36 remained in the NSSL collections by 1980; 7 of 109 varieties of spinach were left; 14 varieties of runner bean had been reduced to 1; and, to return to the tomato, of 408 varieties available in 1903, only 79 different tomato varieties were available in 1980, most of them not grown commercially.

The patenting of genes threatens to make the collapse of diversity even worse, since each gene owner will wish to market as many seeds as possible that contain that company's privately owned genes. It seems like a fist in the face of Nature for any single company to claim it owns genes that are the common property of life on earth. It shouldn't be illegal to save seeds and grow them in your backyard, but to do so when one or more of their genes is patented *is* illegal. So I decided to break the law.

I learned several years ago that if you want to turn tomatoes back into tomato seeds, you have to scoop out the slippery pulp and let it mold for a while. This breaks down the gel around the seeds, and sterilizes them. A few days later, you can wash off all the accumulated gunk and pat the naked seeds dry. For some reason known to Nature (and perhaps, by now, to science, but not yet to me), the seeds do not sprout in that juicy, moldy environment, but only after they have been dried and then made damp again in early spring when Nature wants them to sprout. I have tried this improbable scheme, and it works.

Although I have grown tomatoes from self-saved seed for several years now, I'm not sure when it occurred to me that I might use my newly acquired seed-saving skill to protest the way the food system is headed. But I'm glad I thought of it, since my law-breaking clarified some of the things that were bothering me about the genetic engineering of food.

When I learned that Calgene intended to promote the FlavrSavr by sending samples of the fruit to food writers, I shared with a food writer friend my desire to grow an illegal crop. Several months later she called and announced, "I've got a tomato. What do I do with it?"

"Cut it up, scoop out the seeds, put them in a jar, and let them rot," I said.

"No, you let them rot. I'm sending the jar."

And she did. Inside the jar that arrived, the pulp was already fairly moldy, but I let it sit a few more days, then washed the mess in a strainer, and patted out the seeds on a paper towel. The tomato seeds I'm familiar with are usually yellow. These seeds were bright red. If I were inclined to paranoia, I would imagine FlavrSavr's creators had stuck in an additional gene to make the seeds of these tomatoes identifiable for purposes of prosecution.

In any case, I saved the seeds until the following year—our first full summer in the new garden—and in April, I sowed them in their own little flat to grow indoors under lights like the other seedlings until the weather warmed. The seedlings grew well, and when the weather was warm enough, I set them out—but not with my other plants.

I decided that I should isolate the seedlings and the soil they were planted in, just in case that extra gene I mentioned earlier—a gene that makes the plant resistant to an antibiotic—could transfer resistance to the soil organisms. I had no desire to add unnecessary antibiotic resistance to the planet. So I filled some oblong concrete planters salvaged from the old house with garden soil and planted the Flavr-Savrs.

The plants did well, and in due time I had several tomatoes, glowing red and presumably ripe, although in this situation, it was hard to know what "ripe" meant. As the tomatoes reddened, I realized that my lawbreaking was merely a private protest unless I let the world know. So when the first tomato was fully red, Alan called one of our favorite local reporters. After some discussion on the phone, she decided to come and do a story on my illegal backyard tomato.

The phone conversation took place on August 1. When she said she couldn't come for a week, I reassured her. If the tomato's advance publicity was right, it would still be there ripe on the vine a week later. It was. Whatever it turned out to taste like, the FlavrSavr was obviously ideal for photo shoots that needed advance scheduling.

The photographer took the standard photograph of me picking a ripe FlavrSavr, then a second picture of me holding the freshly picked tomato, with my hand on another one. Then we went indoors to taste. I was tempted to steal a Brandywine from the community garden for comparison, since I had just discovered it to be the best-tasting tomato I had ever eaten. But I decided that wasn't fair, so we tasted one of my perfect palm-sized Donas, which I understood to be a standard French variety.

The FlavrSavr had been on the vine in a state of color-ripeness for almost a week; I felt I was giving it the optimum taste trial. During that week, the acids and sugars should have been increasing and the remaining PG enzyme, which was supposed to soften the fruit eventually, should have begun to kick in. So when I finally cut into it, the FlavrSavr's *taste* should have been thoroughly developed. And no doubt it was. But with its hard skin and unyielding flesh, the tomato tasted artificial. Its taste of semi-ripeness (acid, sort of sweet) conflicted with its unripe texture. Was it ripe? Who can say? Genetic engineering had raised new questions about what "ripening" meant.

What would the FlavrSavr do off the vine, I wondered? Would it eventually soften, the taste and texture combining in my kitchen to make the perfect "vine-ripened" tomato? I left one on the counter marked "FlavrSavr, August 7." I felt I could safety omit the year— surely by December. . . . A month or so later, I threw it away, not yet rotten. I had grown my own FlavrSavr as a symbolic protest against a few giant companies who were using the genes that are the basis of all life for private profit, heedless of the potential consequences. I didn't have to eat it too.

That particular experiment has now vanished into irrelevance. The FlavrSavr was a commercial failure, since consumers apparently agreed that it didn't taste like much. It was, however, the last biotech product to be voluntarily identified in the marketplace, and the tech- nology has moved on so fast that you are regularly eating foods that have been genetically engineered without knowing it.

Meanwhile, I continue to produce glorious and varied fresh toma- toes all summer and fall, and to find interesting ways of storing them for the rest of the year. I have spoken earlier about drying them. One of the varieties I now grow, a cherry tomato called quite grandly Principe Borghese, was a serious disappointment when I first tasted it fresh off the vine, but cut in half and dried on a food drier, it makes an incomparable snack, brightens up cooked sauces, and, if the dill is still standing in the garden, can be used in another of my favorite pasta dishes.

Low-fat Pasta with Salmon

In a 9-inch frying pan melt:
2 to 4 ounces **sweet butter** (*or half oil, half butter*)
Sauté until tender but not brown:
½ medium **onion**, *chopped*
Stir in:
1 ½ cups **half-and-half mixed with skim milk**
Increase heat to high and simmer 5 minutes to reduce by half.

Stir into sauce:

*1 teaspoon **corn starch**, dissolved in 1 tablespoon water (keeps sauce from curdling)*
*¼ cup **Cognac** or **white wine***
*5 **sundried tomatoes**, cut in strips*
*¼ pound **smoked salmon**, cut into 1-by-1-inch pieces*
Simmer for 2 minutes.

Meanwhile, boil until tender:
*½ pound **farfalle** (butterfly pasta)*
Drain.

Toss with 1 tablespoon **salad oil** and add to hot salmon sauce.

Remove from heat and stir in:
*½ cup grated **romano cheese***
Sprinkle with:
***fresh dill**, chopped*

Serve. This is delicious even cold the next day.

In mid-winter, dried tomatoes, softened by heating in a mix of balsamic and red wine vinegars, make a great topping for a cheese sandwich. You can hardly dry too many tomatoes.

I have two other tomato storage techniques to help you get through the winter on the local tomato crop (yours or that of a neighboring farmer). One technique I stumbled on after long experimentation; the other came to me as a recipe, which I have titled Tomato Glut Sauce because it's what you do when you're short of time and the tomatoes are sitting there on the counter looking reproachfully at you as the fruit flies gather round. Or, worse yet, when the fruits are looking so vulnerable with their sunken spots that you have to refrigerate them and thus end forever their future as fresh sliced tomatoes.

Tomato Glut Sauce

(adapted from The New York Times*)*

Preheat oven to 400°F.

Put into a large roasting pan:
> 6 pounds **tomatoes** *(plum are best), cored and quartered*
> 1 ½ cups coarsely chopped **carrots** *(optional)*
> 1 ½ cups coarsely chopped **celery** *(optional)*
> 1 ½ cups coarsely chopped **onions**
> 9 cloves **garlic**, *coarsely chopped*
> 6 tablespoons **balsamic vinegar**
> 1 **bay leaf**
> 1 ½ tablespoons each fresh **thyme**, **oregano**, **basil**, **parsley**
> 1 ½ teaspoons **salt** *(or less)*
> 1 tablespoon freshly ground **black pepper**

Roast for 45 minutes or until vegetables are soft. Process briefly to leave slightly chunky, and freeze in 2-cup portions. Makes 2 quarts (4 pounds).

What you need to know about this recipe is that it is more forgiving than your favorite aunt. The ingredients, other than the tomatoes, garlic, and balsamic vinegar, are pretty much up to you, depending on what you have too much of. I have put in a lot of cut-up peppers. I have used eggplant and zucchini in place of the carrots. And since I never grow celery, only celery leaf, I put some of that in. The secret seems to lie in the balsamic vinegar and the roasting process itself. All the community gardeners who asked me for the recipe came back thanking me for brightening their whole summer.

The most endearing aspect of this recipe so far as I am concerned is that it can be made even in a bad onion year using my own no-fail scallions in place of onions. Decades ago, in Congers, we planted some seeds for what were described in the catalogue as Japanese bunching onions, and have grown them ever since. Used raw like scallions when small, bunching onions get bigger but never bulb, and when they get quite large, both the white base and the green tops can substitute for storage onions in certain cooked dishes.

Although they die down at the first hard freeze, each bunching onion will multiply to come up again in the spring as a bunch of onions, as its name implies—one of the first substantial vegetables of the new season. So persistent are these vegetables that we never again had to plant seed after that first long-ago sowing. Selectively not pulled, bunching onions make themselves into a permanent border, which is how we grew them in Congers. And if the border gets a little thin from overenthusiastic harvesting, the plants obligingly send up stately balls of bloom in June and then reseed themselves; they are entirely self-maintaining.

The bunching onions here in Piermont are descendants of those first seeded onions, dug from Congers and bought down to plant along the north fence shortly after we took possession of the property. When the plants send up flower heads, they are nearly inedible, but after the blossom has gone to seed, new seedlings will appear wherever the stalk has dropped them, and the original plant, now multiplied, will resume its production of tender pungent leaves until the first frost.

My other solution to tomato glut takes a bit more time and attention than Tomato Glut Sauce, but it rewards you with an interesting variety of products. These include, if you choose, an addictive tomato juice that doesn't contain the heart-stopping slugs of sodium they use to brighten up the commercial kind. Just take all the tomatoes, little ones, big ones, yellow Brandywines, red and orange Old Flames, round red Donas, or even Early Girl or one of the other hybrids, not forgetting the damaged ones you've stuck in a bag in the refrigerator and all the bucketfuls of tiny tomatoes, even if they've cracked open, as long as they haven't begun to mold.

Now cut the big ones into chunks, removing the bad spots, and put everything in a big pot (I use my stainless steel pasta-cooking pot). Slowly bring to a boil, smashing the tomatoes down from time to time with a big spoon or a potato masher to help them release their juice. When they're very soft and mushy, put a food mill over a good-sized non-reactive pan (I use the largest of a set of stainless steel bowls), and pour in as much of the cooked tomato as the food mill will hold. Now stop! Don't do anything. Let the liquid run through into the bowl—you can move the solid stuff around a bit to allow the really watery juice to run through, but don't push. When you have let the tomato mush drain for about five minutes, set the food mill back over the cooking pot and pour the liquid in the bowl into a one of those glass or plastic bottles you have left over from buying juice.

If the level in the food mill has gone down enough that you can add what's left of the cooked tomato, you can repeat the draining process before you begin part two. When you're ready for part two, move the food mill back over the (empty) bowl and begin to turn its handle, working the tomato flesh down through its teeth. Reverse it from time to time to get as much of the mash as possible caught under its crusher, and when you think you've got nothing left but skin and seeds, clean them out by reversing the food mill handle and turning it upside down over your compost container (if you don't have a compost container, you're on your own). Remove the tomato purée to a wide mouthed jar. Repeat this process, letting the liquid drain, pouring it into the juice jar, and puréeing what is left until you've used up all your cooked tomatoes and have all the tomato water in bottles and the tomato purée in old peanut butter jars or the like.

Now put all the jars in the refrigerator overnight to settle out. In the morning, the bottles with the puréed tomato flesh in them should have a layer of pinkish-orange liquid collected at the top. Using a baster, suck up as much of that liquid as possible and add it to the jars of tomato water. Then pour the solids into freezer containers, put a basil leaf on top, and freeze. Of course, if you're a canner, you can preserve the purée that way too.

Now you have a choice regarding the jars of liquid. You can simply shake them up and pour yourself a glass of tomato juice, or you can pour off the thinnest part into ice cube trays and turn out the resulting cubes to store in the freezer as stock for winter soups. This leaves only the in-between stuff for tomato juice. I sometimes opt for the first choice, and sometimes for the second. As I said, the tomato juice is addictive, so I find it hard not to drink the whole batch. On the other hand, the tomato liquid makes a lovely soup.

TOMATO AND POTATO SOUP

Bring to a boil:

1½ quarts (6 cups) **tomato water** *(solids removed for freezing)*

Add:

1 teaspoon **salt**

5 medium **potatoes**, *cut in 1-inch cubes*

1 **serrano pepper**, *minced*

1 **chorizo sausage**, *sliced in ¼-inch slices*

Cook until potatoes are almost tender, then add:

2 teaspoons (or less) **ground coriander**

Just before serving add:

1 medium **red onion**, *chopped fine*

Serve over broken **tortilla chips**.

Then, of course, there's the *really* easy way to preserve tomatoes through the winter. The other day, I took out of the freezer one of the tomatoes I had simply thrown into a bag and frozen for lack of time. I thawed it with a little heat, but not so as to cook it, and ate it from a bowl with salt and pepper. Closest thing to a fresh tomato in winter. Tomatoes frozen like this do take up lots of space, so you can also thaw them and turn them into tomato sauce after summer when time allows and space demands.

Sometimes it seems as if it would be lovely to live in Italy, near Naples, where the fresh-tomato season can sometimes last seven or eight months of the year. Lacking such bounty, those of us who live where it's colder need to teach ourselves to put up tomato products for the winter while we encourage our farmers to experiment with season extension. Only then will we be heading for the goal a colleague of mine suggested we should be working toward, a sign next to the road leading into every community carrying a picture of that familiar hard orange globe, and across it, a red slash and the words, "This is a winter-tomato-free community."

14

Is It Worth It?

It is easier to buy your food than to grow it. . . . It is easier
to drink soft drinks and throw the containers out the window
than to practice the difficult disciplines of health and frugality.

—Wendell Berry, *The Gift of Good Land*

THE FOREGOING CELEBRATION of local food rests, admittedly, on the threatening assumption that someone will cook. Judging from their behavior, it looks as if most people in many circumstances don't and won't. They seem to have decided that cooking doesn't pay—although buying lavish cookbooks does. According to time-use studies, what has replaced cooking for females is television and grooming; men didn't have that much cooking to replace. So I understand that growing up before TV, before shampooing more than once a week was even imaginable, puts me at a disadvantage in understanding contemporary life.

In Congers, Alan and I fell into the habit of collecting branches that blew down from our oak trees over the winter and piling them near a crude outdoor fireplace built from stacked cement blocks. On mornings when we had time, we would have fires there—always on winter solstice mornings when I was free for the holidays, sometimes through the long dawns of the summer solstice—and we would drink coffee and talk. And in summer and fall, we roasted chili peppers over the coals so they could be sweated and peeled, and we roasted eggplant. It was hot work and took a while. Later, when the fire had cooled, we used the ashes in the garden. We used the eggplant in Eggplant Bhurta.

EGGPLANT BHURTA

Roast over a fire or in the coals until skins are charred and flesh soft:

*2 medium **eggplants***

Peel, mash, or chop in processor.

Meanwhile, sauté in:

*2 tablespoons **butter***

*1 **onion**, chopped*

*1 peeled **green Anaheim pepper**, diced*

Add eggplant. Then add:

*¹/₂ teaspoon **salt***

*4 tablespoons **yogurt***

The eggplant purée can be frozen for winter use: Just thaw and add the onion, peppers, and yogurt. This is absolutely addictive, plain or over rice, or—best yet—stuffed into a whole-wheat pita bread.

A later recipe that uses lots of fire-roasted peppers will illustrate further how the activity we came to call simply chili-roasting became a ritual step in the production of certain ingredients vital to our meals.

Attempting to explain to my professional colleagues why, even in a world of convenience foods, it might be worthwhile to cook, I once used this activity to show how hard it is to answer a question such as "Does cooking pay?"—the title of an article I wrote for the *Journal of Nutrition Education*. To calculate "scientifically" whether cooking pays requires comparing the costs of cooking at home against the cost of purchasing an equivalent product in the market. This means that you have to place a monetary value on all the home inputs—the cost of raw materials and of heat for cooking, what you'd get for your labor if you were being paid, and so on—before you can ask whether it costs less, the same, or more to prepare, for example, stuffed baked potatoes at home than it does to buy them frozen.

The authors of the few studies of cooking I could find concluded that cooking might not always pay for the simplest canned and frozen foods and the most highly paid women, but that cooking at home was cheaper for most women and many foods. Surprisingly, this proved to be true even if the calculated labor cost was based on the salary of a professional woman at the time the study was done. (For reasons it's probably best not to harp on, the study authors never plugged the salary of a professional man into the equation.)

All these research efforts shared a common problem unrelated to calculating the input cost of home-cooked food, however, namely how to decide whether the outputs—the edibles produced—were equivalent. Although the inputs—the cost of a frozen stuffed potato in the store versus the calculated costs for making a stuffed baked potato at home—could be fairly well equated, the attributes of the foods that came to the table were more difficult to match.

In the studies I reviewed, the authors often accepted as equivalent foods that the careful eater would judge absurdly different: a fresh raspberry and a canned one, for example, or freshly made and instant coffee. Moreover, the authors of these studies often chose products for comparison to which I have never felt it necessary to devote home cooking time, "Hawaiian-style" (?) vegetables, for example. Finally, in duplicating an industrial product with one that was "homemade," these cooks often used such processed ingredients as canned French-fried onions and mushroom soup, which many knowing food preparers might not use in a similar "homemade" product.

What I discovered, in other words, was that when researchers asked whether cooking paid, they either discounted profound disparities in the quality of the resulting foods, or seemed to be asking the wrong questions; that is, is it possible to duplicate the quality of some second-rate commercial product by mixing the appropriate commercial products at home? And, of course, all their questions about whether cooking paid were posed in purely monetary terms. Values did not intrude.

Before I wrote my article, I had been burrowing into the economics of home work. Having convinced myself that we needed to start using food from closer to home, I recognized that doing so would necessitate some cooking. So I was trying to discover whether there might be *scientific* reasons to cook, other than a libertarian desire to save ourselves from slavery to Colonel Sanders and General Foods.

Mucking about in the economics literature, I came across the following sentence in a paper by an Israeli economist named Reuben Gronau that nearly made me get up and dance in the library.

> An intuitive distinction between work at home (i.e., home production time) and leisure (i.e., home consumption time), is that work at home (like work in the market) is something one would rather have somebody else do for one (if the cost were low enough) while it would be almost impossible to enjoy leisure through a surrogate.

Wow, I thought. Anything done unwillingly at home is work; anything done voluntarily is pleasure. So if I enjoy cooking, then my work counts as a benefit, not a cost. Although campfire cooking may be absurdly difficult to evaluate economically, Gronau's distinction helps clarify our chili-roasting scenario.

What are the inputs when we sit by our fire, roasting? Fallen wood is a gift of Nature; the monetary inputs would include a very small cost for seeds and some minute proportion of our gardening expenses. In theory, the input costs would also include our labor in growing the peppers and eggplants, but since we enjoy gardening and would not willingly have it done by a surrogate, that labor must count as a benefit.

What are the material outputs? Roasted chilies and eggplants? We could buy roasted chilies "cheaper" in the store and, given the madness of product-proliferation in the marketplace, we might even find fire-roasted eggplant for a price. Other outputs from our activity can't be compared with anything we could buy in a store. Ashes for the garden, for example, and disposal of our fallen branches. The only imaginable commercial equivalent would be a negative output: a disposal cost for the fancy packaging of the eggplant purée.

And then there are the nonmaterial outputs unique to our homemade product: our sense of closure when the minerals pulled from the soil by the tree roots return to nearby soil in the ashes; our enriched marital relations, or—when we let company play—improved social relationships.

The word *play* here is intentional. I can imagine many ways in which our chili-roasting could be counted as a waste of time. Yet I would not have willingly abandoned this task to—in Gronau's words—a surrogate. Before I retired, my salary certainly paid me more per hour than the peeled chilies were *worth* if they were bought in a can. But I would have grieved if the fire laws were so strictly enforced that we had to abandon our roasting.

Among the non-monetary outputs from chili-roasting for Alan were several delicious flame, green, and eggplant-colored chalk paintings: "Chili Today," "Chili Morning," and "Chili Roasting." And we have the testimony of friends who have savored our eggplant bhurta at dinner and urged us to keep producing it. So when we left Congers, it was evident that we needed to create a place where our roasting could continue.

When we took possession of our new land in Piermont, we found a large outdoor fireplace, once properly laid up with mortar, on which we grilled our first Fourth of July picnic. But that fireplace was in a state of terminal decay and did not survive even the deconstruction of the old house. Those were the remains that "tripped" the backhoe that cracked our brand-new foundation. However, Providence provided a substitute fire site. In the course of cleaning up the backyard, we found a low-lying 10-by-10 foot concrete pad at the foot of the riverbank. Using bricks we had salvaged from around the lot, I "paved" the space to raise it a bit and constructed a crude fireplace with firebricks on the paving, smaller than the one we had at Congers.

It was around a fire built in this little space that we gathered a few of the new community gardeners to share the first winter solstice fire at our new home, just short of a year after we moved in. The previous summer, we had roasted peppers and eggplant there, using construction debris as firewood. But Alan's and my chili-roasting in Piermont lasted only two summers. The second summer, we used river-donated driftwood for the fire; by the third summer, Alan was gone.

It was only after Alan's death that I came to a true appreciation of the social payout of chili-roasting. The task is difficult to do alone. The fire is too hot to stand close to for long, so you need to trade off tending the chilies, and the person who's not tending needs to keep gathering small, quick-burning twigs and branches to create—atop the bed of coals—a flame hot and fast enough to blister the peppers without overcooking them. But solitary chili-roasting is difficult in another way. Like going to the movies alone, it's just not as much fun as when you share its pleasures. As a task for one, the labor associated with chili-roasting might have to count as a cost rather than a benefit.

And that brings me back to the larger question of whether trying to eat locally is, on the whole, worth it. And the answer, I have concluded, is that it all depends. Before I try to explain what it depends on, however, I want to use up those roasted chilies. The obvious way to do that is with chiles rellenos, those fatty, cheese-filled chilies fried in an egg batter and served with hot sauce that are a staple on Mexican restaurant menus.

As a native Californian, I have been a fan of cheap Mexican food since childhood, and when I first moved to New York in 1950 and couldn't find an affordable Mexican restaurant, I tried to make chiles rellenos. But in my kitchen, they never worked. The batter always slipped off the chilies and I was left with naked peppers to fry. My sister finally sent me a recipe that calls for spooning a strip of batter into the frying pan, laying the cheese-stuffed chili on top of it, and covering the whole with batter. You turn the package over when the bottom has browned and fry the other side. It not only works; it produces terrific chiles rellenos. But I am a nutritionist and it soon became evident to me that this is not a health food.

When I fried the batter-dipped cheese-filled chilies, they absorbed a half-inch of fat and inevitably splattered whatever I was wearing with grease when I turned them over. What is more, I never mastered the art of getting onto the table in a timely way two chilies each for more than two people. That's when I came up with Chiles Rellenos Casserole, which uses many more chilies for much less egg and fat, besides being easy and delicious.

CHILES RELLENOS CASSEROLE FOR TWO

Preheat oven to 350° F.

Slit and remove seeds from:
>   *6 to 7 **peeled green chilies** (fresh or canned)*

Grate:
>   *½ cup **cheddar cheese***

Separate:
>   *2 **eggs***

Beat the yolks with:
>   *2 tablespoons **flour***
>   *2 tablespoons **cornmeal***
>   *enough **water** to make thick batter (about 3 tablespoons)*
>   *1 to 2 teaspoons ground **cumin** (optional)*

Beat eggwhites with **cream of tartar** until soft peaks form. Stir a quarter of egg whites into batter and then fold in those remaining.

Heat in 4-by-8-inch baking pan, tilting to cover bottom and sides:
>   *1 teaspoon **oil***

Turn off heat, and cover bottom with one third of batter.

Add:
>   *2 chilies*
>   *½ the grated cheese*
>   *6 **cherry tomatoes**, halved (optional)*

Add another third of batter, two more chilies, and remaining cheese.

Add remaining chilies and top with remaining batter.

Cover, and bake at 350°F for about 30 minutes.

Serve with Tomatillo Enchilada Sauce (see chapter 5) or other hot sauce, and warm tortillas.

We roasted dozens of peppers whenever we made a fire, and froze those we didn't intend to use right away. Once the blistered chilies come off the grill, they need to be sweated in a closed paper bag until they cool, after which their skins can be stripped off and they're ready to use. We used to peel them before freezing. Now I spread the cooled blackened peppers out on a cookie sheet that I slip into the freezer. When the chilies have frozen, I dump them in a plastic bag for storage. Then, in mid-winter, when the day needs a little heat, I take out the peppers I need, run them briefly under warm water, and the skins peel right off.

After thinking about chiles rellenos, it is difficult for me to take seriously the question of whether eating locally is worth the trouble. Clearly it is for me. Trying to understand why, I have realized that my own commitment is probably driven by three things. The first is the taste of live food; the second is my relation to frugality; the third is my deep concern about the state of the planet.

As is surely obvious in all I have written to date, the production and consumption of fresh local food is so rich an experience for me that I find it hard to imagine how I would live if I couldn't grow what I eat and eat what I grow. I was in the hospital once trying to recover from a malaria-induced coma. What the hospital was offering as food almost gagged me, and because I was being infused intravenously

THIS ORGANIC LIFE

with something that affected everything I tasted, I couldn't even tell if the food was as awful as it seemed. Alan, who was ecstatic to have me conscious again, began bringing in home-food: noodles with sautéed snow peas, fresh strawberries, and sundried tomatoes. They didn't taste right either, so I knew I wasn't normal yet, but they tasted so alive that I wolfed them down.

Eating fresh, seasonal food changes you. Many of my friends who can't grow their own—as most people can't—have joined with other eaters in a movement called Community Supported Agriculture (CSA). Invented in Japan in 1965, the CSA idea was first brought to the United States in 1986 by the late Robyn Van En, who gave the process the name Community Supported Agriculture. Members of a CSA get together with a farmer, usually in fall or winter, and having calculated his or her expenses for the coming year, they split those among themselves, into shares that generally cost from $250 to $500. The farmer gets money for the coming year's work, and the members, in return, receive fresh produce throughout the next growing season. In their book *Sharing the Harvest*, Elizabeth Henderson and Van En describe the process that has created community support of an estimated one thousand farmers across the country.

The growing season for CSAs in this part of the country has usually been late-spring, summer, and fall, with no distribution in the winter. Recently, in response to complaints from members that they were "starving" since their shares had stopped, some farmers are adding "winter shares" of squash, root vegetables, and cold-frame crops to their offering. Fresh seasonal food, once experienced, can become a necessity.

As for my helpless frugality, the second reason why I may find it easier than most people to give up out-of-season foods, I have begun to suspect that I have a pathological relationship to the careful use of things. (One can face these things in one's eighth decade.) I could, but I won't, blame my mother for this, or the Scotch lady who taught me to diagram sentences in junior high or even my work at *Time* magazine, where I learned to put a black dot over every uncapitalized word and a red dot over every capitalized one to show that I had checked them carefully—the red ones in an irrefutable written source. I don't think any of these folks did more than exploit my genetically programmed need to get things exactly right. I was pretty insufferable before I learned that.

After spending years mentally denouncing the influence of my Iowa-born Dutch mother, who did housework with ruthless thoroughness though she hated it, I suddenly remembered what I used to do when she asked me and my sister to "clean up your room." I began by emptying out my desk drawers so that for the first hour or two things moved progressively toward chaos. Then I would dust out the drawers (I'm afraid I may even have wiped them out with a damp cloth) and put everything back in order. Only then did I feel secure in having places to put the things she had wanted me to get out of sight in the first place. I seem to have been born incapable of chucking things into drawers and shutting them without noticing whether the contents would shortly need reorganizing.

I am also forced to confess that, as far back as I can remember, I spent much more time washing my dolls' clothes and refolding them neatly than actually playing with the dolls. Since my early memories are—unlike those of my sister—relatively shallow, I don't really remember much about my youngest years, so perhaps I was more fun-loving as a very young child. Fun loving or not, everyone remembers me as happy, so I probably liked making things orderly.

But it wasn't all genes. I was also raised thrifty, although that doesn't seem to explain my ongoing parsimony, because many people raised poor can't get enough when they grow up. Although my father worked in the Los Angeles civil service and remained salaried during the Great Depression, money was always scarce when I was a child, and not-wasting was something of a secular religion. My father regularly stopped along the road during family drives to pick up stray wooden boxes, planks, pieces of metal—and mostly he used them.

One event will give you the flavor. When my parents came to visit after Alan and I first moved to Rockland County, Dad noticed that our

chime doorbell had died. He took it down, took it apart, and concluded that it needed a new part: a little sleeve of metal through which
a small bar, held at one end by a smaller spring, moved back and forth.
When the doorbell was pushed, the contact closed a circuit and
charged an electromagnet. The magnet pulled back the small metal
bar and released it. The spring then propelled it in the other direction
where it hit the chime.

Of course, no replacement part was available. The next step, so far
as the hardware store was concerned, was for my father to buy a new
chime. No way. He made a new sleeve from a small piece of one of
those hollow round curtain rods people used to hang kitchen curtains
on, used the little metal bar from the original doorbell, and fastened
it to a rubber band in place of the spring. I have no idea how it worked.
Fortunately, the rubber band lasted until we moved out.

Since my father had no sons, and my sister didn't like getting dirty,
I was the one who ingested my father's attitude toward salvage and
repair. "Take it apart, and if you can't fix it, *then* you can call someone
to put it back together." But never, never just throw it away.

Given such a history, I suppose it's no surprise that fifty-odd years
later, four different people made sure to send me the *New Yorker* cartoon showing a self-righteous farmwife clothes-pinning plastic wrap
to her clothesline. I recognized the message even before I read the
caption: "Where the ecologically correct meets the pathologically
frugal." That's me. If I end up with a palmful of bottle cap and onion
root when I wipe off the kitchen counter, I have to give myself permission to dump both into the trash, since I know that the little disc
of onion root *should* be salvaged for the compost container.

And perhaps it's the case that some such compulsion may be necessary if one is to make a virtue of non-necessity. Our ancestors, living in leaner times, were told to "make a virtue of necessity," to em-
brace what was unavoidable and enjoy it. But to give up eating the
world in favor of eating one's own backyard is not unavoidable (all
you have to do is go to the store)—indeed it is not always even a
possibility. Maria Lydia Child, who wrote *The American Frugal*

Housewife in the United States of the 1800s, taught frugality because there was no other choice.

More recent generations have been teethed on the obligation to buy the latest, use it briefly, and throw it away, in order to keep the economy running. Unless we're poor or temporarily jobless, we don't see any need to be cautious spenders or cautious users, especially where food is concerned. It's too cheap. Trying to behave differently puts you in conflict with the culture, makes you feel alienated in ShopRite, and often makes you feel that you're wasting your time.

But my assumption about consumption has always been that it was better not to. Not buying, I was convinced, was more righteous than buying. If you could grow it or make it or remake it you were a better person for it. Forty years of marriage to an artist, too much of whose work remained, alas, in our collection, did nothing to stimulate any latent consumerism. By the time my job, his parents' deaths, and the sale of our now-valuable Victorian house gave us financial elbow-room, I had learned to be content with having little to spend. So I began my relocalization effort with the deep conviction that making do with what you have is a good thing. Which means, of course, that all this effort has been a lot easier for me than it would have been for most people.

Despite my admitted parsimony, however, I'm not really cheap. I've simply hyper-internalized the lesson that everything counts because everything is connected. I've been teaching about this for almost thirty years. I wrote about the web of connections between food production and the planet more than twenty years ago in *The Feeding Web*, a book that reflected what was then a newly acquired understanding.

> Although it is a fact we often lose sight of, humankind depends wholly on growing plants as the primary producers of foodstuffs (and oxygen). It is not true, as our supermarkets insinuate, that we depend on the beneficence of General Foods or Kellogg's. Once we have firmly in mind our dependence on plants in nature (and not in White Plains or Battle Creek), we can begin to under-

stand how important it is to look critically at all the things that interfere with the growing of plants—and to examine ways in which a variety of our consumption "needs," apparently unrelated to eating, have begun to compete with food plants and the inputs required to produce them. . . .

If advertising fans our desire for things (and it does), and if production of these things (disposable bottles, aerosol cans, second homes, plastic bags, green lawns, white laundry) begins to use up pieces of the world important in food production (energy, ozone, open land, petrochemicals, phosphate rock), then excessive demand for anything may have an impact on our food-producing capacity. And if our food supply is . . . not only unnecessarily using up resources, but is cutting us off from an awareness of what we are doing to our food-producing environment, then clearly our food supply is part of the ecological problem, is part of the interconnected web of causes and effects that will ultimately determine the sustainability of human life on earth.

Which lands me in the middle of what is the most abstract and certainly the least comfortable reason for trying to eat locally: a profound concern for the future of the planet.

I was recently asked to speak at a conference on responsible eating about the barriers to getting people to begin to eat locally. The first one, I said, was that people didn't know why they should do it, and the second—and most important one—was that they didn't want to know. I know they don't because I keep trying to tell them.

As a consequence, I have learned that in a society where thoughtless consumption is the norm, you can not only drive yourself crazy trying to live responsibly, you can easily make yourself a pain to others, especially others whose well-intentioned efforts you find misdirected. A neighbor once offered me some organic tropical juice canned in Patagonia. "This is from *Patagonia!*" I said in a shocked tone of voice. "That's at the foot of Latin America! What an incredible waste of resources to ship it all the way here." She was offended, of course, and rightly so, since her organic juice was intended to please. Another friend once told us well after the fact that when Alan and I were coming to dinner, she was careful to have only white toilet paper in her bathrooms since we were environmentalists. Colored paper was thought at the time to cause more pollution than white.

So it does not come as news to me that my message that we are killing the planet's ability to support us is often seen as a burden. The ten-year-old son of a friend made that evident years ago. He was asking for some food object that his mom didn't want to buy him and when he kept nagging, she said, "Joan thinks that's junk." He looked her in the eye and pronounced his verdict: "Someone should stop that woman!"

But what is one to do? How should I behave when I am at a local restaurant with a friend and the menu features salmon baked in horseradish? And I'm just back from a meeting where I learned that it takes three pounds of wild-caught fish to raise one pound of farmed salmon? Should I go ahead and order the horseradish-crusted salmon, which sounds delicious? I suppose my one salmon wouldn't matter in the overall scheme of things. Should I refrain from ordering it even though I want it, and just shut up? Or should I not have it, and explain to my dinner companion why I'm having vegetable tacos instead, thereby making her feel defiantly guilty if she orders salmon, and—even if she doesn't—annoyed with me for telling her something she was happier not knowing?

Like other threats to our food supply, the ongoing collapse of global fisheries from pollution and overfishing is not on most people's everyday screen. "All-you-can-eat" seafood restaurants shout a message of abundance. The farmed salmon on restaurant menus seems an indicator of progress, a sign that we're belatedly shifting from fish hunting to fish growing just as we moved long ago from hunting and gathering to agriculture. We don't depend on wild game; why should we have to depend on wild-caught fish?

Where salmon are concerned, of course, the answer is that *they* are living on wild-caught fish. Raising salmon for humans to eat, as someone said, is like raising tigers for meat. They're at the top of the food chain. They're fish eaters. And fish is what we're running short of. Fisheries are closing because their fish stocks are depleted, or contaminated, or both.

And so it is with the soils, the waters, and the air. They too are threatened by human demand. We consume as if a great food-producing machine were just over the horizon, just out of sight. But it is not; someone, somewhere, has to grow our food. While I was hunting for the frugal housewife cartoon in my files, I came across another cartoon of an angry housewife holding a bag of groceries and shouting at a man in a cowboy hat, "What do I care if a bunch of farmers go broke? I buy my food at a grocery store!" The conviction she's expressing is close enough to how most of us act that discomfort makes us laugh. Most of us buy food as if the only question that needs asking is whether we have enough money to pay for it.

I learned early on from the community gardeners that everything but gardening was "politics" and off limits. I had become disturbed by the trash barrels full of plastic that appeared at planting time in the community garden. So I gave a little educational talk about how everything counted and if we wanted to be sustainable and not just organic, we should try to reduce our impact by returning plastic plant containers to the nursery, growing our own seedlings, and so on. One of the gardeners raised his voice in protest. "I don't think we ought to get into politics here," he said. "I just want to come down and garden."

I tried to protest that environmental awareness is not politics, but it didn't fly. So from then on, my educational talks have stayed on safe territory: boosting fertility, keeping weeds from going to seed to make next year easier, and other nonpolitical topics. But just the other day, I was approached at our winter potluck by a gardener asking me whether I would talk to the group about genetic engineering, because some of the seed companies are selling genetically engineered seeds. I surely will—and it will be political. Readiness, as they say, is all. And meanwhile, I take heart from the fact that the gardeners are learning to love the taste of their own produce. It's a beginning.

15

What a Sacrifice?

> Everyone who is so happy as to live in the country, and can gather
> vegetables daily from his own garden, knows the difference between them
> when gathered thus and properly cooked, and those which have been picked
> and kept for market even one night.
>
> —Solon Robinson, *Facts for Farmers*, 1866

TWO YEARS AFTER ALAN DIED, the second year the peach tree bore—
the year after the squirrels got them all—I bit into the first home-
grown peach I had tasted since the Congers peach keeled over and
killed itself. There were twenty-five fruits on the tree, and I plucked
and ate a single ripe one the morning before I found two chewed-up
ones on the ground. I knew better this time than to dicker with the
squirrels about their plans, so I picked the whole crop, put them in the
refrigerator, and brought them out a few at a time to warm and fully
ripen over the next few weeks. The first one reminded me that it was
. . . a peach. It had a velvety skin that I didn't have to peel off for fear
its fuzz had trapped pesticides. It dripped peach juice down my chin
and hand when I bit into it. It wasn't brown and fibrous at its center.
I used the others slowly, relished every bite, and reluctantly shared a
few with friends.

When I concluded many years ago that eating locally was a morally responsible way to use the planet's resources, I also assumed it
would mean sacrifice. I was ignorant, but ready to put my ethics into
practice. My peaches are among the many things that have convinced
me that deliciousness is the best reason to eat food grown nearby and
in season.

Describing the way that air freight has allowed us to consume
"fresh" food from all over the world, a shipper once remarked to the

New York Times that we were a "spoiled" country. "You go to a place in Europe and order a salad, and you get whatever's in season. Here, you always get tomatoes, you always get peppers, you can get whatever you want, any time of year." Some of us who have learned to lust after fresh foods in season read a lot of learned tastelessness into that statement. A nation *spoiled* by a steady supply of cottony orange tomato-units instead of a few months of the stunningly delicious fruits of late summer? *Spoiled* by giant perfect-looking strawberries that taste like Styrofoam? And—unless they grow them—who except the rich can afford raspberries, an occasional treat of my Depression-era childhood?

What seems to have spoiled over the last decades of "progress" in the food system is our memory of how things ought to taste. Philip Wylie, who is remembered if at all as the assaulter of "momism," was even angrier about what other people had done to our food:

> For years I couldn't figure out what had happened to vegetables. I knew, of course, that most vegetables, to be enjoyed in their full deliciousness, must be picked fresh and cooked at once. I knew that vegetables cannot be overcooked and remain even edible. . . . The Parisians manage by getting their vegetables picked at dawn and rushed in farmers' carts to market where no middleman or marketman delays produce on its way to the pot.
>
> Our vegetables, however, come to us through a long chain of command. There are merchants of several sorts—wholesalers before the retailers, commission men, and so on—with the result that what were once edible products become in transit, mere wilted leaves and withered tubers. . . . I have long thought that the famed blindfold test for cigarettes should be applied to city vegetables. For I am sure that if you puréed them and ate them blindfolded, you couldn't tell the beans from the peas, the turnips from the squash, the Brussels sprouts from the broccoli . . .
>
> It is only lately that I have found how much science has had to do with this reduction of noble victuals to pottage . . . What

they've done is to develop "improved" strains of things for every purpose but eating. They work out, say, peas that will ripen all at once. The farmer can then harvest his peas and thresh them and be done with them. It is extremely profitable because it is efficient. What matter if such peas taste like boiled paper wads?

. . . Personally, I don't care if they hybridize onions till they are as big as your head and come up through the snow; but, in doing so, they are producing onions that only vaguely and feebly remind you of onions. . . . [I]f people don't eat onions because they taste like onions, what in the name of Luther Burbank do they eat them for?

And that was more than fifty years ago!

While all this scientific fooling around has been going on, we've been convinced that our lives and diets have steadily improved as refrigeration and air freight have eliminated our dependence on what can be produced near home. And it's true that any season of the year, vivid mounds of cosmetically perfect fruits and vegetables, brought from every region of the planet, fill the supermarket produce sections. But most of them have been made tasteless by breeding and too much travel. Watching the man just ahead of me in the checkout line buying tomatoes, celery, and "fresh" sweet corn in frigid mid-February, I grieved at the thought of how unlikely it was that those chilly well-travelled objects were going to delight his palate. And I silently cursed my inability to protest his choices in any way that he would understand. No wonder Americans must be nagged to eat their vegetables.

Although I myself never knowingly eat fruits and vegetables shipped by air freight, I know how bland they are, because when people eat what we grow, they are always knocked over by the intensity of the taste. I don't think the variety of strawberry we grow tastes like much, but not long ago, when I had a massive California strawberry at a public luncheon, I realized what "don't taste like much" really meant.

So I guess I wasn't surprised—although I was delighted—when I received a letter from a well-known writer on gardening telling me science was on my side. He asked me if I knew whether much work had been done on chilling injury. I said I didn't, except that my generation learned from Carmen Miranda to keep bananas unrefrigerated. My correspondent informed me that chilling is the enemy of more than bananas. When a tomato or a strawberry is chilled, he explained, the mix of chemicals, and therefore the taste, changes entirely. I was glad to have scientific confirmation of what my taste buds had already taught me. I avoid at all costs putting tomatoes in the refrigerator, and if I have to refrigerate one from which I've cut out a bad spot, as I mentioned earlier, I use it only in cooking.

Strawberries undergo the same taste transformation when they're chilled; so do raspberries. My taste buds tell me it's okay to chill a blueberry, an admission I hope does not brand me taste-challenged. But where certain fruits are concerned (tomatoes included), it's hardly worth eating them if you have to refrigerate them before you do so. So when you're eating produce shipped from Israel or Chile or South Africa, much of its flavor will have been chilled out of it before it reaches the supermarket.

But what choice do we have? Praising the taste of local summer fruits and vegetables in season can only depress anyone whose real worries hover around what to eat when neighborhood tomato plants have been blasted by frost and strawberry plants are under ice. What about winter? Well, there's always cabbage. I say this partly in jest, because I mostly don't like cabbage. Coleslaw bores me; stuffed cabbage seems to me to be delicious solely because of its stuffing and sauce; and at Christmas I used to flee outdoors (in California, fortunately) from the smell of my mother's sweet-and-sour red cabbage. As for sauerkraut. . . . When I had lunch recently with two people who were talking excitedly about sauerkraut, I found the conversation genuinely astonishing.

So I'm not a cabbage fan, and I mention cabbage to prove that the depths of winter can be amazingly tasty even for cabbage unbelievers like me. Here's a recipe that led me to grow that stolid winter ball. I learned this recipe from a Sri Lankan scholar who was, like me, attending a January meeting in Norway, so I can affirm that this dish warms up even a Norwegian winter.

SRI LANKAN CABBAGE
(Kumar Rupesinghe)

Thinly slice:
   2 or more **onions**
Sauté in:
   1 to 2 tablespoons **butter** *or* **olive oil**
Add:
   1 teaspoon **turmeric**
   several **whole cardamom pods**
   several **cloves**
   2 to 3 cloves **garlic***, finely cut*
When onions are soft, add:
   1 head **cabbage***, thinly sliced*
Stir fry until tender.
   salt *to taste*

Will convert even non-cabbage eaters!

It's not only more delicious to avoid summer foods in winter, it's also more interesting to build meals around different foods at different times of the year. As anyone knows who has had the chance to feast in parts of Europe where the locals still eat seasonally, eating only foods that are in season can be a delicious adventure. I remarked to a friend recently that our local Italian restaurant turned out better meals in the summer and fall when the tomatoes and eggplants and other foods they depend on were in season locally. He replied, "But

Joan, you have to have fresh tomatoes all the time if you're going to be an Italian restaurant." I reminded him that cooks in Italy don't do that. Out in the country, and even in the city, lots of them still live by the seasons—and winter isn't really *fresh* tomato season anywhere. The tomatoes Italians use then are canned or dried.

Meal planning is simply more exciting and less bewildering when you wait for fruits and vegetables to come into season, eat them steadily when they arrive, and say a reluctant goodbye for another year when their season has passed. When you've done this for a while, you lose your taste for out-of-season produce. I remember one time when some friends came to visit in mid-winter with a lovely basket of fruit: peaches, grapes, plums. Alan was pleasant enough when they were here. But after they left, he expressed real offense, as if they had missed the point of our lives, and refused to eat any of it. I don't remember whether my food-waste avoidance drove me to eat the fruit regardless, but my experience with winter fruit warns me that if I did, it didn't taste anything like it looked.

Some of the fresh foods I eat a lot of in winter are storage vegetables such as white and sweet potatoes and carrots and parsnips. Carrots are of course easy. Almost everyone likes carrots, raw or cooked, and I'll get to them in a minute. Parsnips are something else. I'm certain that there are entire neighborhoods in the United States where no one would recognize a parsnip if it bit her—and would hesitate to bite back if it did. Where people give a thought to parsnips, they may recall them as vaguely unhappy-looking, hairy white carrots—old-fashioned root vegetables—not at all the sort of thing one might pleasurably anticipate for dinner. At least that's how I thought of parsnips before I grew them.

My mother, being from northwest Iowa, knew about parsnips, but as the youngest of six, she admittedly didn't know much about cooking. As far as I can remember, she sliced parsnips like carrots and boiled them a long time, which is what you did with root vegetables in Iowa in the early twentieth century. Accordingly, I thought parsnips ought to taste like boiled carrots (just as I thought coffee with cream ought to taste like hot chocolate and disappointingly didn't), so when parsnips didn't imitate carrots—and they don't—I gagged on them as I gagged on many other foods in my picky youth.

I learned to like black coffee in college because it was cheaper than hot chocolate, but it took me a lot longer to learn to like parsnips. Until we grew parsnips, I hadn't tasted one since childhood, and we didn't start growing them because I wanted to eat them, but because they were available at the right time of year. For those trying to eat food as fresh as possible year-round, parsnips are like kale, a gift of Nature and of human ingenuity in plant selection. Parsnips are often ready by December, but if you still have lots of other things to eat then, as we always do, you can put off digging them until the January thaw or even into February. You just need to get them out of the ground before spring pushes them into growth, after which they can get hairy and fibrous.

When I had made my vegetable charts and could see which months were especially devoid of anything fresh to eat, I noticed that parsnips could be dug in the very months when little else was available to be harvested. So I decided that we should grow them and I would force myself to like them. Alan had never met a vegetable he didn't like, so he didn't even have to be convinced. Growing parsnips turned out to be harder than liking them; the seeds will not germinate at all unless they're very fresh, and even the freshest seeds are slow to sprout. Moreover, our schedule requires them to be planted in the heat of the summer when it's hard to keep them damp, and the seedlings start growing very slowly even though they will have produced impressively large plants with massive roots by the time winter slows them down.

Given my prejudice against those hairy roots, you can imagine my surprise when, following instructions in the *Victory Garden Cookbook*, I lightly sautéed sliced parsnips in butter and olive oil and discovered them to be spicy, aromatic, and delicious. This was when I learned that the similarity between carrots and parsnips ends with the shape. To begin with, parsnips give off a tangy aroma as the knife goes through them, a promise of things to come. And parsnip slices are generally larger—some parsnips are at least twice the diameter of our biggest carrots. But they cook in a flash—five to seven minutes maybe—in a sauté pan. You don't need a recipe. You just scrub the parsnips well, and slice them about ¼-inch thick. Then you put them in a large hot frying pan with a teaspoon or so of oil and as much or as little butter as you think you ought to eat, and fry them a few minutes until they're tender. They brown beautifully and smell the same. I slice and cook every part, even down to the tiny roots. Cooked that way, they have a sweet spiciness that cannot be matched.

For those who still find it hard to believe that a fried parsnip is one of the compensations of eating locally in a cold climate, I offer two remarkable things I have learned. The first is how to make parsnip pancakes, a dish one of my favorite farmers once served me for breakfast. No batter, just great big parsnip slices sautéed in butter (he believes in butter therapy for everything) with maple syrup. I know. But try it. They're delicious.

I learned the second remarkable thing just recently: Some people love parsnips enough to import them out of season! Reading a review by Malcolm Baldwin of a book about eating locally in Britain, I followed the author through her argument about the true costs of technological advance in the food supply before stumbling with astonishment on the following statement:

> Sure enough, I can buy out of season parsnips from Western Australia but do they taste as good as those grown on the nearby organic farm? Certainly the supermarkets have devised a wonderful system to put fresh produce on the shelves all year round, but is all this jet-lagged food as nutritious as that picked in the morning and sold at the corner shop later on the same day?

I admit to wishing I had made up the term "jet-lagged food," but what really delighted me was learning that someone would lust for an out-of-season parsnip. Here am I, anxious to convince you that you should just brace up and try parsnips when they're available, and out across the ocean people are so fond of parsnips they import them!

Even as I have been writing this chapter, however, I have had to acknowledge that my high school Latin teacher was right, appetites cannot be disputed. What I think of as absolutely irresistible examples of how you could eat if you decided to forego long-distance produce may not excite your taste buds, although I hope you will try some of the recipes in this book and give winter a chance. If you're accustomed to getting through the cold months on well-travelled produce, it's understandable that you might dread a season absent familiar fruits and summer vegetables even if they're "fresh" in name only. So it's up to those of us who eat locally to invite the rest of you to dinner on occasion and begin re-educating your taste buds.

I myself would serve you carrots. When you are trying to live as much as possible on your own produce, there is no doubt that January, February, and March are the hard months. Carrots usually make a big difference, unless the weather has lured me to leave the carrots uncovered in the ground through December and a sudden hard freeze renders them undiggable. January is only the first of several months when it dawns on the person who wishes to feed herself in the Northeast that it's going to be a long winter. January is challenging, although it is more likely than it used to be—given planetary warming—that the ground will be free of snow sometime during the month, and even thawed enough to dig.

Recently I've been able to dig carrots in January, although it used to be February before I could get a spading fork into the ground. I always mean to dig them before the ground freezes, since their shoulders are either near the surface or out of the ground and I have worried that the frost would damage them. But I worked out a theory as I dug them last January—almost freezing my fingers in the process. The carrot, I realized, is a biennial. If I didn't dig it, it would send up leaves in its second year and go on to produce pretty flower umbels that look something like those of its close relative, Queen Anne's lace. And if the carrot plant had to keep itself strong for another year, I reasoned, it would need to protect its own roots over the winter. So I could be less careful about when I got the roots dug, as long as I got them out of the ground before they sent out little hairy roots in preparation for their flowery second year. This interesting theory was not confirmed, however. Lots of the carrots I didn't get out of the ground before a week of really hard freezes simply rotted.

Assuming, however, that you have dug in time, what can you do with that hydrator drawer full of carrots? To start with, there is the raw carrot. If you have not recently had a raw carrot fresh pulled from the ground in January, if you have convinced yourself that those bags of over-bred, over-travelled, lathe-turned, thumb-sized carrots sold in the produce section of your grocery store are raw *carrots*, then you won't believe how easy it is not merely to tolerate, but to enjoy having carrots as your only significant source of fresh produce for a few weeks every winter.

I know I'm not the only one who thinks of carrots as a winter treat because a few days before Christmas one year, I received a phone call from a farmer friend who asked if I was going to be home for a few days. I said I was. The day before Christmas, I got a Federal Express package filled with succulent winter mesclun and sweet slender carrot roots. Eliot Coleman, who sent them, grows these and other crops in an unheated greenhouse on the coast of Maine, where the ground freezes two feet deep in winter. All of them are sold within ten miles of his home, and he reports that one day when he was delivering an order, he overheard a child urging, "Mom, let's get some more of those candy carrots."

After the raw carrot comes the steamed carrot. Simply sliced, with the largest roots perhaps cut across to make half-circles, carrots can be steamed in one of those fold-up chrome-plated steamers in any pot with a lid. When a fork slips in easily, they can be lightly buttered (*buttered!*) and salted, and treated with a bath of various spices. When you have lots of carrots and when for a long season they're one of the few fresh vegetables you have to eat, it's nice to find different ways to fix them, but I offer a single two-choice recipe so delicious that it's difficult to move beyond; you can eat these carrots night after night.

STEWED CARROTS WITH DIFFERENT FLAVORS

Scrub, trim, peel, and slice or julienne:
> *1 pound* **carrots**

Put carrots in collapsible steamer in small saucepan. Cover, and steam until tender (10 minutes).

Drain water, return carrots to saucepan, and stir briefly over low flame with:
> *1 tablespoon* **butter**
> *¼ to 1 teaspoon* **ground cumin**
> *2 tablespoons chopped* **fresh coriander** *or* **parsley** *(not available in deep winter unless you've frozen herb sprigs)*

Or, for a different flavor, you can add the cooked carrots to a mix of:
> *melted* **butter**
> *1 tablespoon* **light brown sugar**
> *1 tablespoon cracked* **coriander seeds**

Season both of these to taste with **salt** and **pepper** before serving.

Sticking to my principle of not buying vegetables, I'm always hard pressed when I have house guests or need to take food to parties. But I've taken a baking dish of my cumin-seasoned carrots to many pot-lucks with no complaints.

Steamed carrots lend themselves to so many seasonings that it's hard to get tired of them, but my third evening I'd have carrots browned with oregano.

CARROTS WITH OREGANO

Cut lengthwise into ½-inch strips:
   6 *carrots*
Put in heavy pan with:
   2 to 3 tablespoons **butter** *(or half butter, half olive oil)*
   1 tablespoon **water**
   2 teaspoons dried **oregano**

Cover, and steam until carrots are tender. Remove cover and caramelize slightly.

Then there are grated carrots. Try carrot latkes; I have sweet potatoes all winter, and Curried Sweet Potato Latkes (chapter 3) are so incredibly delicious that I don't see why I should take the trouble to try latkes with carrots. But you can. And baked carrots are something different, tart and delicious.

BAKED GRATED CARROTS

Preheat oven to 350°F.

Place in a casserole:
   3 to 4 cups **grated carrots**
Pour over them:
   2 tablespoons melted **butter** or margarine
   1 tablespoon **lemon juice**
   ¼ teaspoon **salt**
   1 tablespoon chopped **chives**
   1 tablespoon **sherry** *(optional)*

Bake for 30 minutes.

You'll notice that I haven't even talked about carrot cake, or grated carrot salad with raisins, or all those other things you associate with carrots. You can have those too in winter.

Back in chapter 3, I mentioned that potatoes and kale were early mainstays of Alan's and my winter diet. Along with sweet potatoes and carrots (and the tomato sauces in the freezer), potatoes are still the foundation of many of my winter meals. We progressed from growing one variety to planting several, many of them in colors not associated with potatoes in my childhood. The ones with yellow names like Yukon Gold or Yellow Finn tend to be as buttery as their yellowish flesh implies. But I don't find blue potatoes especially tasty unless they're very fresh. I do, however, have a recipe that can turn All Blue or Purple Peruvian into the most beautiful potato salad you'll ever see.

BLUE AND GREEN POTATO SALAD

Boil in their skins:
*8 to 10 **blue potatoes** (they are usually small)*
Drain, and cut into ½-inch cubes.

Peel and cut into similarly sized pieces:
***cucumbers** to make an amount roughly equal to potatoes (1 large or 2 small)*
Meanwhile, roast on top of the stove in a heavy pan, stirring constantly until aroma emerges:
*1½ teaspoons **cumin seeds***
*1½ teaspoons **coriander seeds***
Then grind roasted spices in spice grinder or crush in small mortar and pestle.

Put potatoes and cucumbers in a nonreactive bowl, and toss with:
*1 teaspoon **kosher salt***
*2 tablespoons **lemon juice***

Add:

> ¼ *teaspoon* **black pepper**
> ¼ *teaspoon* **red pepper**
> ¼ *cup firmly packed* **fresh mint leaves**, *coarsely chopped*
> *roasted spices*

Toss gently. Let cool but do not refrigerate.

Note: This is a late-summer dish; cucumbers are not a winter crop.

I don't grow blue potatoes just to make Blue and Green Potato Salad, however; I have two other equally important reasons. First, in years when wet weather wreaks havoc with the potatoes, the blues always produce, reminding me that they are still close to their Peruvian peasant origins. Farmers who must live on what they grow value reliability.

The second reason we have blue potatoes every year is not unrelated to the first, namely their determination to persist. The spring after the first autumn we harvested Purple Peruvians, potato shoots popped up all over the plot from which we thought we had removed every last spud. By late spring, the supposedly empty garden bed was covered with lush potato foliage. So I don't plan to grow blue potatoes. They emerge, knowing I can't kill a volunteer, and I move them around to where I can accommodate them!

Potato volunteers don't show up the following year because they "go to seed." Potatoes do bloom, beautifully—they're one of my favorite vegetable flowers—but they rarely produce seed; what are called "seed potatoes" in the catalogues are really just small (or sometimes large) potatoes raised by seed potato companies for the rest of us to plant. Spuds are one of the few vegetables we eat (garlic is another) that are normally planted as miniature versions or pieces of what they will produce.

When you plant a single clove of garlic, you get a head. When you plant a small seed potato, or a piece of a larger potato with one or more eyes, you harvest five to fifteen whole potatoes. The eyes usually get cut out when you peel potatoes, and they are the source of the shoots that come up to start the whole process over again. I once buried a lot of eye-filled potato peelings in the garden and in no time at all, I had a mass of potato shoots.

Once potatoes had been discovered in the New World, potato-growing caught on in Ireland and elsewhere because potatoes could be planted on rocky or uneven ground where plowing was not feasible; a farmer could just dig a series of holes and drop them in. Living where the land has a tendency to flood, we find the process trickier—as did the Irish when they had a very wet year and lost their whole crop to potato blight (which produced a famine that drove them to the United States in large numbers). The terrible consequences of this poverty- and politics-induced dependence on a single variety called "the lumper," which made all the plants vulnerable to a single disease, are still cited as a warning of the hazards of genetic uniformity.

Since potatoes form as starchy lumps around shoots that grow *up* from the piece you plant, the "seed" must be planted deep enough to leave room for new potatoes to form above it. That's why you hill soil up around the neck of a potato plant. If you plant too deeply, however, your seed may rot in cold spring soil before it ever sprouts. So you need to prepare a well-dug bed, make a trench, insert your seed potato rather shallowly, and then, when the eye has produced a good healthy shoot or two, fill in the trench, heaping earth up around the neck of the plant. This creates a layer of soft rich soil in which the potatoes can form. If the soil is too wet, the potatoes don't like it; our soil is, alas, often too wet.

But the old blues seem undaunted by even the worst weather. Their ability to reappear spontaneously is the result of their tendency to produce lots of pebble-sized potatoes in addition to the regular crop of lumpy three-inch "fingerlings." Since their skins are very dark, and since I seem always to be digging them as dusk approaches,

I invariably miss some of the tiny ones. And next year, there they are.

I haven't spent much time so far talking about how I use potatoes, because most people can think of lots of ways to cook them without help. I can't wind up a chapter on taste, however, without including the recipe for a potato dish I eat at least once a week in the winter, usually at breakfast, with leftovers for lunch or dinner later in the week. It's a seriously modified version of an egg and chorizo specialty Alan and I used to order at Felix's, an Orange County, California, restaurant where we regularly took my mother in a wheelchair after her stroke. Our version was concocted by Alan, who had a much more adventurous way in the kitchen than I do. When we got back home, Alan convinced himself that the dish was made with potatoes (I think he was worried about his cholesterol) and experimented until he got it right. This wonderful dish is what resulted.

MEXICAN BREAKFAST POTATOES À LA FELIX
(Alan Gussow)

Cube and steam until almost soft:
>   *1 pound **white potatoes***
>   *or*
>   *½ pound **white potatoes** and ½ pound **sweet potatoes***

Lay on top of the potatoes to steam for five minutes:
>   *1 **chorizo** or other spicy sausage*

Remove and cut into chunks.

In a frying pan heat:
>   *1 tablespoon **corn oil***

Add:
>   *2 teaspoons **cumin***
>   *½ teaspoon **chili powder***
>   *½ cup or more puréed **tomatillo or mild tomatillo sauce** (both the sausage and the chili powder add heat!)*
>   *½ teaspoon **salt***

Stir to mix, and cook briefly to blend. Add potatoes and sausage.

Mix thoroughly, and bring to a boil. Add water if sauce starts to dry out. Serve with warmed fresh tortillas.

You can also start at "In a frying pan heat" and cook the potatoes in the sauce if you cut them into ¹/₂-inch cubes and add enough water to the sauce to keep it from drying out as the potatoes cook. In that case, cover the pan for the entire cooking time until the end when you can let it thicken up a bit.

I have made this for vegetarians without the chorizo; just add a little more chili powder.

As a Mexican food addict, perhaps my happiest winter surprise—was the discovery of an enchilada made with two of my winter mainstays, carrots and potatoes. I have no idea where I came across this recipe years ago. But a chef told me only recently that this dish is named after a plaza in Mexico, where it is the featured food. I can see why!

Enchiladas Tapatias (Enchiladas de Guadalajara)

Boil in salted water:
    6 **carrots**, *peeled and sliced*
    2 *large* **boiling potatoes**, *peeled and sliced*
Drain each, fry briefly in hot **oil**, and keep warm.

Coat with enchilada sauce (see below), fry briefly in oil, stack and hold:
    1 dozen fresh corn **tortillas**

Have available:

> *¹/₄ cup cooked **chicken** or leftover **turkey** (vegetarians can use small amounts of grated cheddar or pieces of potato as filling)*

Put a small amount of poultry or other filling down the center of each tortilla, then roll up and keep warm in ovenproof dish.

When all tortillas are rolled, top with remaining sauce, carrots, and potatoes, and sprinkle with:

> *¹/₃ cup grated **Parmesan cheese***

Return to oven briefly to get thoroughly warm. Serve with garnish of:

> *8 sliced **radishes** (if in season)*
>
> *4 shredded **romaine lettuce** leaves (or shredded kale if garden is frozen)*

Enchilada sauce may be purchased or prepared from dried ancho chilis, which are much easier to find now than they used to be.

This recipe can be made with no meat, and no garnish.

Enchiladas Tapatias is probably the most complicated recipe in this book, but on a cold winter day, you'll thank me for including it.

16

Heat, Rats, and Despair

> . . . amidst the Hesperian gardens, on whose bancks bedew'd
> with nectar and celestiall songs aeternall roses grow . . .
> the scalie-harnest dragon ever keeps his unenchanted eye . . .
>
> —John Milton, *Comus*, 1634

> Ever notice that "what the hell" is always the right decision?
>
> —Marilyn Monroe

JULY—IT'S HOT. It's been hot and it's going to be hot. It's already broken all records for 90- and 95-degree days—the hottest and driest July on record, they say. In the early morning before the temperature starts climbing up from 80, you go out to the garden not to pick vegetables but to rescue them. And it's dry. Sometimes at 5:00 A.M. before it's even light, you can see a bit of moisture on the leaves, picked up from the river and then dropped. But it's gone by 8:00 A.M. (There's no moisture left to pick up from the garden).

And the river rats are as crazed as the rest of us and are eating every one of my tomatoes that gets ripe. The plants, usually covered with scarlet globes from the bottom up at this time of year, show nothing but green almost to their tops. I sent this note to a friend.

> Rats climb up my vines and eat tomatoes right off the stem. I have
> lost *all* of my ripe tomatoes, even in the cages I surrounded yester-
> day with netting! Meanwhile, outside the fence in the community
> garden, nothing much is touched. Tomatoes hang ripely off the
> vines. I'm unbelievably frustrated. What scares me is whether or
> not it will continue even if the weather isn't so dry. I suspect the
> heat and drought is making it worse, but who knows. It's enough
> to make one give up farming. I've re-anchored the netting, and
> will surround the rest of the cages as well, but I don't think I'll

win. I'm going to try fox urine this evening, just to give them
something to think about!

My great grief is for Nature as a whole *and* that I can't get a
ripe tomato away from the rats.

Roger the exterminator, whom you met briefly in an earlier chapter, is paid to keep the riverfront free of rats for the village. He scouts
the community garden out of generosity, and, since I'm next door, he
fits me in too. He came in response to my alarmed call telling him that
I had not a single ripe tomato unchewed, and that a rat had dashed
over a visitor's foot in the community garden. I shared his diagnosis
and some of my own spleen with the community gardeners by e-mail:

Fellow Gardeners:
Just thought you'd like to know that I haven't harvested a ripe tomato yet. The rats have gotten them all. Roger came and announced that there were no rat burrows on either my property or
in the community garden so he couldn't put poison down the den.
He said he would put out bait stations but then he said, "Joan,
vegetables and fruits are rats' favorite food. They're going to stand
here," he looked back and forth between the bait station and the
tomatoes, "and they're going to say 'chicken or sirloin? chicken or
sirloin?' and they're going to choose sirloin."

So if you find chomped tomatoes, don't, don't throw them on
the ground but remove them to the compost pails, pick up and
compost all dropped tomatoes, surround your plants with netting
if you can, stake them high, get a little rat doll and stick pins in it,
and hope that Roger's bait is more attractive than he thinks!

Frankly, it's in my interest to have the community garden become more rat-attractive than my yard—it clearly isn't now because there are all sorts of ripe tomatoes dangling out there—but I
feel compelled to be helpful. My tomatoes are now surrounded
with polypropylene netting, and even I can't get in to eat them.

And if you ever wonder why rats will outlast us on the planet, just remember they don't contribute to global warming by driving to the store in a Humvee, and they love fruits and vegetables.

Cheers, Joan

Some of this was probably hysterically bad advice, since if the tomatoes were left lying about the rats might have finished the ones they'd already ruined instead of starting fresh ones every night.

Ever since Sir Francis Bacon introduced the notion that science would let us control the natural world for the benefit of *mankind (sic!)*, our species's relationship with Nature has been driven by the illusion that we will ultimately break her to our will. (Bacon's operative phrase was something like "rend her limb from limb"—a formulation some of us find especially disturbing.) So the scientists keep burrowing away, the technologists keep applying their discoveries, and we in the bleachers are supposed to cheer all of them on in the hope that if they keep attacking Nature's secrets, they'll one day "get it all under control," and our lives will be effortlessly satisfying.

Nature will have none of it, of course. And when we ignore our dependence, she swats us with a season that dries up our water supplies and kills crops, livestock—and people. Hot, dry summers, like the ones we seem to be encouraging as we smother the planet with industrial off-gassing, are sobering reminders: Nature is still in charge; science can't fix everything. Money can't either—and driving a Humvee down to the store is nuts.

What's a gardener to do? We're in a phase 2 drought emergency— no lawn sprinklers ("I'm not watering my *lawn*, officer, just my vegetables"), no open hoses, just handheld hoses with nozzles, and buckets. On a long narrow lot full of vegetables, that means a lot of hose-dragging and a lot of time put into watering. But my crops have proved surprisingly durable. I've regularly watered the fruit trees— allowed because they were transplanted this spring—and I just finished harvesting a nice crop of peaches.

As for the other fruits we call vegetables—the tomatoes, peppers, and eggplant—I had decided this spring to imitate one of the community gardeners and sink plastic flower pots in the ground among the plants. As I fill each pot, water runs six inches down and pulls the plant roots down to find it. Surface watering encourages the roots to come up to get wet and makes the plants more vulnerable to drought.

The potatoes were planted under a heavy mulch of leaves and salt hay and managed to flourish and bloom before the heat and drought got bad, so I've had good yields from the ones I've harvested so far. The chard, kale, cabbages, and broccoli have grown so vigorously that their crowns overlap and their leaves shelter the ground; they seem happy with an occasional drenching. I regularly hand-water the green beans and the carrots that I sowed in all this heat. And since the tomatoes are bearing (it's not *their* fault I don't get to pick any), everybody's doing fine.

Except the farmers, of course. It's not the lawn owners, or even gardeners like me we need to worry about, but the professionals who grow our food. As I sat eating a bowl of homemade granola with my delicious peaches the other day, I saw a picture in the newspaper of dried-up peaches hanging on a branch at a local orchard. It was probably a dramatization featuring an isolated dead branch; an established peach orchard is unlikely to die, even in a month like this. But field crops are not so durable. Local corn is unavailable. It wouldn't pay the farmers to irrigate. Usually they don't have to. But this summer's weather is ruining them, as it is ruining farmers across the country. I have an American Farmland Trust bumper sticker on my car that says NO FARMS, NO FOOD, but nobody has ever commented on it, as they comment on my GARLIC license plate. People just don't get it—yet.

For relief, I'm putting in the recipe for the granola I was eating with my peaches, though it's not local.

CRUNCHY GRANOLA
(Michele Bremer)

Preheat oven to 300°F

Mix in a large bowl:
3 to 3½ pounds **rolled oats**
1 cup **wheat germ**
1 cup **sesame seeds**
1 cup **powdered milk**
12 ounces **almonds**, *sliced*
10 ounces **filberts**, *ground in blender*
Warm together:
1½ cups **honey**
1½ cups **oil** .

Stir honey and oil mixture into cereal mixture (with hands if necessary to get it evenly distributed). Spread no more than 1/2-inch thick on cookie sheets or in aluminum baking trays, and bake in a 300° oven approximately one hour or until golden brown. Stir frequently while baking to keep edges from burning. Cool and store in an airtight container.

My own inability to ignore the connection between food growers and weather makes me uncomfortably sensitive to my neighbors' ability to do so. Most Americans have been taught to ignore Nature—except when it gets really violent or interferes with their holidays—and their lives allow such indifference. Even in a heat wave, we coddled Americans look out on a parched world from air-conditioned comfort. (The poor notice the weather, of course, even die of it, but they're not making national policy or writing life-style stories.) Admittedly, the street's hot, which spoils outdoor activities and makes the dash from auto to building uncomfortable. But once the weather cools a bit, as it always eventually does, things get "back to normal," and the city weather man has trouble not sounding happy when he notes that the weekend to come will be rainless and sunny.

But the dryness, the dryness. The drought threatens to be the worst of the century in the northeast. And all the measures we are asked to take to conserve water—showering with a bucket, keeping another in the sink to collect rinse water, turning off the faucet as we brush our teeth—are presented as *emergencies*, the implication being that this weather pattern should be looked on as short-term and our conservation temporary. So we face the water shortage as a crisis. Or we don't face it at all. Like the man being interviewed on the radio the other day who said laughingly that he normally took a half-hour shower every morning but would *try* to cut back.

For a while after my New York county declared a drought emergency that prohibited lawn watering, New Jersey homeowners were still allowed to pour water on their grass. Brown-grassed Rocklanders just north of the state line were resentful that we were sending *our* water south. Then New Jersey's governor got on board and the suburbanites watched their lawns die in synchrony. As if lawns were the issue. The unmentionable fact is that we need to behave today, tomorrow, and forever as if water were a precious resource that ought never to be wasted. Because it is.

The local paper reported that some northern New Jersey homeowners had pumped their wells dry and were hiring well diggers to go deeper; one man had gone down 550 feet without finding water. There was some subdued muttering about the fact that *all* the Jersey water tables are dropping, and that no one knows the real condition of the groundwater reserves. Given our ignorance, it's remarkable that all of us, officials and civilians, continue to behave as if there will always be more.

Growing up in what should have been the Southern California desert, I've known since childhood that water was precious and scarce. But California is also the state that was convinced, and remains so, that any desert can be made to bloom, for a price. My father

helped bring water down to thirsty Los Angeles from parts of the
state that didn't have the power to say "No." (The movie was called
Chinatown.) But Southern Californians always paid for water and we
were careful with it because it cost money.

Even when they live in deserts, however, Americans expect to
have the amenities they have come to believe are their privilege, no
matter what. I remember reading several years ago the shocked comment of an Arizona homeowner alerted to the possibility that water
for lawns might not be available in that desert state. "I wouldn't want
to live here if I couldn't have a lawn," she said. The East Coast has no
history of being a desert, and no practice imagining that water conservation should not be an emergency measure but a way of life. But
I hope that pretty soon we'll start wondering—when the weather is
dry—if there isn't some way we can use less and give more to the
farmers.

I'm not a farmer, just a gardener attempting to self-provision, and
even I have found this year's weather a source of real despair. The
drought turns out to be the reason for my rat problem. The Hudson
is a tidal river, with a wedge of salty water flowing upriver under the
surface to north of where I live. When no rain comes downstream to
dilute it, the river becomes increasingly salty. Well into my rat crisis,
I learned from the mayor, a former fisherman, that the rats can't
handle the salt. They are eating my tomatoes for liquid. I was really
glad to learn that because my journal was getting increasingly de-
spairing.

> AUGUST 3 — Where the rats come from, God knows, but they are
> wiping out every single tomato that gets ripe. I have wrapped the
> cages on the north with black netting, and this morning in one of
> the south-side beds, three tomatoes on one plant were destroyed.
> It's like a picnic ground for rats, I guess. What can I do? Anything?
> Tear out all the plants? It's so deeply disturbing . . . I could stop
> growing tomatoes. Do I have to? I'm just glad I didn't go ahead
> and toss last year's tomato purée when I cleared out the freezer!

But back to the drought. It's difficult to concentrate on other things when Nature is suffering so. And my back yard looks relatively lush. I can't really complain about that. It's just the uneasiness of knowing that where you haven't watered is dead dry, ground-shrinking dry.

Little did I know that worse was yet to come. On August 25, with a serious rain forecast, I worked outdoors preparing the garden for its much-needed shower. What came was a deluge. The following morning, I woke up to pouring rain and to a flood in the garden that extended from the high-sitting shed to the low steps leading to the riverbank. By early afternoon the garden was still mostly drowned under a gray sky. The rain had stopped a couple of hours earlier, but New York City remained paralyzed. I was listening to the every-ten-minute traffic and weather station, and there was so much traffic disruption and so much weather that one ten-minute segment ran into the next! The railroads stopped cold, subways flooded out, cars were stranded in the medians of highways all over the metropolitan area.

Late in the afternoon, I went up to look in a bucket sitting on my terrace. It was half full. I put in a stick and made a mark; when I measured, it was 6½ inches! The flooding was explained, and the water was slowly receding, but its consequences were still to be measured in my weather-stressed garden.

Six days later, on the last day of August, I began to plant for fall, even as I measured my flood losses.

AUGUST 31 — I put in Provider bush beans, Cook's Garden tangy mesclun mix, and mizuna in the former potato bed where I planted peas just before the flood. I also planted Brune D'Hiver romaine lettuce, and Lollo Rosa cutting lettuce in the cold frame where lettuce seedlings are coming up on their own from last year's crop. I relaid some brick edging and swept off the wood chips and other flotsam that had accumulated on the paths from the flood. But the aftermath of the flood is everywhere. Lots of plants—tomatoes, basil, zucchini—are dying from being drowned at the wrong time. Even after the great flood of '94 when all the tomato cages went over, the plants lived to produce. I don't know what's wrong. Were they already weakened by the drought? Was it something washed down by the rainwater that didn't suit them? Is there simply more disease in the soil from heavy use, or what? I have to think about it. If I have wilt in the soil, it's going to be damn hard to get rid of. The tomatoes were already looking not so hot. What could it be?

The rhubarb looks terrible, but will recover [it didn't]. . . . The peppers don't seem to have been damaged, nor the eggplant. The sweet potatoes look excellent.

A growing season like this one pounds in the lesson that finding things to eat year-round isn't the most daunting obstacle to eating locally. The seasonal limitations are actually fun when you can treat them that way. (Lunch in the aftermath was two salvaged red peppers chopped, with New York State goat cheese, homemade tomatillo and serrano salsa, and almonds, grilled under the broiler. It was delicious!) If you can take the cooking lightly and enjoy it, you can celebrate the taste of the produce, whatever it is, and have a good time.

What's hard is accepting Nature's terms. What's hard is having your crops suddenly wilt and die when you've counted all year on harvesting them. What's hard is working to have a perfectly producing garden, only to discover that one or another crop will fail, sometimes for reasons that are less obvious than this year's meteorological catastrophes. So much varies from year to year. This year the potatoes were as good as I can remember them in the bogs of Piermont. But the drowned, rat-bitten tomatoes were, of course, a disaster. This year the zucchini—which I started late deliberately in order to avoid the vine borers—produced early and abundantly, while last year they took forever to begin to fruit. The butternut squash seems indomitable, rambling all over the garden; it just doesn't happen to be my favorite vegetable.

I've had good beets this year, and I can plant more beets and tur-nips for late-fall harvest. I trimmed back the rosemary and it will probably survive. The raspberries (the fall ones are bearing gener-ously right now) seem to have come through unscathed, although last year's flood killed a third of them; of all the garden plants, they were longest under water since that area is so low. Of course, they're heaped with wood chips, and that may help.

And so I tidied up the garden, tried to help the few surviving toma-toes recover, hovered over the wilting rosemary. Two weeks after the first storm, Hurricane Floyd came hurrying up the coast. I had been in the city for a two-day meeting, without an umbrella, so when I got home—after a drenching walk to the subway, a train ride, another sodden walk from the subway to my car, and a driving adventure that took me far afield trying to get back across the Hudson to Piermont—I was so happy to be home that I hardly cared that the garden was completely flooded all the way up to the high ground of the toolshed. I dressed for the weather, and went outside to walk the brick edge and see what had happened. The water was absolutely clear—I could see the clover floating down there on the path. Then I came back in, let down the blinds in my office so I wouldn't have to watch, and began to work. Later, when I went upstairs, I noticed that the water in the yard had turned brown, and muddy water was pouring through the next-door parking area into my driveway. Then the lights went off, my office window and the bedroom ceiling were leaking, and when I gave up and went to bed, the foot of my bed was wet from a new leak. The forecasts were for the rain to cease. I could only *hope*.

SEPTEMBER 23—The morning dawned spectacularly brightly, showing the water to have very largely receded, leaving exposed my mud-covered yard and an inch or so of extra soil on top of my whole driveway (a blessing, I needed the extra height). That morning, I wandered around clearing up the stuff from the leaks indoors, venturing outside only briefly to survey my by now pretty well demolished garden. The tower on which scarlet runner and

Mortgage Lifter beans had been growing really well was blown over and the wind had whipped the leaves to death (the vines are now clearly dead) and the tomatoes that had survived the *last* flood gave up the ghost. They stand this morning with a few ripening fruits but no leaves at all. They're finished.

The new sugar snap peas have been whipped by the wind and then inundated by wood chips, which covered them almost completely, so God knows whether they'll survive. The newly emerging seedlings of mizuna, etc. were drowned, though the self-sown salad greens in the cold frame survived, despite being entirely smothered by wood chips. How did the chips get in there? I don't understand why the peppers are still flourishing. And the sweet potatoes appear to be ready to produce a tremendous crop. I went out this a.m. and dug one for myself for breakfast, though it seems to be taking an astonishingly long time to bake!

It never baked. It was resolutely glassy. And when, a week or so later, I finally dug the rest of the sweet potato crop—for years my winter mainstay—many were rotted, and most were gigantic and cracked as if during the drought the plants had said to themselves, "Let's not start another one, let's just keep growing." Then, having dryly expanded, they were drowned, absorbed water, and cracked open. The crop looks hideous, giving new meaning to the term Frankenfood. I may have no sweet potatoes through the winter, and the butternut squash, which has always played second fiddle in my winter orchestra, will reap the rewards of its utter reliability through everything.

Now there's a moral to all this and I can't put it off. It is this sort of summer—when the rats eat the tomatoes, when the lawns dry up, and the park trails close because a spark would start a brush fire—that forces me to understand how disconnected our thinking has become. If I can't produce my own food, it really doesn't matter, since I have a market within walking distance and can afford even their high prices. But the same cannot be said for the crops of my fellow farmers, the ones who feed you, and provide for me when my own crops fail. No divine dispensation shelters their crops from the sorts of devastation mine experienced.

No sensible farmer would choose my flood-prone land, of course, and they're better at what we both do. But when I bought peaches at our local farmers' market in September, after the great flood, I mentioned to the grower that all my tomatoes had simply collapsed. He said, "Mine, too." And in the narcissism of relief, I said, "I'm so glad." But I caught myself, apologized, and said, "I thought it was me." And he smiled for the first time since we began dealing with each other weeks before and said, "No, when full-grown plants are suddenly hit with stress, they just collapse." So it's not my soil, or my skills, or wilt from the manure I brought in this year. It's the weather.

Blinded by the supermarket cornucopia, most of us need to be reminded that food is the generous result of a collaboration between our species and the rest of Nature, not simply another product of industrial civilization. Driving home from a Sunday breakfast early enough in the year that the summer's heat and the floods that followed it were unimaginable, I was propelled into steering-wheel-banging outrage by an interview on my favorite radio station. It reminded me of the disinterest and ignorance with which those who ought to know better are afflicted.

The interviewer observed that the year had ended with another record high for the stock market, and asked his financial-expert guest: "Are we refusing to accept the fact that this really is a sustained bull market, or are we headed for a fall?" With the glib confidence of one in a profession that is always consulted and seldom right, his interviewee replied, "I think it's the former." He then went on to talk about the fact that in addition to the buoyant stock market, holiday sales had been excellent, unemployment was low, and all the indicators were good—despite some meltdowns in the global economy. Then he added, "Of course, there are problems in some sectors. If you're in the export sector, you will be feeling this. Agriculture, for example."

That's when I bruised my hand on the steering wheel. *Agriculture for example*. Sure. Agriculture's in trouble, but it's sure to be better next year, or the next. Like the auto industry or textiles or electronics, agriculture can bounce back. Really? What if farmers get discouraged by the kind of weather that sideswiped me this year and stop farming because they can't make a living—as too many can't? Who will feed us then?

For years I have quoted poet-farmer Wendell Berry's comment that we are eating more thoughtlessly than any people in history. By now our thoughtlessness about the soils that support us is complete. Unlike cars and clothes and computers, food must be produced year by year, by year, by year . . . forever, as part of a functioning ecosystem. The vintage cars on the streets of Havana are a demonstration that automobiles can be kept running for half a century or more, but "pre-owned" food is not an option. Food gets used up every day.

The inability of economists to recognize this uniqueness is exquisitely demonstrated by the ruminations of Yale economist Richard Nordhaus, who has argued for years that it isn't cost-effective to worry about greenhouse warming. A doubling of atmospheric carbon dioxide—more than enough to drown thirty-seven island nations under icecap meltwater and other ocean-raising events—would reduce U.S. gross national product by only one-fourth of one percent. The economic impact would be so trivial, Nordhaus concludes, because warming would affect only those parts of our economy that interface with the environment. Want to guess which parts those are? Right! Agriculture tops the list. And since agriculture is only two percent of our GNP, the economic impact of its destruction would be minor even if Miami moved to Michigan.

This summer we've been going up in both smoke and steam. Smoke when the parched grasses and shrubs catch fire at a spark. Steam when the ground dries so much that the tight root balls of newly planted shrubs rise up from the shrunken soil. I live without TV and air-conditioning, so what's perhaps most upsetting to a planet watcher like me is the unchanged media focus on celebrities, sports, scandals, wars, and endless political campaigns—all in the service of

selling things. After more than two centuries of American excep-
tionalism, after a hundred years of awe at the astonishing changes
science has wrought, after fifty years of being convinced that we need
the latest version of everything, most of us just don't get it where our
relationship with Nature is concerned.

As for our relationship with people who grow food, the *New York
Times*, my newspaper of record, often runs stories suggesting that
farmers are ripping off consumers. I myself recognize the truth in the
joke popular in farming country. "So what would you do if you won a
million dollars?" "Oh—probably just go on farming until it was
gone." In this time of changing weather and bankrupt farmers, it does
seem risky to be ignoring the people who produce our food, counting
for our dinner on people who must be willing to lose money to keep
growing it.

17

California and the Rest of Us

> It's not written anywhere that irrigated agriculture
> is a perpetual source of sustenance for a civilization.
>
> —Jack Norlyn

IN THE FALL OF THE YEAR when the rats ate my tomatoes, I began the last of these chapters in an extraordinary writers' haven called Mesa Refuge, just in from the San Andreas fault and the Point Reyes National Seashore on the mid-north coast of California. The three of us in residence were given two weeks of absolute quiet, near total lack of communication with the outside world, perfect accommodations indoors and out, and local organic food. Most of the fruits, vegetables, meats, and dairy products that filled the well-stocked refrigerator-freezer during our stay came from nearby farms. All the foods in the dinners prepared for us five nights a week were also local and organic. Did they know when they invited me what I was writing about? Actually, I suppose they did. But I didn't know they knew and I didn't have any idea what I would find when I got there.

Being there, it was tempting to imagine, as I often do when I am privileged to drop in on the still-blessed state of Northern California, that the triumph of local eating is at hand. The meals we ate were proof, if any were needed, that living on local food is not a sacrifice but a privilege. Of course, I was feasting in October—harvest season—and I was in that unspoiled fragment of California where a week or so of residence always convinces me that putting everything right will be easy.

It will not be easy, however, to put even the food system right—

even in California. It will not be easy, but it no longer seems absurdly wistful, as it did twenty-five years ago, to imagine that eaters might begin to question the sanity of eating food more travelled than they are. Many people have begun to seek out foods grown near home, even without a serious interruption in the flow of bounty from the West. The need to support local growers will likely become more evident as Nature forcefully reminds California of the fragility of an irrigated agriculture.

In September of 1977, in the midst of a cost-price squeeze in farming not unlike the present one, President Carter's newly appointed Secretary of Agriculture, former farmer Bob Berglund, called a meeting in Downingtown, Pennsylvania, which was attended by the secretary himself, all of his assistant secretaries, and fifty-odd citizens interested in U.S. food and agriculture—including, to my great surprise, me. This remarkably diverse group of professionals—agricultural economists, crop and livestock specialists, nutritionists, farm labor representatives, hunger activists, and others whose affiliations escape me twenty-three years later—met together in small groups to address fundamental questions about where the U.S. food system ought to be going. It was a heady time in which any sort of answer to that question seemed possible.

The discussions were vigorous and enlightening, but what sticks most in my mind from that weekend was a conversation I had with one of the assistant secretaries over a glass of beer at the end of the first day. I don't remember what we were talking about when he suddenly said, "Well, in his second term, the President's going to let the price of California water rise to its real cost." I don't know if he had his facts straight. Carter didn't get his second term, and Reagan, who succeeded him, was not eager to challenge the water barons of his home state. So taxpayers continued—and continue today—to pay for California water as part of the price of their "cheap" food.

But all that disappointment came later; at that moment, standing at the bar with an authoritative stranger, I took a very deep breath. Raising the price of California water could change everything. California crops would cost more. Local agriculture could be competitive again. There was a chance for the Northeast to become less dependent on food from two thousand miles away.

The oil crisis that helped drive Carter from office had already taught us Northeasterners something about the energy cost of our import dependence. When fuel prices rose, making truck transport expensive, the price of local produce became briefly competitive. A rise in the price of California water could make a permanent change.

It is easy now, when so many people's connection with food is limited to what can be found packaged in the supermarket, to take the triumph of California for granted, to assume, as the state's boosters urged more than a century ago, that California's "natural advantage" made it the obvious place to grow food for the rest of the nation. When I first became curious about why it was so hard to find a New York State apple in New York City, one of my students came across a 1910 booklet on the city's markets. The booklet made it clear that by the turn of the century, apples from the West Coast were already seriously competing with local fruit for the New York trade.

But it was not until I read Steven Stoll's book *The Fruits of Natural Advantage*, that I understood the origin of the forces that had pushed local fruit out of local markets. Stoll wonderfully describes the convictions that drove the process, the belief that California's "natural advantage" in climate could overcome its vast distance from the major population centers and turn the West Coast into the fruit-growing center of the nation. But to succeed in exploiting California's "natural advantage," as Stoll demonstrates, required the invention of industrial agriculture: huge waterworks, a pesticide treadmill to protect the vulnerable crops, a cheap and docile temporary labor force, and a marketing system that could both convince people to want fruit all the time, and get it to them from a distance. The actual fruits of natural advantage were, in brief, some of the industrial food system's worst characteristics.

But in the beginning, water seemed the only serious barrier to California's farmers. On the continent we presumed was meant to be our nation, Nature had goofed. She had left the western third short of rainfall, an oversight California's visionaries were confident they could remedy. Here is one of them, the Reverend Thomas Starr King, speaking to the San Joaquin Valley Agricultural Society on 11 September 1862. (My choice of King as a spokesperson is entirely idiosyncratic; my junior high school bore his name.)

King was speaking to a bunch of discouraged farmers at the end of what historian Donald Worster in *Rivers of Empire* describes as "another long, hot, rainless, dusty summer." Miners, using torrents of water to strip the foothills to their layer of gold-bearing ore, had helped make the state an "abomination of desolation." But that was not, as King saw it, what "God has in mind for it."

"The earth is not yet finished. . . . It was not made for nettles, nor for the manzanito [*sic*] and chaparral. It was made for grain, for orchards, for the vine, for the comfort and luxuries of thrifty homes. It was made for these through the educated, organized, and moral labor of man." And, of course, through water.

And so the water came, diverted first from such watercourses as there were, then pulled up from underground with wells and pumps. And when more was needed, and the price of the canals and dams and tunnels was more than private enterprise could handle, federal money was brought in to move the water from the wetter north to the great San Joaquin Valley and south, to tame even the mighty Colorado River, turning California into an agricultural dynamo.

Farmers in the rest of the country were not unaware of what California water would do to them. As Worster explains, on the day in January 1901 that the House of Representatives began debating the bill that would put federal money to work watering the west, a Congressman from Pennsylvania "rose to denounce the bill as a poisoned chalice pressed to the lips of the farming classes." Eastern farmers had seen their land values fall "50 percent in a generation, they suffered from overproduction of crops, they were working sixteen hours a day to make ends meet, across states like New Hampshire their farmhouses and barns stood empty, the brush growing up to the eaves."

Now irrigation of the arid lands would be added "to the eastern farmer's woes.'"

"So long as we have a large exportable surplus of agricultural products," the Congressman asked, "let the farmer meet, as others must, private but not governmental competition." But farming was never the point. Conquest was. The legislation passed, and the money started flowing west.

The results were awesome. Go a little east of Point Reyes Station on the mid-north coast where I sat writing, and you can see the reality of what cheap water has produced. There, running north to south in the state's vast Central Valley between the mountains of the coast and the Sierra Nevadas, are a series of landscapes utterly different from the cattle-dotted scrub I looked out on through the windows of my writing shack. Here, points out Ann Foley Scheuring in *A Guidebook to California Agriculture*, is almost half of the agricultural land in the state, almost two-thirds of the cropland, and nearly three-quarters of the irrigated land. Here, on "farms" that cover thousands of acres, precious and over-committed water produces bounty in a landscape that was never intended to be a garden.

By the middle of the twentieth century, California had become the leading agricultural state in the nation, a distinction it still holds half a century later. Its farmers grow with irrigation things that could be produced as well, or better, elsewhere with rain—alfalfa for example—and they also grow things produced almost nowhere else in the nation. For 12 of the 350 different crops it produces, California is essentially the only U.S. source.

When I was growing up in Southern California, I didn't know I lived in a farming state. Farms, as I knew them, were in places like Iowa, and produced things like corn and alfalfa and hogs and milk. We saw these farms—not very prosperous during the Depression—when our family drove Route 66 "back east" to visit our Iowa relatives.

But California oranges I knew about. One of my vivid childhood memories is of riding in the family car to the citrus packing plant in San Dimas and buying for $1 a shopping bag full of oranges as they tumbled off the sorting line. California was an agricultural colony even then. The best, most perfect oranges were sent east, and those of us who lived where they were grown got what was left over. In compensation, we southern Californians could get freshly squeezed orange juice, "all you can drink for 25¢," at stands along the back roads of Orange County.

And we had peaches. At the right time of year, after Mom had received a postcard announcing, "The peaches are ready, Mrs. Dye," our family would drive east from Alhambra to pick up several boxes of "clingstones" that Mom canned or made into my father's favorite pickled peaches. My father also used to inundate us with berries when they came into season. We didn't have much money when I was a child, but in those days ordinary folk could have seasonal fresh berries—even raspberries and blackberries—without going into debt.

Blackberries were the inspiration for my mother's best dessert. My father claimed his sister used to make this dish, but he didn't bring a recipe to the marriage. So he kept nudging my mother—who wasn't much of a cook—to work it out. He never conceded that she had it exactly right, but my sister and I thought it was heavenly. Dad called the dish Apple Pan Dowdy, but other recipes for apple pan dowdy that I've seen weren't anything like his. You can only make Dad's APD in late summer (August where I am), when both apples and blackberries are in season. But it's worth waiting for.

Dad's Apple Pan Dowdy
(Joyce Fisher Dye)

Preheat oven to 350° F.

Grease an 8-inch square baking pan, and cover the bottom with:
   *3 to 4 large **apples**, peeled and sliced*
Sprinkle with:
   *½ cup **brown sugar***
Set aside.

Put in bowl of food processor with steel knife:

2 cups **flour**

4 teaspoons **baking powder**

¹/₂ teaspoon **salt**

2 tablespoons **sugar**

¹/₂ cup **shortening** *cut into 7 or 8 pieces*

Process 5 to 10 seconds until mixture has consistency of coarse meal.

With machine running, pour through feed tube:

³/₄ cup **cold milk**

Stop processing as soon as the dough forms a ball. (Dough may be used immediately or wrapped in plastic and chilled if desired.)

Cover apples with pastry, and bake in a preheated 350° oven for one hour.

Turn pan out with apples on top, and cover with as many **sugared blackberries** as you can pile on.

Serve warm with cream and get fat.

We sometimes had Dad's APD topped with Rudolph Boysen's invention, the boysenberry.

Where boysenberries were concerned, we were pretty much in at the creation. Going to or returning from our hand-built cabin at Lytle Creek in the San Bernardino Mountains, we used to stop for lunch or supper at a little place along Route 66 where the Knott family grew poultry and boysenberries and served crusty fried-chicken dinners in a small dining room—with homemade boysenberry pie for dessert. In the 1930s, Knott's Berry Farm was just that: a berry farm with attached restaurant. It wasn't yet part of the depressing Orange County "amusement complex" that has since swallowed Southern California. The family gave us fair warning when in the 1940s they set up a fake "jail cell" holding a papier-mâché "prisoner" to attract tourists.

So I knew that there were orange groves and peach orchards within driving distance of where I grew up, but I don't remember hearing about the vast watered deserts where so many of the nation's crops were even then being grown. I do remember my mother complaining about the way vegetables declined in quality during World War II when the Japanese farmers were taken away to internment camps. But where the Japanese and their successors on the land grew our vegetables remained unspecified.

My father worked for the Los Angeles Department of Water and Power in the years when they brought the water down from Owens Valley (stole it, many would argue) and tamed the Colorado with what was then called Boulder Dam. So I always understood the importance of imported water to the dry south of the state, but my father talked about water to quench the city's thirst, and about the electricity the water generated as it fell, not about the crops that thrived on these projects' outpourings.

When, as a grown-up Easterner, I became interested in where our food was produced, I assumed that my childhood unfamiliarity with California's farms was accounted for by distance—the Central Valley was a long way northeast of where we lived, the Imperial Valley was southeast, and the gasoline rationing of World War II limited our mobility. But I have since learned that as I was coming of age in the 1940s, Los Angeles County, my county, "led the nation in farm income." So neither distance nor gas shortages account for my ignorance of the origin of that glassy iceberg lettuce I grew up hating. My family, like most eaters across the country, probably thought little about who actually grew our food, so long as there was food on the table.

Which raises the critical question: Dare we persist in our ignorance? Can the system that now puts food on our tables continue to do so? There are many threats to California's continued fruitfulness—soil erosion, air pollution, salinization of irrigated land, the invasion of exotic pests, and land subsidence are among them. But the two most worrying are the disappearance of farmland and the competition for water.

Several years ago I went back for the first time in fifty years to Alhambra, a small town when I was born there, now part of the eastern flank of Greater Los Angeles. Everyone's hometown changes, of course, as humans overrun more and more of the planet, but if you were born in Southern California before the Depression, before the first "free"way was built, when you could walk to a trolley line that would take you from wherever you lived to downtown Los Angeles or to the beach; if you're that old, then your birthplace has not changed, it has disappeared, mostly under concrete.

The San Dimas packing plant where we used to buy our oranges is history, and I read not long ago that the last lemon grove in that onetime lemon capital of the U.S. has also fallen to progress. Knott's Berry Farm is a full-fledged amusement park. Orange County, named after what used to grow there, is zoning out its last few agricultural acres. It's now a depressing landscape of run-together condos, houses, and strip malls laced by macadam parking lots and eight-lane highways and pocked by tall office buildings, garish tourist hotels, and entertainment complexes. Everywhere, little technicolor hummocks of flowers, pushed up, I have always imagined, by a hummock-making machine, attempt to belie the flatness of the land. Everything seems to have been built yesterday. The critical issue, however, is neither authenticity nor aesthetics; it is permanence.

Although the lands that feed us are disappearing everywhere, the paving of California takes on special significance because of its unique Mediterranean climate. You can't grow oranges in Iowa. Even now, according to Marc Reisner in *American Farmland*, California produces "almost all of the nation's kiwis, almonds and dates," and most of our "grapes, navel oranges, asparagus, tomatoes, lemons, carrots, lettuce, walnuts, celery and pistachios—just to name a few." Yet, "California's Central Valley, which produces over two-thirds of California's farm products . . . is the most threatened agricultural land in the nation." And fifty years after it led the nation in farm income, Los Angeles county "is virtually bereft of farms."

Some of California's most productive land is no longer threatened because it has been entombed. The beautiful Santa Clara Valley was once producer of nearly 50 percent of the *world's* prunes, apricots, and cherries. Aaron Sachs tells us it took only four decades to transform this "Valley of Heart's Delight," with its 132,000 acres of flowering trees, into Silicon Valley.

What is using up all this farmland is people. California's climate not only coddles crops, it lures immigrants, domestic and foreign. As Rick Standiford reports in a recent issue of *California Agriculture,* "California is home to one of the most rapidly growing human populations in the world." Its average annual rate of growth since 1850 is 3.4 percent, bringing it from fewer than 100,000 people in 1850 to more than 31 million in 150 years, with a projection of 52 million by 2030. All those folks need to be housed, and the easiest land to build on is the same flat land that's good for growing crops. According to Steve Sander, the estimate is that from 50,000 to 100,000 acres of California farmland have been urbanized annually since the early 1970s.

Obviously at some point the state will run out of places to farm. Yet despite the continued loss of some of its best croplands, California's total agricultural acreage remains high, as irrigation brings new, less-fertile land into production. And that's the second squeeze. Those newcomers not only want homes, they want them with flush toilets and showers, with lawns and swimming pools. So the threat to California agriculture is not merely that new construction—homes for newcomers and factories to employ them, and hotels and diversions for visitors, and roads to carry everybody from one place to another, and parking lots to hold their cars when they get there—is covering over some of the state's best cropland. The threat is that there's simply not enough water to meet the needs of both agriculture and industry, and to allow these newcomers to live as they feel they are entitled to, now that they've arrived in paradise.

The competition over water will not be a pretty one. Efforts to make agriculture pay a fair price for its water are long-standing—beginning with the first 1902 Reclamation Law, which said that no one farmer could irrigate more than 160 acres with federally subsidized water, a rule flagrantly disregarded ever since. Intermittent efforts to enforce the law, or some more liberalized version of it, have consistently gone aground on the outrage of the powerful California agricultural lobby. But fair pricing may not in the end be the linchpin. If there's just not enough to go around, the lobby may lose. When push comes to shove, it's hard to imagine a politician who would challenge the urban homeowning majority to restrict themselves for the sake of keeping agriculture alive.

What does this mean for the rest of us? Would we have enough to eat if California stopped feeding us? In a thoughtful book titled *Reclaiming the Commons*, Brian Donohue looks at the potential for reviving New England agriculture by examining what he calls the unravelling of "the sensible regional food system of a century ago" in the face of competition subsidized by cheap water and energy.

> The reorganization of nature to support industrial farming . . . required unprecedented amounts of earth-moving engines and earth-replacing concrete—it all ultimately rested, and still rests on fossil fuel.
>
> Cultivation on such a scale was beyond the reach of animal muscles and organic manures; it required gas-powered tractors and inexpensive petrochemical-derived fertilizers to really take off. It was possible to grow hundreds of acres of the same vegetable in one place only with the help of powerful new pesticides, and harvesting those vast acres of produce took armies of underpaid migrant farmworkers or new machines. Market gardeners in the suburbs of Boston were up against a new capital-intensive,

highly mechanized mode of vegetable production. . . . Generation after generation, local growers were worn down by this competition until they all but disappeared.

But "food produced in this way," Donohue notes, "will remain economical only so long as energy remains cheap." And energy will not in the long run—perhaps even in the short run—remain cheap.

So it's only sensible to assume that a time may come when California agriculture will be unable to indulge us as it has. Can the rest of us learn to feed ourselves again? Probably. The eastern two-thirds of the country where there is usually ample rain for agriculture still has more than enough cropland.

Twenty-odd years ago, when the first energy crisis awoke the Northeast to its dependence on food brought in from elsewhere, activists in a number of northeastern states did studies examining the capacity of their respective states to replace imports with locally grown food. The studies concluded that much, though of course not all, of the food imported from points east, west, and south was producible in-state. Much more recently, a colleague of mine calculated that even New Jersey, the most urbanized state in the nation, could grow much of its own produce.

Donohue's thoughtful analysis concludes that New England "ought to be able to provide the great bulk of its vegetables and fruits from its own soil," though he doubts that we northeasterners will ever produce the largest part of the grains, oils, and meat we need. Those, of course, could come from the great middle of the country where they are mostly produced today, though some of us would argue that if we ate flesh more moderately, much of that could be raised locally.

Meanwhile, a number of states are finally undertaking serious efforts to preserve farmland from development or sequestration; unprecedented (and unequal) affluence is causing land to be eaten up more rapidly by grandiosity than by numbers. In parts of the Northeast, McMansions gobble up farmland to surround themselves with country "estates." Between 1994 and 1997, according to George

Lardner, Jr., land in the United States was consumed at twice the rate of population growth.

But if farmland is saved, and if California's problems begin to reduce the push of its crops into the rest of the nation, allowing for more local self-reliance, will eaters be willing to make some changes in the foods they expect to have across the year? There is reason to hope that they might. The changes need not be draconian, as I have tried to demonstrate, since "the most important issue is not whether people have oranges to eat in cold climates," as Helena Norberg-Hodge writes, "but whether . . . their basic food needs should travel thousands of miles when they could all be produced within a fifty-mile radius."

Although we're all consumers where food is concerned, we are primarily citizens of the world, and a surprising number of us appear to have concluded that there may be problems in the food system that our food dollars could do something about. I am obviously one of them, although most people aren't trying to grow much if any of their own food. They are, however, beginning to ask where their food comes from and how their choices might help to reward its producers.

Many of these people shop at farmers markets and farmstands where farmers sell mostly what they grow, some of them belong to CSAs where the grower's risk is reduced and consumers know personally the farmer growing their food (see chapter 14). Some of them find farmer-identified food in food co-ops or even supermarkets that distinguish themselves by featuring local growers. By shortening the chain that links them to the farm, these eaters hope to assure themselves of healthful food, while simultaneously assuring the farmer a living wage. To keep the next generation from falling into our culture's blindness about food, children in many places are being taught about the possibility and promise of local eating through schoolyard gardens and other projects where they learn to grow, cook, and share food.

It's important here to deny the too-common assumption that this safe, fresh, local food movement is only for the well-off. If we argue that in order to have sustainable agriculture everyone must pay more for food, we throw away the game. "This approach marginalizes the poor," points out Norberg-Hodge, "and opens [us] to charges of elitism." Community Supported Agriculture has proven amenable to support by low-income communities in New York City, and if we can do it here, you can do it anywhere. This is not to deny that it's harder to eat locally if you are not well off. The restaurants that make a point of serving local food are, almost universally, expensive. Mass-marketed prepared food thrives on, demands, a delocalized uniformity. But if we take away the subsidies that support the present food system—cheap fuel and water, public funding of high-tech agricultural research, massive public investments in infrastructure, including overbuilt highways to handle giant truckloads of travelling food—we can invest them in a food system that conserves soil, water, air, and human resources, *and* produces reasonably priced food.

All these possibilities hearten me as I tend my mini-farm. I wouldn't expect many people to limit their choices as I do; it's not even necessary, but I would hope that they would begin to think of the weather not just as an inconvenience but as a force in whether they eat. I would hope that they would remember that rain falls on farmers and their land, and succors, or drowns, their food. I would hope that eaters would learn to prefer the tastes of simple fresh foods grown close to home to the taste of the flashy produce that travels so long to reach them. And I would hope that they would begin to nudge themselves toward eating even more locally, asking where their grains and milk and meat and eggs come from. To become connected with food in such a way is to change the meaning of one's ingestion.

My passionate support of the idea that the food system should be relocalized may have exposed me to more local feasts than anyone now alive, including one in Alaska when the energy crisis of the 1970s battered the state with alarming transportation costs for imported food. My history may thus induce me to believe that the movement is bigger than it is. Admittedly, the threat to McDonald's is minimal at present. But I am cheered to realize how much attitudes have changed in just a quarter of a century. And, as record-breaking weather forcibly reminds us of our dependence on Nature, I am confident that eating from closer to home will come to seem increasingly attractive.

DECEMBER 30, 1999—I realize today as I wash the last of the just-dug carrots in the sink—cleaning up even the littlest ones because the crop was so bad this year—that what this is all really about is using up, making do, cutting down, even more than it's about eating locally. It's about fighting to model self-restraint in a society built upon encouraging lack of it. Why are we surprised when our children shoot each other over sneakers when we, their parents and grandparents, have been trying to live out the lesson that we must yield to our impulses because if we don't the economy might falter? Who but me would clean these tiny carrots? Who would try to salvage every last one against the winter that is coming and will come, and will require me to buy food in order to get through it? Does it make sense? If meditation makes sense, I suppose. If reflecting on the meaning of things makes sense. It is my meditation, my learning, my caring for each thing the earth has produced as if my life depended on it, because of course, in a larger sense, it does.

Bibliography

Baldwin, Malcolm. "Delicious Ways to Save the Planet." Review of Kate de Selincourt's *Local Harvest* (London: Lawrence & Wishart, 1997). *The Ecologist* 28, no. 1 (January/February 1998): 44.

Child, Maria Francis. *The American Frugal Housewife*, ed. Alice M. Geffen. New York: Harper & Row, 1972.

Donohue, Brian. *Reclaiming the Commons: Community Farms and Forests in a New England Town*. New Haven and London: Yale University Press, 1999.

Farmer, Fannie Merritt. *The Boston Cooking-School Cook Book*. Boston: Little, Brown and Company, 1920.

Fowler, Cary, and Pat Mooney. *Shattering: Food, Politics, and the Loss of Genetic Diversity*. Tucson: University of Arizona Press, 1990.

Given, Meta. *Modern Encyclopedia of Cooking*. Chicago: J.G. Ferguson and Associates, 1954.

Gronau, Reuben. "Leisure, Home Production and Work: The Theory of the Allocation of Time Revisited." *Journal of Political Economy* 85 (December 1977): 1099–123.

Gussow, Joan Dye. *Chicken Little, Tomato Sauce and Agriculture*. New York: The Bootstrap Press, 1991.

———. "Does Cooking Pay?" *Journal of Nutrition Education* 20, no. 5 (October 1988): 221–26.

———. "Why Cook?" *Journal of Gastronomy* 7, no. 1 (Winter/Spring 1993): 79–88.

———. *The Feeding Web: Issues in Nutritional Ecology*. Palo Alto: Bull Publishing Company, 1978.

Hage, Dave. "Bitter Harvest." *The Nation*, 11 October 1999, 5–6.

Henderson, Elizabeth, and Robyn Van En. *Sharing the Harvest: A Guide to Community-Supported Agriculture*. White River Junction, Vt.: Chelsea Green Publishing Company, 1999.

Jeavons, John. *How to Grow More Vegetables Than You Ever Thought Possible in Less Space Than You Can Imagine*. Berkeley: Ten Speed Press, 1995.

Kander, Mrs. Simon. *The Settlement Cook Book*. Milwaukee: The Settlement Cook Book Co., June, 1934.

Lardner, George, Jr., cited in Edward Thompson, Jr. and Timothy W. Warman. "Meeting the Challenge of Farmland Protection in the Twenty-first Century." *American Farmland* (Summer 2000), 14.

Madison, Deborah. *The Savory Way*. New York: Bantam Books, 1990.

Maranto, Gina. "A Once and Future Desert." *Discover*, June 1985, pp. 32, 36–39.

.McCarrison, Robert, and H. M. Sinclair. *Nutrition and Health*. London: Faber & Faber, 1936.

Morash, Marian. *The Victory Garden Cookbook*. New York: Alfred A. Knopf, 1982.

Mowat, Farley. *Never Cry Wolf*. New York: Bantam Books, 1982.

Norberg-Hodge, Helena. "Think Global—Eat Local! Delicious Ways to Counter Globalization." *The Ecologist* 28, no. 4 (July/August 1998): 209–14.

Pelzman, Helen, ed. "Water Policy and Farmland Protection: A New Approach to Saving California's Best Agricultural Lands. Highlights of Marc Reisner's Discussion Paper for American Farmland Trust." *American Farmland* (Winter 1998): 4–6.

Richards, B. N. *Introduction to the Soil Ecosystem*. London and New York: Longman Group Limited, 1976.

Root, Waverley, and Richard de Rochemont. *Eating in America: A History*. New York: William Morrow and Company, 1976.

Sachs, Aaron. "Virtual Ecology: A Brief Environmental History of Silicon Valley." *World Watch* 12, no. 1 (January/February 1999): 12–21.

Sander, Steve. "Statewide Farmland Protection Is Fragmented, Limited." *California Agriculture* 5, no. 2 (May–June 1998): 5–10.

Scheuring, Ann Foley, ed. *A Guidebook to California Agriculture*. Berkeley: University of California, 1983.

Standiford, Rick. "U.C. Research Can Foster Science-based Land-use Planning." *California Agriculture* 54, no. 3 (May–June 2000): 2.

Stoll, Steven. *The Fruits of Natural Advantage*. Berkeley and Los Angeles: University of California Press, 1998.

Toussaint-Samat, Maguelonne. *A History of Food*. Oxford, U.K.: Blackwell, 1992.

Tudge, Colin. *Future Food*. New York: Harmony Books, 1980.

Wilson, E.O. *Biodiversity*, Washington, D.C.: National Academy Press, 1992.

Worster, Donald. *Rivers of Empire*. New York: Pantheon Books, 1985.

Wylie, Philip. "Science Has Spoiled My Supper." *Atlantic Monthly* 193 (April 1954): 45–47.

Index

Put $50 out there and just see what comes back from

the Invisible Universe

THE INVISIBLE UNIVERSE is a virtual and virtuous "place" for people who want to be on the leading edge of sustainable living. For a $50 membership fee (annual), you receive the following benefits:

SOLARFEST

1. A free book. (Our selection will change from time to time, but at the moment new Denizens receive *Slow Food: Collected Thoughts on Taste, Tradition, and the Honest Pleasures of Food*, a $24.95 value.)

2. A free trial subscription to (your choice) *Natural Home Magazine*, *Mother Earth News*, *Permaculture Magazine*, or *Resurgence Magazine*. A value of up to $25.

3. A one-year membership in Co-op America, entitled to their full benefits, including a copy of their indispensible reference *The Green Pages*. A value of $30.

4. Free admission to Convocations, festivals that celebrate sustainability. These carry a dollar value of $25, but how do you really attach dollars to learning and fun?

5. The Hub enewsletter and *The Junction*, Chelsea Green's print newsletter.

6. Access to the unpublished Invisible Universe Web site, where Denizens are encouraged to mount the soapbox, show off, or just noodle around.

7. A free gift anytime you visit the Solar Living Center or Terra Verde. Just identify yourself as a Denizen of the Invisible Universe and show them your invisible membership card.

8. Free shipping on all Chelsea Green books—for Denizens only!

...and much more

Midwest Renewable Energy Association

Co-op America
building an economy for people and the planet

The HUB

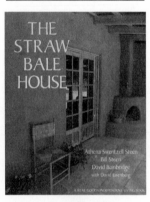
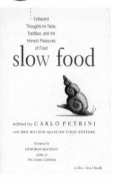